THERE ARE SOME who remember their schooldays through a rosy haze, some who look back on them (apparently) through a thunder-cloud. But Dom Hubert van Zeller is one of those rare people who remembers them exactly as they were: the misery of nearly always being cold, for instance, nicely balanced by the pleasure of nearly always being interested and amused.

School life at Downside, the masters, and the boys appear as clearly as though one saw them in a movie; many a reader's own boyhood will suddenly return to him as he reads of the amount of energy cheerfully expended on avoiding a little work, and the painfully accurate (though never unkind) portraits of the masters who endured the author and his companions.

As for his fellow-students—no doubt boys are boys the whole world over, but a more pleasantly absurd collection of them can seldom have existed in one school at one time. The illustrations make one almost wish the author had not had a vocation but had given his whole time to art. Almost, but not quite, for how many superb spiritual books we should have missed if he had!

…AN ZELLER is now sta- …e Abbey. His life as a …assignments as headmas- …nd teacher of painting …has also given many re- …ngland and the United …s book because "someone …ould write a novel about school life and I felt that the truth about it might do instead."

Willingly to School

Willingly to School

by

HUBERT VAN ZELLER

•　•

". . . creeping like a snail unwillingly to school."

—*As You Like It*, Act II, Scene 7

Preface

IN THE KIND of open-air photography which this book amounts to it is not always easy to keep one's own shadow from spoiling the picture. So the only thing to do is to admit frankly that the work, though hopefully biographical, is for the most part an autobiography . . . and to trust that the groups and views which have come before the camera are of themselves sufficiently interesting to distract from the same head-and-shoulder outline which keeps getting into the foreground. You may say that there is no necessity to tell beforehand what sort of book this is going to be, that it is for the reader (or publisher or reviewer) to decide whether the result is to be labelled biography or history or essay or whatever else, and that it is a weakness for an author to have to explain what he has written. Yes I know, but in this particular case there happens to be a reason. Since I am not writing of a school for the sake of the people who have been to it, but am writing of a period —out of school as well as in it—which is meant to appeal to men and women who have never heard of Downside and who have no particular concern with monks or me, I feel I should bear the major responsibility myself and not saddle my community with it. These pages are censored by, but do not necessarily reflect the assessments and memories of, my Gregorian brethren. Any other member of the Downside community who happened to have been in the school would make different selections, pass different judgments. Those here expressed are, for what they are worth, mine.

I must thank my fellow monks of St. Gregory's Downside, for having read the script and made suggestions. One such suggestion, ventured at the moment of going to press, is certainly to be followed up. I must make it clear, accordingly, that the standard of living which obtained in the more spacious days of which I write does not, in the Downside of today, obtain still. It must not be thought that only the leisured—if such exist—have access to the benefits and luxuries which I, all unquestioning in the days of my youth, enjoyed. The benefits which are enjoyed by the boys of the present generation are doubtless of a higher order. Doubtless. I speak only for the bad old days of plenty. And the benefits which we enjoyed then, I am glad to say, I enjoyed a good deal.

DOWNSIDE, 1951

Contents

	PREFACE	V
I:	PRE-PREPARATORY	I
II:	JUNIOR SCHOOL	22
III:	MIDDLE SCHOOL	93
IV:	FAG YEAR	108
V:	PRIVILEGE PERIOD	146
VI:	THE LAST YEAR	190
	EPILOGUE	254

Illustrations

M. Cartel   facing page 20

Herr Heronberger   53

Sgt. Instructor Bastable   84

Dr. Pollard   117

W. R. Lush, Esq.   148
(from a drawing by Tristam Hillier)

Capt. Le Seur   181

F. Moorat, Esq.   212

Adolphus ("Dolly") Vane Tempest   229

(The illustrations, except that of W. R. Lush, Esq., are by the author.)

Willingly to School

I: Pre-Preparatory

IF LENGTH OF TIME spent in the same school justifies writing about it, then my nine years at Downside give me the excuse I want. It is true that the excuse does not arise in the case of the only other school which I attended, because I was there for only a few hours, but I mean to write about it nevertheless.

My first school, the one which served me so briefly, was in Alexandria. It was a day-school. I was just seven when my name was printed on its lists, and I suspect that the reason for this early start in education had as much to do with getting me out of the house in the mornings and until three o'clock in the afternoon—for I was becoming a nuisance at home—as with the need to have me well grounded in classics and mathematics before my entry into Downside, which was to take place in two years' time.

Looking back, I feel that the whole of this opening experiment in school life was badly stage-managed. Had I been simply taken off one day after breakfast and put in a classroom with instructions to stay there until I was fetched in the afternoon—as if it was the most natural thing in the world—it might have worked. I would have been suitably subdued during the first few lessons, and would have asserted a naturally gregarious nature by about lunchtime. Instead there was talk, almost in a whisper and for weeks beforehand, of "going to school". It was looked upon as a venture (which indeed it turned out to be) and was treated *en grand sérieux*. I was rehearsed in the correct decorum to be observed towards authority; I was given textbooks, exercise-books, a blotter, and a rectangular wooden box which divided horizontally into two (if not three) parts and which contained pencils, pens, clips, nibs and rubber bands. I was told (all this long before the great day) that since the carriage would be taking me there each morning I would be wearing my indoor shoes, but that I would be taking my outdoor shoes as well—in case there were games or in case the other boys wore them. It was explained that I would be bringing my luncheon in a small wicker basket, and that I would not be eating with the rest of the school but apart, in another room, in the company of the lady who taught geography. But above all —and this was the real weakness in the preparation for my pre-preparatory school career—I was able to see that my mother was dreading it every bit as much as I was.

Then dawned the day itself. My father in over-boisterous humour, and inclined to slap one's back. My mother smiling bravely, but looking the picture of misery. I, noncommittal, glad to be the centre of interest, but hesitating between the role of martyr about to be flung to the lions— which would mean a strong resolute face—and the possible wisdom of insuring against the future by exhibiting uncontrolled grief. Perhaps the thought that my father's bluff determination would be impervious to tearful demonstrations inclined me finally towards the more dignified part of martyr, for I set off (as I learned long afterwards) with an expression of calm resignation on my face. Considering that I was due to be back in the house shortly after three o'clock on the same day, my composure does not now surprise me. Nor, knowing what my mother was like, does it surprise me to hear that my father extracted promises that there was to be no ringing up the school during the morning to find out how I was getting on.

I do not remember anything about the look of the

school, or about the grounds, or whether there were such things as a theatre and a gymnasium. Apart from the class-room in which I sat for my one sole lesson, and to which I was led by the lady who taught geography, all I can remember is the sound of a piano-practice coming through the open window from another part of the building. For once my visual memory is a blank, and I think I can account for this by the discovery which I made on arrival that it was a school for girls as well as for boys. I had not been prepared for this, and I regarded it as an affront. Psychologists would probably agree that surprise and indignation are quite enough to fill the mind to the exclusion of all other impressions. Certainly I recall little else, before the class began, than the feeling of having been tricked. A woman's place, I felt, was in the home, and if she needs must learn to read and write and cast accounts, let her do so in a region apart, with others of her kind, but not, Oh not, with men.

Consequently when placed at the side of a little girl who was sitting on a window seat (the desks were already allotted by the time we arrived, the new pupils forming an overflow line under the window), I was in no mood either to learn or to weep or to play the martyr. I wanted to show that this sort of thing would not do.

Fortune, as alas it so often does in the beginning, favoured me. The cord which hung from the upper windows was within easy reach, and to this I attached the little girl's plaits. In order to follow the subject and see the blackboard we had to sit diagonally on our crowded window-seat, so the undertaking presented no difficulty. I suppose there was some sort of scene when the bell went, because after a surprisingly short space of time I found myself in the carriage again—with my outdoor shoes, my luncheon basket, my schoolroom gear on my lap as before, and with the lady who taught geography at my side. Glad as my mother was to see me back, it was a mixed reception that I got on my return. My father, when he came home that evening, was at first furious. "Flung out," he shouted, "O my God, flung out on the first day." But he very soon calmed down, and was even, I venture to think, rather proud of my anti-feminist flourish.

The blotter and exercise books were put away, the pencil-box was given as a birthday present (a rather dull one I thought) to a small boy called Bridge Snow who was a neighbour of ours, and the wicker basket came in useful for my roller skates. But it was not an auspicious beginning. Expelled at the age of seven.

II

The second move in providing for my studies followed shortly afterwards. If the abortive experiment at the day-school had proved anything, it had shown that the great thing to be avoided was anti-climax after a too elaborate preparation. The fact that I had been led to expect a mix-ture of Dotheboys Hall and Dr. Arnold, and in the event had found Beatrix Potter, was taken into account by my parents when planning what to do next. With the result that about the arrival of Mr. Carter, who was to be my tutor for the next two years until again I went to school, there was maintained, right up to the day of the first lesson, the strictest secrecy. In this decision to spring Mr. Carter upon me, in letting the curtain go up to reveal the man of discipline and learning already solidly planted at the desk in my father's study, my parents showed—for being some-what spoilt I had views about most things, and would cer-tainly have had views about Mr. Carter—an admirable discretion. And as it turned out, Mr. Carter was an unquali-fied success. Even I—in spite of disagreements on subjects as varied as religion, times for beginning and ending studies, and the best way of washing paint brushes—was ready to admit that Mr. Carter could not have been bettered.

Long ago, in some remote past, Mr. Carter had been to Cambridge. It was probably his good degree and his precise donnish voice which had impressed my father. "Scholarly chap, old Carter," my father used to say, "best brain in Alexandria." This opinion, like so many of my father's opinions, changed later on, and poor Mr. Carter was looked upon as a joke, but certainly to start with there was no want of homage on my father's part.

Conscientious to a fault, and therefore prepared to keep my nose as well as his own to the grindstone, fully equipped with the kind of knowledge which I was likely to want, possessed of a pronounced—if a fastidious—taste, Mr. Carter succeeded in bringing to our peculiarly unbookish household in Alexandria some slight sniff of the University. My father, who never called people by their proper names for very long, referred to Mr. Carter as "Pericles." "Old Pericles is in the garden spouting Greek" or "No good asking old Pericles for tennis; he'd much rather read the Georgics to the bees." Mr. Carter, incidentally, played tennis remarkably well, which shows that he could not have been as old as he seemed to my youthfully measuring judgment. He was bald, he wore a thick moustache, his complexion was blue and red (like a map only darker), and he carried himself so straight that his stiff walk and upright sitting position were a gift to the caricaturist. His clothes were severe in cut, and he never took off his coat even in the greatest heat. His high starched collar emphasised his rigidity, and he had a way of holding his stick or umbrella as though it were a halberd, vertically, in front of him. People used to turn and look at him in the street. Even when alone he appeared to be walking in procession. His expression was one of such abstraction that one wondered how he was not run over, and even when he was talking across a table one felt that his eyes were on some distant horizon. This quality of appearing not to focus would lull the inadvertent hearer into a false state of security, and often during our sessions I would be surprised into renewed activity where I had thought the field was clear.

Mr. Carter was a non-smoker and, despite his rich colouring, a non-drinker. A bachelor of the kind whom one could not imagine even considering the married state, he disliked women, was shy in their company, and never mentioned them if he could help it. Though lacking in humour, he was neither a pedant nor a martinet. The deficiency as regards a lighter side was made good by his oddness of manner and appearance. I found him alarming at first, but not when I got to know him. He had evidently been told of my expulsion from school for rowdy behaviour, because for a week he assumed an expression of such ferocity, and exacted a discipline of such strictness, that I feared we should never get on. But when very soon he found out that my unfortunate lapse in early life had been due not to hooliganism but to wounded pride (which is much worse, though not, by most, judged to be so) he relaxed the tension of our meetings, and nothing could have been easier than the relationship which sprang up between us. Severity was as alien to Mr. Carter's nature as practical joking was alien to mine, so it was a relief to both of us when we found that we need not live up to our reputations.

My tutor was fond of cricket. In fact it might be said that cricket was Mr. Carter's obsession, his life. He followed it in the papers from England, he read books about it, he wrote articles about it, he knew the history of every player of any standing whether alive or dead, and on the least pretext he would be prepared to demonstrate a stroke with his umbrella. But it seemed that he had only rarely in his life actually played it. The enthusiasm was communicated to me, and we talked cricket whenever we could decently shed our Latin and mathematics. To this day I keep up with the literature of the game, and the only thing that dulls the delight which I derive from Mr. Cardus, Mr. C. B. Fry, Mr. Blunden, and Mr. Robertson Glasgow is the fact that I cannot exchange quotations with Mr. Carter.

My father, needless to say, approved strongly of our interest in cricket, and I imagine that it was only his sense of responsibility as a parent which kept him from insisting that we drop Latin and mathematics altogether, and concentrate on the game. Apparently the Headmaster of Downside, Dom Leander Ramsay, had impressed upon my father the necessity of having me grounded scholastically before I should come, at the age of nine, under his care at my first boarding school. Father Ramsay had said nothing, alas, about cricket. Though in the event it would not have mattered a great deal if Mr. Carter had spared his classical sensibilities and indulged his fancy, for when I came to Downside it was assumed that I knew nothing and I had to begin again from the beginning. In later years I was able to note that whatever Dom Leander Ramsay considered to be important *was* important, and so could well appreciate my father's insistence, maintained against his own inclination, upon laying solid scholastic foundations. It is gratifying to think of my father, an outwardly more forceful personality than Dom Leander, bowing before the other man's rare and secret power—secret, anyway, to characters like my father.

So long as the weather was at all suitable we had our lessons in the garden. The fiction that it was cooler outside was kept up for the two years that the tutorship lasted. We knew, both of us, that it was really much hotter out of doors, but smilingly we would collect our books and pencils each morning and trudge out into the shimmering heat. "So stuffy in the house," we lied encouragingly as we plunged into the airless little arbour which I had hollowed out for myself some time before. The Lair, or the Hidden Lair as it had been called at first, was hardly more than a deep recess in an overgrown pergola. It was roofed and backed by trellis-work which was covered with a matted creeper. Strands of unattached foliage had originally hidden the entrance, but now that the place had lost its specifically private character it at least had the advantage of being open on one side. Since the day when the Snow children had followed me to the Hidden Lair, there had seemed no point in retaining the fourth (the hanging creepered) wall, so all effort at further concealment was flung to the winds.[1] That particular spell had been broken. My Lair it remained, however, though the significant adjective had to be dropped.

Here, then, Mr. Carter and I pursued our studies. Being bitten by gnats away from the house was vastly preferable to being seated at a table inside it. Schoolroom atmosphere was uncongenial to both of us, and in the Lair we had our setting for Kipling and Rider Haggard. Also there was plenty of distraction in the shape of lizards, ants, and insect life.

One of the things which Mr. Carter insisted upon was punctuality. He used to carry two watches, and was for ever checking one against the other. Both these watches were placed in front of him on two inverted flower pots— since there was not room in the Lair for more than one small table, and that was supposed to be for me—while on a third inverted flower pot there would be a handbell of the kind used in side-chapels. How long the lessons

---

[1] Colonel Snow, the father of the boy and girl who were my friends, was treacherously shot in the back after conducting a peace parley with a tribe of the Senussi. He was my father's superior officer, and ours was not the only family which mourned his death as a personal loss.

lasted I do not remember, but four minutes separated the subjects, and the bell was rung at the beginning and end of each. As it happened, the four-minute break was for one reason or another hardly ever observed—either we had to "make up" for an interruption or else we simply went on with the same book but took it to be altering its scheduled direction—but the bells were punctiliously rung nevertheless. "It will get you into the habit of it for your public school," Mr. Carter would explain.

Interruptions were fairly frequent. How Mr. Carter viewed them I can only guess: certainly he never expressed annoyance. My brother, then aged two, used to be brought along by his nurse to see how we were getting on. By the time he was three he used to come on his own, and eventually had to be discouraged from the practice or we should never have done any work. The nurse, Josephine Tonitz, was an Austrian, and Mr. Carter amused her a good deal. Vienna and Cambridge—at all events Mr. Carter's sort of Cambridge—do not mix, and to the gay, Catholic, young, high-spirited Josephine, Mr. Carter's hard-hatted, Anglican, nineteenth-century correctness was a huge joke. She teased him to his face—heaven knows what he made of it—and imitated him behind his back. It was particularly the bowler hat which delighted her, and I can remember her marching in the nursery like a puppet soldier with my brother's little tin pot on her head. Mr. Carter had arrived only a day or two before, so it was quick of her to remark his possibilities. Elbows well in to the sides, forearm at right angles to the body, a broom held tightly upright. Josephine was, and is still, an original person.

If Josephine had not been a woman, Mr. Carter would probably have liked her. As it was, he shrank from her, backing into the spiders and cobwebs of the Lair whenever she invaded our seclusion. Blinking and staring down into

the thicket of his moustache, Mr. Carter used to look the
picture of polite misery until she went back, usually singing,
to the house. She told him once that he was a pagan, and
that I must be allowed holidays on the feast days of the
Church. It was in this way that I came to know what were
the feast days of the Church. Mention of religion was, to
Mr. Carter, painful: it sent him into paroxysms of embarrassment. The blues and reds of his face would become almost purple, and his long legs would wind round each other.
Until I saw that it really distressed him, I often raised the
subject of religion. Though I never discovered the exact
nature of his beliefs, I am sure that so much goodness and
kindness could not have been mere natural virtues; certainly
he showed all the signs of being a deeply religious man.

One interruption of our studies which I remember particularly was an occasion when my father came home unexpectedly, and called in at the Lair on the way towards
the house. There was a deckchair just outside the entrance
(there would have been no room inside it), and he sat
down. By this time my father had already, I think, begun
to lose confidence in "the finest brain in Alexandria."
Already he had begun to refer to my tutor as "Pumpernickel" instead of "Pericles." (Years later, when travelling with my father in Germany, I discovered Pumpernickel to be a variety of dark, dry, rather heavy bread.
Evidently Mr. Carter had reminded him of Pumpernickel.
When I told my father that I had always imagined the
name to have been given because it sounded like "nin-
compoop," he admitted tersely: "Bit of both.") From his
deckchair in the garden, my father, who had probably
spent an idle morning in a classical library, plied Mr.
Carter with questions which my unfortunate tutor found
himself unable to answer. Far too honest to bluff or evade,
Mr. Carter had to keep on saying "I'm afraid I don't

know . . . I'll look it up . . . dear me, my Catullus has got so very very rusty," until it was quite clear, even to me, that my father, whose knowledge of the classics must have been slender, was doing the whole thing on purpose. Curiously enough my own confidence in Mr. Carter was not in the least shaken by this incident, and I probably thought the more of him for sparing me the Latin and Greek authors whom he had largely forgotten, and for giving me instead an interest in a wide range of English literature which he had at his finger tips.

On another morning my father visited us in the same way at the Lair, and again sat in a deckchair just outside the cordon of watches and flower-pots. He had not been there many minutes when he broke off what he was saying, and glared through his eyeglass in the direction of the house. "Good God, look what they've done—how perfectly frightful." Hoisting himself to his feet he bounded over the flower beds and paths, shot through the hall door, and in a moment or two appeared again on the first floor balcony looking like the Angel of Vengeance. By this time Mr. Carter and I were outside the Lair, and could see what it was that my father had objected to. Apparently the hairbrushes of the household had been washed that morning, and were now spread out in a line on towels to dry. Seizing one after another, my father hurled the whole collection high above our heads and into the road behind us. I can remember the thrill of seeing a silver-backed brush catch the light of the sun as it spun in a great curve against the cloudless blue of the sky.

My mother was furious about the brushes, and sent a boy at once to get them back. All were recovered except one ivory pair which must have been picked up before the boy arrived. This surprised everybody, because it was thought that if there had been time to walk off with one pair there had presumably been time to walk off with the lot. "I expect old Pumpernickel has pocketed them," my father said.

III

Having mentioned Mr. Carter's practice of carrying over from one lesson to another with the same book, I must add here that this was not a form of laziness on his part: it was a deliberate feature of his teaching, and a very successful one. Looking back at the two years before I went to Downside, I am amazed at the amount of books which we must have got through and at the number of sidelines which our reading caused us to investigate. Nor do I remember that all this called for anything very much in the way of hard work. Or if it did, I must have enjoyed it.

Mr. Carter's method was this. He would start, for example, with *The Jungle Book*, and this would be called the English class. Then he would go on with *The Jungle Book*, and by the end of it I would know enough about India to enable me to answer reasonably difficult questions in a Geography paper. Or we would be doing Harrison Ainsworth, Kingsley and Scott for History as well as for recreation. (True, I had a certain amount of Ainsworth and Kingsley history to unlearn when I came to take the subject in a Catholic school, but so far as the general setting went I was well enough equipped.) Fiction, whether in English or French, seems to have provided the basic material of Mr. Carter's teaching. Sometimes it was the short story, but mostly it was the novel. I learned more French from *Marguerite de Valois* and *Les Misérables* than I would ever have assimilated direct from the grammar and the prose translation book. It showed imagination on an elderly tutor's part to try out Dumas, Victor Hugo—intermixed with Stevenson, Marryat, Ballantyne as well as those already mentioned—on a small boy who could only just write. The pity of it was that the same method could not be applied to the teaching of mathematics. Nor was I able to learn the rules of Latin syntax by listening to Mr. Carter's soft spinsterish voice reading *Treasure Island*. It was a pity too that neither of us much cared for Henty, who at that time was generally considered the ideal writer for boys of my age, because if we had I can see that no corner of the Empire would have been left untrod.

Another way in which my tutor showed an ingenuity the astuteness of which I was too young to appreciate was in the matter of our out-of-school activities. Most afternoons we would go for a walk, and it became our habit to look out for people in the street who resembled characters about whom we had been reading. "Oh look, there goes d'Artagnan talking to Florence Nightingale." "Is that Roland riding along at the side of the tramlines? Or do you think it's the Black Prince who has just borrowed Veillantiff for the afternoon?" Once when my mother asked at tea where we had been for our walk I am alleged to have replied promptly: "We got all the way to Shalott, and on the way home saw two Sancho Panzas playing dominoes outside a café with Sam Weller." Shalott was the fort, almost cut off from the mainland, at the other side of the bay. But I suspect the authenticity of this story, and see in it a trace of my father's hand, because for some reason Dickens does not seem to have figured in our reading. It was my aunt, Yolande, who introduced me to Dickens later on in my literary wanderings.

Often on our walks, Mr. Carter would refer to a passerby as a character of whom I had never heard. This meant that he was disqualified and that I had won the game. But it also meant that I would want to know the story. That the game was partly for his own entertainment as well as for my instruction is suggested by an allusion which he once made to Trilby, and which, though pressed, he would not follow up.

It was of course the story and not the style that chiefly interested me in the literature which Mr. Carter taught so admirably. The feeling for style comes later. To the aunt mentioned above do I owe this more strictly cultural taste, for when I left Mr. Carter's hands and came to England it was Yolande's choice which guided my reading. Here again I was fortunate, since not only was I put on to authors whom I was quite able to understand, and who otherwise would have been kept back from me until I was older, but I was also initiated into the drama. Of this I shall have more to say on a later page. It is strange to look back now and to find that I was reading at the age of eight and nine (or having read to me, presumably with expurgations) books of which my much more intelligent companions at Downside were ignorant at a considerably later stage. The advantage of always being a few years ahead in the matter of books and plays and pictures was, for a non-intellectual person like myself, enormous. For one thing, while all the junior boys around me—and I was the most junior of them when I first went to school—were emptying the shelves of Henty and adventure stories, I had the whole section of Conrad, Robert Hugh Benson, Wells and Arnold Bennett to myself. I must have been somewhat objectionable with this unexpected precocity, because masters used to say to me during English class: "But I suppose you've read all this before?" "Yes, sir."

IV

To come back to Mr. Carter, and our off-duty pursuits. Once a week we used to take a tram to the harbour, and I would have my diving lesson. Mr. Carter did not bathe; he merely handed me over to a certain Mr. Martin, my

diving instructor, and then picked me up at the tram ter-
minus two hours later. When it was very hot, Mr. Carter,
who felt the heat, put a large white handkerchief over
his head and under his bowler hat in such a way that, seen
from behind, he looked like a bride with a truncated veil.
A bowlered and trousered bride. So long as our excursions
took us to the less populated areas of Alexandria I never
minded this protection of his against the heat; but alighting
from a crowded tram into a throng of waiting people, I
felt it acutely. Especially did I feel it in the presence of Mr.
Martin.

The tutor and the diving master could hardly have been
more different in character, appearance, background, and
general outlook. Though they never quarrelled—because
if they possessed one thing in common it was kindliness—
they never mixed. I was impartially fond of both of them,
but I never felt ashamed of Mr. Martin in the way that I
am afraid I sometimes felt ashamed, although I owed him
far more, of Mr. Carter. It was that wretched handkerchief and hat.

Mr. Martin, a cashier at the Bank of Egypt in the Rue
Sherif Pasha, was a big easy-going smiling man in the late
forties. He had won international diving competitions, and
was more at home in midair (where he spent a considerable time each season) than in his office. The heights from
which he flung his great body, and the evolutions which
he performed with it before he plunged with the neatness
of a greased torpedo into the water, were unpredictable. He
also played, captain of the side, in first-class water polo,
and could outlast much younger men in long-distance
races. More impressive even than the sight of his massive
shape heaving out of the water like a porpoise was the way
in which he could keep perfectly still with only his head
showing above the surface, upright and with his arms
folded. This accomplishment fascinated me, and I asked

my father about it. "Sheer will power," he said, "or else
perhaps he waggles his toes and we can't see it from where
we are." My father greatly admired Mr. Martin, who in
any case was much more his type than Mr. Carter, and I
think envied him his facility in the water—especially, as
I did too, that ability to float standing up.

Mr. Martin had taught me to swim when I was six, and
though I had learned to dive long since (but not as
quickly or successfully as Mr. Martin had predicted) I was
still keeping up with the lessons for the sake of the bathe,
the use of the boards, and the company of Mr. Martin.
These weekly visits to the Swimming Club brought me in
touch with a kind of person who was quite new to me, and
whom I have hardly ever come across again. All were experts, all were single-minded in their pursuit of physical
fitness, and all were rather dull. That is why Mr. Martin,
who scorned the idea of keeping in training and who was by
no means dull, remains in my memory as perhaps a more
dazzling light than in actual fact he was.

Mr. Martin drank beer. I do not mean that he drank
it to excess, but merely that he drank it in quantities. I
mean that he was not like Mr. Carter. A distinct picture
remains with me of an occasion when the three of us,
seated at a table outside a café, were waiting for a tram.
I can see Mr. Martin's comfortable roomy frame clothed
in a tropical suit of cream tussore silk, against which the
dark ramrod form of Mr. Carter looks like a withered
tree. The one is a shiny, cleanshaven, laughing John-
sonian figure with a right arm that makes sweeping movements in the air and yet spills nothing from the large glass
tankard which he holds. The other is a dusty, dry man
who wears a forbidding expression and who holds no glass.
Both are misunderstanding one another. Yet each is being
sincerely himself. It is a bewildering study. Possibly if Mr.
Martin had joined me with my modest lemonade, and if

Mr. Carter had removed the handkerchief and bowler from his head (to reveal, incidentally, a whiteness of skin on top which always came as a surprise after the rich tones lower down), there might have been a common platform for the good which each man, in his particular way, had to give. But it obviously never crossed the mind of either of them to be other than what he was. So we were left, three-cornered and with great gulfs fixed between us, at that round table waiting for the tram.

v

With regard to my religious education during these years, I have—apart from Josephine who, as we have seen, taught me the days on which I might demand, on conscientious grounds, a cessation of studies—two people to thank for their explanations of Catholic doctrine. One was the seamstress at my grandmother's house in London where we spent summer months each year; the other was Father Dunstan, a Franciscan in Alexandria. About the seamstress I have written at length elsewhere, so only the Franciscan need be drawn from his self-chosen obscurity here. In case it might be wondered why the duty of religious instruction was not discharged by my mother, I must explain that though we made a start in this direction the attempt was abandoned. We both of us laboured under a delusion about the Catechism: in her case that she was unqualified to teach it; in mine that I was unqualified to learn it.

My father's approach to the same question was different but no less typical. The line he took was that since the van Zellers had kept the Faith for eight hundred years they could be assumed somehow or other to know it without having to learn it. "Our ancestor, Arnald de Zellaer, was a good enough Catholic to help in founding a cathedral," was the argument, "so we have obviously got it in the blood." But to have it in the blood is not the same as to have it in the head, and Father Dunstan was just the man to correct this idea of an infused knowledge.[1]

The instructions took place in the Friary. It was my first contact with the conventual life. But I cannot claim that my religious vocation dated from this time, because I connected the interviews with the purely intellectual process of learning lines from the Catechism by heart. Father Dunstan, in spite of the Catechism, became a great friend of mine, and I had a letter from him on the day of my ordination twenty years later. He was the only English member of a community which numbered Italians, French, Germans, and one Maltese lay-brother who opened the door and who cracked walnuts between the point of his chin and his collar-bone. Father Dunstan must have found things in that mixed community very hard. In fact I know he did, because he told me how he welcomed talking in his native tongue to Mr. Carter, who used to bring me with evident distress to the doors of this Papist stronghold, and to me. If this was really the case, I thought, it seemed a pity to spend the whole of our time when Mr. Carter was not present talking the words of the Catechism. It seems that I had no natural piety, or I must surely have acquired at least a reflected devotion from my Franciscan expositor.

Like Mr. Carter, but unlike Mr. Martin, Father Dunstan was a precise man. His was not the precision, the prim Carteresque precision, of the cultured don, but rather that of the trained theologian. Perhaps that is why I found a pedagogue when what I needed was a mentor or a mis-

---

[1] So fond was my father of citing the name of Arnald de Zellaer that when once, at the age of seven or thereabouts, I said "Ancestor Arnald is only a silly old Dutch cheese" there was the most awful row. It was even in all seriousness pointed out to me that the illustrious relative belonged to a period before the Dutch were strictly Dutch at all. "That part of the world was then called the Low Countries or the Netherlands," my father explained. Dull as I was, I felt of course at once that to substitute "silly old Netherland cheese" would not be worth it.

sioner. Though he prepared me for Confession, Holy Communion, and Confirmation—it was my father's idea, once he had decided that I should be instructed at all, that I should receive the three Sacraments before going to an English school—Father Dunstan was either too far above my head or too much on his guard against an assumed sanctity to give me any sort of real impression as to what religion was all about. That he was himself holy I have no doubt whatever—and indeed others have told me that he was—but that I derived any direct good from his holiness is not so clear. This, however, was presumably more my fault than his.

One thing I certainly failed to learn in my visits to the Friary, and I would have given much for the knowledge, was how to crack walnuts between the collar-bone and the point of the chin.

VI

Before closing this chapter and transferring the scene from Egypt to England, from blistering sunshine to yellow fog, it is worth noting the little that subsequent history has to record about the people mentioned so far.

Mr. Carter stayed on in Alexandria after leaving us, and though I believe he retired eventually and came back to England I am afraid we lost touch with him. The last I heard of him was that he was "keeping himself from running to fat" (the phrase was my father's) by doing odd reviewing jobs and acting as a publishers' reader. This is just the sort of work which would have suited him. One of my lasting regrets is that I did not take the trouble to write from school to tell him how well he had prepared me for the awful ordeals which were mine. His was a friendship which I valued more in retrospect than at the time, and I can see now that this dry reserved man, in allowing me the freedom of so much of his composition that was normally shut off from his fellow men, not only paid me a compliment which I was then too young to be aware of but also, which was more important, left with me a standard which proved invaluable later on.

Mr. Martin's end was a sad one. He was killed in an accident outside the Bank where he worked. This was while we were still living in Alexandria, but I was not told of it in case I should be upset. My father went to the funeral, and told me years afterwards that it had moved him more than he would have believed possible. "Poor old Martin with his slow fat laugh and his white suit of clothes."

Josephine left us for a time, and another Austrian girl took her place. She too was *fröhlich, lebendig*—but not as *fröhlich* and *lebendig* as Josephine. Nor was she as clever. Sophie (*die Sophie*) was her name, and though not from the right country she looked exactly like a picture by Renoir. There was the fringe, the peach and cream skin, the not very reliable expression. Mr. Carter could not make *die Sophie* out at all. Again, as in the case of Josephine, if she had not been a woman (or young, or *frölich* and *lebendig*—in fact if she had not been *die Sophie* except for her innocence and frankness) Mr. Carter would have liked her. Perhaps the truth about Mr. Carter was that he was not so much a misogynist as a gynophobe. But to leave Mr. Carter and *die Sophie*, that ill-assorted pair, and to return to Josephine. Josephine's departures were fairly frequent but never lengthy. In the end, after my brother was old enough to do without a nurse, she came to be accepted as a necessary though undefined part of the household. But she is strictly my brother's friend more than mine, so I had better say no more about her here in case he should feel moved to write about her himself.

Turning from people to places, I discovered when, at the age of eighteen and after a ten years' absence, I returned to Alexandria for a holiday, that the school which I had

M. CARTEL

attended for only one day had changed hands and was now receiving boys only. This somehow made me feel that my honour had been vindicated. The Swimming Club had not altered in the least. The same damp towels, the same peculiar smell which is proper to wooden floors that are being rotted by salt water, the same sound of water dripping from bathing suits, the same eager one-subject conversation from what appeared to be exactly the same people with different names and faces. Today whenever I drink tea made with condensed milk I am back again among the pontoons and the springboards and the covered stands of the Swimming Club. I can feel my clothes sticking to me where I have failed to dry myself. My eyes smart, and there is water in my ears. My wet hair is standing up under my panama, and Mr. Martin is signalling to me from my father's launch to hurry up. The exhaust is popping away as the trim little white craft rises and falls with the pontoons on the heaving swell of a larger vessel and in a few minutes we shall see Mr. Carter on the harbour quay waiting for us to arrive. He will have a watch in each hand, and as the spear of white foam subsides when we draw alongside he will say: "Nicely timed . . . can I give you a hand?" Condensed milk in tea can do every bit of that.

And as for the Friary, that too was the same after ten years away from it. But then you never expect religious houses to change much. You would be bitterly disappointed if, on entering the cloister, you were unable truthfully to say "Heavens, how the smell of soft soap and incense comes back to me." On entering the Friary in 1923 to call on Father Dunstan the first thing I remembered was the smell. My friend with the walnuts, however, had in the meantime been transferred to another house of the Order. Perhaps with the Franciscans it is the same as it is with the Benedictines—the only thing that changes being the personnel.

II: Junior School

I

MY DOWNSIDE CAREER opened in September 1914, six weeks after the outbreak of war. I was brought from London to the school by my parents—we drove up from the station in a cab, with my new trunk leaning perilously from the box—and I cried all the way. They went back to London next day and sailed the following week to Egypt. I was not to see my mother for two years, my father for three. I did not cry for the whole of this time, but I cried a good deal. I was so homesick at first that I got ill, and had to be taken into the Old House.[1] If it had not been for the kindness of Father Austin Corney I would have run away during the first week.

Father Austin was in charge of the Junior School, Father Leander was Headmaster. My mother told both of them that she was leaving me in a prison, and my father said "Knock some sense into him, because I haven't been able to." Despite this not very promising beginning I somehow got through the term without feeling that those in authority were warders or that that knocking-in of sense was a drastic process.

No sooner had I said goodbye to my father and mother than I learned the first lesson of school life—namely that the three things which mattered most to small boys were food, exchanging one possession for another, and getting off work. A boy called John Phillips, a newcomer like myself, was an adept in each of these departments, and

[1] Infirmary.

before I had been twenty-four hours at Downside I was shown where I might hide a parcel of provisions, was relieved of a box camera in exchange for a fountain pen, and was pointed out some highly promising weaknesses in the school timetable. John Phillips had been to school before.

Another new boy was Bernard Lane, and with him I struck up on the first day a friendship which was to last for four years. Four years, incidentally, almost to a day. He too had the question of food much at heart, and there was nothing which even John Phillips could teach him about the hazards of barter or the possibilities of juggling with the curriculum, but with him there went a more mature outlook as well as a more subtle sense of humour. For my part I found, after the first agonies of homesickness had spent themselves, that there was one consideration before all others which dominated one's time at school—and that was how to deal with one's chilblains. I had never spent a winter away from Egypt before, and already at the end of September my fingers were red and itching. By October I had chilblains on my toes, and throughout November and December I was wondering what I could do about my ears. After that, it was the same each year. Except for about a month in the summer I do not think I was ever really warm at school, and the fact that there were so many taboos regarding what one wore—whether underneath or on top or in bed—made it impossible to circumvent the cold at that age in ways which would have been easy enough had one been older.

Unlike most small boys, I preferred time spent in the classroom to time spent outside it. Not that I felt drawn to work, or that I did very much when I got there, but that I felt less at the mercy of circumstances. As eager as John Phillips to evade the course laid down, I was nevertheless hard put to it to find an adequate substitute. I had

not yet got into the way of the library, and there was nowhere except in the dayroom where I could paint, so it
meant that the long stretches of free time had to be spent
either in the company of my fellow new boys or in running
away from them. I was not as gregarious as I might have
been, and I was far more at home with grown-ups. So I
welcomed the bell for class.

The thing which I most looked forward to in the day
was going to bed. For one thing it would probably be
warmer between the sheets than anywhere else, and for
another it meant talking to an understanding adult like
Dom Paul. Also there was every chance—even if it was
not one's proper night for it—of a bath. Dom Paul Brookfield was the son of Charles Brookfield the actor, dramatic
critic and playwright, and he was also a person who went
to endless trouble over the more misfitting boys in his
dormitory. The Bungalow was the most junior dormitory
in the school, and Dom Paul was in charge of it. On one
side of the dormitory the windows were kept open all
the year round. I was on that side. In the bed next to mine
slept Alick Dru, who is now an authority on the Danish
philosopher Kierkegaard, and on the right of me was
Paddy de Bromhead, who accused me once (wrongly as
it chanced) of reading a postcard addressed to him by an
aunt. There was always this about school life, I discovered,
that no matter how adroit one was in keeping out of the
trouble which one deserved, there was the constant danger
of being involved in a trouble which one did not. Crises
of this kind were precipitated much more often by the
boys than by the masters, and it was the element of chance,
of insecurity about everything, which spoiled my first
few terms at Downside.[1] Which is another reason why
I liked class and going to bed: in both places one was

[1] One of my letters home at this period ends with the phrase "so you
see things are not exactly *sturmfrei*."

more or less untouchable. One was untouchable also in church, and it was probably this tendency to escape which gave me my first real taste of religion.

For evening prayers, Dom Austin used to herd us up to the Abbey, where we normally arrived a few minutes before the monks came in to recite Compline. There were no set prayers which we had to say, and we could kneel where we liked in the darkened nave. The combination of this informality about religion, the mysterious goings on in the choir, the feeling that one was extra-territorial so far as the school was concerned, and the general sense of being for a little while in a world which was at once a strictly private world of one's own and which was yet a traditional world, evidently had its effect upon me. I used to linger as long as I dared, and then grope my way out on tiptoe while the psalms were going on in the dark. Later on, this arrangement for night prayers was changed, and even the smallest boys in the school like ourselves, who went to bed earlier than the others, said specially selected prayers out loud in the dormitory. I am glad that I was in time for the older system.

Sometimes, on birthdays and special occasions, Dom Paul brought out a gramophone in the dormitory and we had music. It was a very early model with a great green horn and a wheezing rasping delivery. The records were not new nor cultural. The songs we liked best were "Straight on and up the Stairs," "I'm Henry the Eighth I am, I am," and one which contained the line "Oh by gosh you are, nicer than lemon squash you are." Dom Paul had got, and I am glad to say still has, the *genre* of the music-hall at his finger-tips, and I imagine that he looked forward to an excuse for putting on these old variety favourites.

Another dormitory memory which remains with me is one which is connected with the weekly distribution of pocket money. Small silver rained down upon our beds

on Saturday evenings, and it was Bernard Lane's unpleasant custom to place a threepenny bit in one nostril,
press a finger to the other nostril, and blow. This was
thought highly diverting. One Saturday a boy called
Hodgkinson, not to be outdone, placed a threepenny bit
in each nostril, and blew. But though he blew harder and
harder, becoming very red in the face, there was no tinkle
of threepenny bit upon the dormitory floor. We all gave
advice (for what it was worth), and rather than invoke the
aid of authority, Hodgkinson was persuaded to suspend
his attempts at freeing the threepenny bits until after
lights-out when there would be less likelihood of attracting attention. This, had we known it, was a bad move, for
even with the help of an electric torch it is no easy matter
to extract coins from a person's nose in the dark. At the
point at which nail-scissors were brought to bear, I with-
drew my services. And it was as well for my sake that I
did, for when the unfortunate Hodgkinson was finally removed, bleeding and screaming, to receive professional
attention, there was an enquiry into the business, and
those who had taken an active part were punished. From
that day onwards, pocket money was given out in shilling
and two-shilling pieces.

II

Among the other things which I was persuaded by John
Phillips to take up in the interests of evading the more
regular subjects, was carpentry. As I was already taking
drawing and riding—though in fact the "mounts from a
nearby livery stables" which figured in the prospectus
never seemed to figure anywhere else—the only remaining
alternative to carpentry was music. I knew that for me
music lessons would be hopeless, so, since these decisions
were left by my kind parents to my choice, I opted for
carpentry. Like music, drawing, mythical riding, and milk

and biscuits at eleven, carpentry was an extra on the bill. My father estimated that the three objects which I made in the carpentry course (four, if you count a fire in the carpenter's hat which I made towards the end of my time at the bench) were worth fifteen pounds each. A boat, a tray, and a box (or small chest) were the finished achievements of the carpentry classes which livened the greater part of my Junior School career.

At first for our instructor we had a fine craftsman called Walter Maggs, who was reputed to treat the spikes of his moustaches with carpenter's glue, and after him came Mr. Robins. Walter Maggs left us for the forces, and after fighting at Salonica and the Dardenelles was wounded and invalided out of the army. His military career was packed with interest and incident—as I came to know when, as an Old Boy, I used to visit the inn which he bought himself on the Nettlebridge hill. He had swiftly risen to the rank of sergeant (which was only fitting, in view of the moustache) and had never had any regrets about leaving the dusty disorder of the carpenter's shed.

Mr. Robins was of quite another order, and it was in his hat that we made our fire. Harry Cryan, Tristram ("Birdie") Hillier, and Gerald Kilkelly (who became a Lieut. Colonel during the last war and was killed) were my companions in this enterprise. The shavings were lying to hand, there were matches for the lighting of the gluepot, and there was methylated spirit for cleaning the surface of the wood. By punching a hole in a hat and blowing through a length of lead tubing, you can keep up an effective blaze: it will be the smoke and the smell of burning felt that will give you away.

The results obtained from Extra Drawing were hardly more satisfactory than those which represented the apprenticeship with chisel and saw. We had our lessons from a Mr. Whitcombe who, though a qualified painter, was not good at keeping discipline. This was a pity because there were three of us in the class who were anxious to draw. Tristram Hillier has since become a well known name in both the English and French painting world,[1] Arthur Woods left Cambridge with a reputation for stage design which he subsequently developed and extended to décor for the film,[2] so it was not surprising that the Art Prize went to one or other of us each year. Though we learned little or nothing from Mr. Whitcombe, we owed it to his intervention on our behalf that a classroom was allowed us to paint in during our free time. This made an enormous difference to my happiness at school, because I felt that here at last was something which I could do in a place where there was an opportunity of doing it. The dayroom had been too noisy and public, and it was not until I got almost to the top of the school that I was given a room of my own.

My father, who exhibited regularly, had taught me to draw from the moment I was old enough to hold a pencil, and Mr. Carter had helped this on with a pretty little skill in polite water colour, so by the time I was a new boy at Downside I must have been better equipped than most. The first commission which I received was to draw pictures of a certain pacifist mathematical master who had been unwise enough, in those first months of the war, to speak on a platform in the nearby town of Midsomer Norton. His was an easy face to draw, and I am afraid I must have contributed to the mortification of his last weeks at Downside.

Orders for caricatures came also from Old Boys on leave, and I look now with a pang at the photographs of

[1] Two of Hillier's pictures hang in the Tate. I was glad to find, when preaching in America last year (1950), that critics were praising his work highly in the States.

[2] Arthur Woods was killed in the Second World War.

those who were killed at the Somme and on the Marne: a
number of their faces I had studied with a draughtsman's
interest at the age of nine. Today when I am asked to
draw young men in the service dress of the Brigade of
Guards, my mind leaves the autograph book under my
hand and I remember Johnnie Dame, Desmond Butler,
Wilfrid Cary-Elwes and others.

To be asked, as the youngest boy but one in the school,
to limn the features of the great is test enough for anyone's
humility, and I imagine I became objectionable. My
greatest painting success of this early period was when a
boy called Dwight Taylor demanded a picture of his
mother, who was taking London by storm in musical
comedy. Fortunately I had seen Miss Laurette Taylor on
the stage, and was able to remember her fairly accurately.
So when she came down during the term to see her son,
she asked to see the boy whose drawing had been given to
her by Dwight. She looked relieved when she discovered
that the artist was a child and not a member of the Sixth
Form or First Fifteen, and told me that she had shown
the picture to her producer who said "We'd better book
him later on to do our posters." This may have been only
a tribute of hers made up on the spur of the moment, but
whether it was or not there can have been few more ardent
admirers of the American actress, Laurette Taylor, than
the boy with chilblains and the ill-fitting Eton collar.

The stage, in one form or another, seems to have received a good deal of attention from us nine- or ten-year-
olds. Not that the walls of our lockers were adorned with
the kind of pictures which the sound-screen has since
popularised, or even that the Hippodrome predominated
noticeably over the Court, but simply that the boys of
my year seemed to have had the theatre in the blood.
Bernard Lane was an authority, established as such by
universal consent of the lower forms, on revue and light

comedy; Napper Dean Paul knew more than anybody of
our age about opera and the ballet (he and his sister entertained the school one evening with the performance of a
dance from a composition of their own); Arthur Woods
had visited a film studio, and was therefore the accredited
cinema critic. Even my own humble experience under
tutelage from an uncle whose interests I have described
elsewhere[1] was not, in matters histrionic, to be despised.
Bernard Lane lived in London, and during the holidays
we used to do the rounds of the theatres. Sometimes we
were accompanied by Alick Dru, whose tastes were severe,
and by Arthur Woods, who was more concerned with the
technical and decorative side than with the plays themselves. Fortunately I was provident enough to make a list
of all the straight plays which I saw between the time of
leaving Egypt and the day of entering Downside as a
monk. I had been urged to do this by Mr. Carter, who
advised me also to keep a diary and to write down my
impressions of every book I read.

These farewell injunctions of Mr. Carter's were, like
most of the advice he gave me, observed at least inter-
mittently and selectively. That is to say I kept a diary
for the first and last years of my time at school, wrote
what I thought of the books which I liked—merely making a list of the rest—and recorded the plays. Pantomimes,
musical comedies, ballets and revues were not for some
reason put down. Looking back at the dramatic catalogue
I cannot but be surprised at some of the plays which I saw.
I suppose I understood them; certainly I enjoyed them. It
was mostly my aunt Yolande who told me what I should
see, and more often than not it was she who took me. Her
knowledge about everything to do with the theatre was
phenomenal, her taste unerring. Had I followed all her

[1] The allusion is to Marcel van de Velde, a short biography of whom
appears in *Family Case-book*.

suggestions, instead of only about two thirds of them, I should not have missed some of the most notable performances of that time. As it was, I saw some of her favourite actors and actresses during my first year at school, and thereafter they became my own. Among them were Arthur Wontner, Sir George Alexander, Marie Löhr in *Kings and Queens*; Dennis Eadie, Malcolm Cherry, Mary Jerrold in a gripping spy play, *The Man who Stayed at Home*; Henry Ainley with Godfrey Tearle and Sydney Fairbrother in what I suppose was a revival, *Quinneys*, and which had a deservedly long run; Sir Herbert Tree in both *David Copperfield* and *Henry IV* (in the former supported by Nigel Playfair, Leon Quartermaine, Sydney Fairbrother, and in the latter by Matheson Lang, Owen Nares and Basil Gill); James Welch in *When Knights were Bold* and *The New Clown*. Also, and this was all the more memorable because it was occasioned by a flying visit to London during the Lent term to see a doctor, there was Charles Hawtrey as a young peer selling cheese and bars of soap to Fay Compton in *A Busy Day*.

During the war years which followed I saw Gerald du Maurier playing all his best parts. H. B. Irving as a seventeenth-century knight one holidays and a Harley Street surgeon the next, Irene Vanbrugh in a Pinero play with George Alexander, Gladys Cooper with Malcolm Cherry and Weedon Grossmith, and a host of others. I know that Dom Austin and the Headmaster were amazed at the number as well as the kind of plays which I was allowed to see during the holidays. Dom Paul Brookfield, on the other hand, was not in the least amazed: he approved.

It is not surprising, then, that the conversation at our end of the table in the Junior School refectory was largely about the theatre. So eager was I to see everything that came out, and so envious of what others had seen and I had not, that for months I could not get over the disappointment of having missed a musical production called *Business as Usual* which had apparently been a great success. I heard so much about it that for a little while I think I managed to persuade myself that I had, after all, seen it. But it was no use: the imagination was still questioning, and, despite the information which I had about the piece, I had to admit that I had not sat before the curtain of *Business as Usual*. I have since felt much the same about *The Arcadians*, which I know inside out and which represents to me more than any other musical production the spirit of its period, but here too there is the disqualifying accident of never having been to it. So in case I have ever, reeling off the names in the original cast, given to people the impression that night after night I witnessed *The Arcadians*, let me now acknowledge frankly that I have not once been present at its performance.

In the twenty-five years that I have been a monk, I have not of course seen any plays, but to judge from those that I read and from the reviews, I should imagine that the standard of acting is as high now as in the days of Tree, Alexander, Bancroft and the Vanbrughs, and that the standard of playwriting is very much higher. This quite arbitrary opinion at least gives me the right to feel that the giants of the theatre whom I saw then in their most famous roles would have made an even bigger thing of the plays which could be written for them now. And here we may leave the subject of the stage—anyway until further mention is made of the person who gave a new impetus to my theatre-going, namely my uncle Marcel.

III

To do with performance, though not strictly with dramatic performance, was the appearance at this period upon the Downside scene of a man who bore the unlikely name of Sep Flake. Not often did Mr. Flake appear—perhaps not more than once a term—but when he did, he was welcomed by the junior boys with an acclaim which was hardly accorded to other and more important visiting notables. Mr. Flake was an organ-grinder and the proprietor of a performing monkey. There was another itinerant musician who used to visit us, but of him, a concertina-player, I have only the haziest recollections; it is the memory of Mr. Flake that seems particularly worth preserving. What Mr. Flake's monkey was called I cannot now remember, but I seem to connect the name with a town—it might be Karachi or Lichfield—and was certainly not a name which suggested any particular gender. Dom John Kane, who will be mentioned later in this book as teaching Sixth Form Classics, called the monkey Domitilla and its master Flaccus. "Isn't it about time," Dom John would say about half way through the term, "that we had a visit from Flaccus and Domitilla?"

Mr. Sep Flake, or Flaccus Septimus as we may now call him, clearly felt that he and his performing monkey were a survival of a vanishing era. He acted up to this, wearing somewhat peculiar clothes—even for an organ grinder— and speaking in the fashion of a generation back. He would, for instance, when speaking of us to Domitilla, refer to "the young masters." There was something self-conscious in the manner adopted, and one cannot but feel, looking back, that Flaccus was not so much deferring to *us* with his courtly flourishes, but to a conception of his own . . . to an old-world picture. "Take round the tambourine, Chichester," he would command (or it may have been Nepal), "and see if one of these good young masters hasn't got a sovereign or two in his purse." Few of us had ever possessed a sovereign in our lives, and some had probably never seen one.

The monkey who, thanks to Dom John, was to us not a town but a Roman matron, had a perpetual cold in the head. It wore, not in order to keep warm but for gaiety's sake, a red flannel cap and a red flannel skirt. The cap masculine, the skirt feminine; the result, in Flaccus's eyes evidently, neutral. I remember particularly about the skirt, because a boy called Couban, a Northerner and a nephew of one of the monks, took it off and was sharply bitten for his pains. To me, watching the scene from the fringe of the crowd as befitting a new boy, it came as a surprise that the monkey should resent Couban's action. Were not a cap and the petticoat symbols of bondage? Did they not, every morning when they were put on, humiliate? You would have thought that an elderly and intelligent ape—and little Domitilla was not young nor stupid—must prefer to walk as nature had arranged. Not a bit: Domitilla, forgetting the dignity of its proper kind, fancied the trappings which the impresario had provided. I am grateful now to the boy Stephen Couban for his ill-starred pleasantry; it has taught me how insidious can be the influence of vain things. Finery corrupts.

Though Flaccus was undistinguished enough, his performing animal was at once repellent and appealing. I noticed that the main interest always went to the lesser member in the partnership. Fascinated, we used to watch the change which came over Domitilla the moment the music began to play. The tired, dejected, listless body which had dragged itself, hands trailing in the dust of the road, from goodness knew what home along the Somerset and Dorset Line sprang suddenly to life as if injected with notes from a syringe. Then would Domitilla dance and caper and rattle the tambourine. Then would Domitilla, spry as you please despite its years, climb up the stick which supported the organ, and finally sit, shivering somewhat, upon Flaccus's shoulder. No wonder Domitilla—what with the pathetic expression, sneezes, the enormous appetite, the hairy hands with their wrinkled indigo palms which seemed to retain the frosts of innumerable English winters, the sense of great age and the general air of mustiness and patched carpet—left an indelible impression upon the memory. I can see now that long upper lip —the characteristic of the professional humourist—and those heavily lidded eyes. I can hear the bang and tinkle of the tambourine.

The tunes which were released from Flaccus's instrument ring also in the ears. They were not many, but they were varied. The repertoire included "The Cachucha," "Hold your hand out, naughty boy," "Yip-i-yaddy-i-yay-i-yay," one or two melodies from *The Dollar Princess*, and, most heart-rending of all, "Won't you buy my pret-ty flowers?" There were probably others—polkas almost certainly—but I have forgotten them. The trouble was that the tunes had to be played in their proper order . . . so that if you wanted Flaccus to play "Won't you buy etc." you had to persuade him to turn the handle at a brisk pace in rendering the pieces which intervened. This, as a true artist, he was not always willing to do, and more often than not you would hear the bell going for class before you had heard your "Won't you buy."

To conclude this section on Flaccus and his monkey, it may be added that the boys seem to have felt too, with Flaccus, that the day of barrel-organs and performing monkeys was fast drawing to a close. Many, accordingly, were the photographs taken of the pair, and some of these photographs exist still. Indeed it was only when Flaccus was asked to sign a print which is now barely decipherable that we learned of his inability to read or write.

The last I saw of the two of them was in 1915, when I watched from a classroom window (for I was still eager to be first in the classroom) a crowd of my fellow juniors escorting Flaccus and his companion across the Ballplace in the direction of Chilcompton Station. It was like the

Pied Piper. Through the window I could hear shouts of "Come on, Flaccus, give us 'Hold your hand out' . . . I say, Flaccus, let me take another in case that one doesn't come out . . . look here, Flaccus, it isn't nearly time yet . . ." Then Domitilla's sneeze, like someone quickly crumpling tissue paper, and down would go the little cocoanut head with a jerk which set the bells tinkling on the tambourine.

Another suggestion of antiquity was conveyed—and to a larger public as well as over a longer period of time than was conveyed by the Flaccus visits—by the existence of a tinker's shed which lay on the road between the Romantic Valley and a little hamlet called Gurney Slade. This workshop was called by the school "Cyclops." In it were to be found treasures more varied than anything to be seen in Aladdin's cave. The blazing furnace, the great water wheel, the piled up heaps of scrap metal which ranged from tobacco-tins to bedsteads and the chassis of old motor cars, the enormous tongs and pincers and above all the huge and almost fairy-tale hammer from which the place got its name, delighted generations of small boys who were taken there on days when it was too wet or too cold to play games. The noise in the workshop was deafening. Everything seemed to be jumping about, and as most of the things were red hot the general effect was that of a Wagnerian opera or of an Inferno taken from Dante's control and reshaped by Disney. Gigantic bellows puffed and blew, sheets of metal clanged and changed colour, heavy chunks of coal glowed and fell about into trays or baths of water with a great hiss and clatter, pots and pans and kettles seemed to turn into one another almost while you watched, and before you had been in the place five minutes you were covered in a fine dust which was partly ash and partly metal. The man who presided over this splendid pandemonium was old and bent and silent. At least I have always assumed that he was silent: certainly he would never have been heard if he had chosen to speak while Cyclops was in operation.

His hair, moustache, shoulders, chest, arms and trousers were all one colour, all one texture. He was as rusty as the scrap heaps which collected everywhere around him.

How the owner of Cyclops managed to keep the place together, working at such high pressure, was a mystery. Everything was patched and tied to everything else, and all the bolts rattled. Eventually of course it fell to bits. Not all at once, but a wall here and a piece of roof there. In an incredibly short time there was nothing to show for the Cyclops that had been. Today you cannot even be sure of the site where it stood. Not a bedstead, not a pudding basin . . . only the stream which originally worked the wheel. But though the great hammer is stilled, and the giant bellows—asthmatic in sound and pantomimic in appearance—have ceased to blow, though the tinker is dead and the scrap iron has probably gone into armaments, there is never the least doubt as to what you mean if you say today that you are going for the Cyclops walk. There may be nothing left except the name, but let us hope that this will go on being used for longer than any of the pots and frying pans that were fashioned in that place—for as long as there are Gregorians who will remember what it stood for. Few things so impress upon us the mutability of human affairs as the complete disappearance of familiar landmarks, the utter silencing of great and sustained dins.

IV

It is time that more was said, in a book which is supposed to be about school, on the topic of work. Form One, the lowest class, was my *habitat* for all except French and German. For French I was attached to a form which was three stages higher on the list, and for German I was one of a small group which received separate tuition from an almost legendary figure called Herr Heronberger. All three positions in the curriculum suited me perfectly, and in each of them I would have been happy to remain for the rest of my school career. In fact had it not been for considerations of age, and the desire to have greater freedom for painting, I would probably never have moved.

Since classroom competition interested me hardly at all, and since I have never felt the least curiosity about the sheer mechanics of acquiring knowledge, I can remember little of what went on in the classes at which I assisted. This is only another way of admitting that I was shockingly lazy—bored equally by the grammar of learning and the whole silly business of marks. I can remember the masters, the boys, the smell of the nictating gas, the noise of the lawn-mower in summer and of the straining hot-pipes in winter, can recall the feel of the desk on one's knees when one pressed forward in a game of "taxi," can live again the agonies of trying to keep awake in Mr. Wylie's class, and the punishments. But I cannot remember what we did the whole time.

There were only two subjects that I cared for at all: Scripture and English. Biblical history was read to us by Dom Austin on Sunday evenings, and my imagination was so fired by the drama and violence and language of it that I borrowed the book to read during the week and to copy out the passages which I liked. Later, when I had to take Scripture as a subject for the School Certificate, I enjoyed it even more. It was Dom Rupert then who stirred my interest, and I have never really lost it since. Under him, Maclear—even Maclear—rose up and sang.

The English faculty, anyway so far as we juniors went, was divided. From one source we had parsing and analysis, from another we had dictation and "English book."

Needless to say I scorned parsing, analysis, and spelling, and have been paying the penalty ever since: I still waste hours of time substituting my own patent methods of parsing and analysing, and I can never be sure how to spell. With regard to "English book" I was on safer ground.

It is characteristic of our national approach in matters of education that the only English book which we did in my first term was a German one. And I had done it before—in German. At my father's insistence, Josephine had read to me, in the intervals of looking after my infant brother and imitating Mr. Carter, *Baron Münchausen*. In German it had sounded mad and romantic; in English it was archaic and flat. When Father Walter, who took us for this subject, asked me why I looked so indifferent I replied "the gallop has gone out of it," and thereby acquired a reputation for pertness.[1] Father Walter also asked me one day why I never put up my hand either to ask or answer a question, and it turned out that I was not doing this because I was pert or indifferent but because I was always sitting on my hands to keep them warm.

As a by-product of English book was English essay, and here I needed no exhortation from Father Walter to remove my hands from underneath me. On one occasion the subject proposed for our essay was: "Describe some incident from your past life which has really happened." In Form One we numbered some whose lives had been crammed with vivid incident, and we set to work with zest. Only one boy in the class chewed an idle pen, and this was all the more surprising because he had been born in China, had travelled with his parents in India and the Near East, and had finally come on to Downside from a school in Switzerland. "Surely there must be *something*

[1] It is humiliating to reflect that *Baron Münchausen* was first written by Rudolf Raspe in English, and then only in his own language. Even so, the German is better than the English.

you remember happening," insisted Father Walter. No, apparently there was nothing. The rest of us stopped our feverish scratching with pen and ink, and turned round to look at this tall fair boy who sat at the back of the class and who could not remember any single incident of interest in the past. "Think, boy," urged Father Walter five minutes before the end of the period, "just *think*." Inspiration must then have come to the writer, for on the paper which he handed up when the bell went were the words: "Once my father's nose bled and he had to lie down."

For mathematics we were taken by the W. E. Campbell who later became an expert on Thomas More, saint and chancellor, and who must have found teaching small boys very trying indeed. However, he initiated me into the mysteries of long division, and there, for many years, I stuck. Less tranquil than Mr. Campbell's classes were the various branches of mathematics taught by Dom Aidan Trafford, but of these I shall have occasion to speak in their chronological place.

French, in that more advanced form to which I have referred, was taught by a succession of masters. To me the great charm of belonging to this exalted group lay in the fact that one never knew from term to term, or even from week to week, whom one was going to get next. The war, with its consequent shortage of masters, was responsible for this state of continual flux, and not until Dom Gregory Quinlan was reluctantly drawn from his retreat in the monastery did the form possess a master who showed any sign of staying. Thus during my first year, when presumably the pre-war modern language professors were censoring letters and acting as interpreters in government offices, we had one man who was sick out of the window into the quad, another who, though living in the village, used to come up to the school in a red dressing-gown to have his bath, and yet another who averred that he was being pursued by ladies in the pay of the Spanish secret police, and who, in order to scare away these foreign adventuresses, used to conduct his classes carrying a sword-stick. So of course it was well worth belonging to that particular class.

With the arrival of Dom Gregory came a temporary lull: excitement dropped sharply. But though we no longer enjoyed the constant change of method, we enjoyed, under Dom Gregory, an absence of method of any sort. He was much too good and kind for the particular group which he was expected to teach, and often I would be sent out to receive punishment which I richly deserved. In those days almost all offences were dealt with by the Headmaster, so I had frequently to explain my frivolous behaviour to a man whom already I admired and whom later on I frankly venerated. He was to be my Abbot for the first four years of my religious life, and when he died I felt that a great current of power had ceased to run through the wires of Downside's life. But at the time of which I write, Dom Leander Ramsay was still Headmaster of the school, and as such he had to listen to me and administer correction when I was sent out of class by Father Gregory. Here is a specimen of one of our interviews: the first part is representative of many such, the last a verbatim account as I remember it.

"Well, what is it now? Father Gregory?"

"Yes, sir; fooling, sir."

"And he sent you to me?"

"Yes, sir; I'm afraid so, sir."

"In the middle of class?"

"Well yes, sir; just now, sir."

"Very good. Go and fetch the weapon, and get it over."

The 'weapon' was the instrument, whichever it might

be, of correction. On this particular occasion I fancy it was
the cane. After the formalities had been observed and
I got my breath back, the dialogue continued as follows:

"You should not fool in Father Gregory's class. He
dislikes it, and his sister has written a book about Damien
the Leper."

"Is it a good book, sir?"

"Not very. But her name is May."

"Is it in our library, sir?"

"Probably not, probably not. Because you see she lives
in Chilcompton. And keeps chickens."

"Oh."

"And the frontispiece is a picture of Father Damien
painted by a very famous Pre-Raphaelite."

"Is it like him, sir?"

"No."

Such, with its deliberate *non sequitur*, was the quality
of Dom Leander's humour.

But Dom Leander was far from being a humourist, and
it was only on rare occasions that we saw his lighter side.
With his set mouth and firm chin, with a relentlessly penetrating focus of vision, with the suggestion of intense
mental and physical energy in every line of his taut body,
Dom Leander was held in great awe by us small boys. But
though we were afraid of him and puzzled by him, we
saw enough of him to realize that he was probably a saint.
We felt very clearly—and this is not simply my idea, but
one which is confirmed by contemporary Old Gregorians
—that here was someone quite out of the ordinary, and
that holiness was his distinguishing mark. On days when
the Upper School had its "long sleep" the boys of the
Junior School used to serve the Masses in the Abbey, and
I shall not forget the impression which Dom Leander's
Mass left on me when it was my good fortune to serve
him. The concentration, the characteristically deliberate

yet quick movements of the hands, the hissed whispering of the prayers, the careful genuflexions, the jerk of the head which looked as if he were shaking distractions out of his hair—all this must be remembered by his Old Boys. Certainly Dom Leander's Mass, and the sight of his rigid, absorbed, fierce thanksgiving afterwards, marked a further stage in the development of my religious vocation.

At Downside the Headmaster was not the distant figure-head which he is at most large schools. Even apart from being punished by him and assisting him in the Abbey, we juniors saw a certain amount of him in the ordinary run of daily life. For one thing he used to meet us in the Study Room (now a House Dayroom) every Sunday morning while the rest of the school was attending High Mass, and give us half an hour of semi-liturgical, semi-devotional, semi-exegetical, semi-moral-and-disciplinary instruction. Much of what he told us at these gatherings went clean above our heads—Tertullian was quoted every now and then, and once we were treated to an outline course on Modernism—but much of it stuck. Particularly I can remember the subjects which he chose for Lent: humility, hardness with oneself, love of Christ's Passion, not grumbling. One Sunday he made us stand up, row by row, and recite a variant reading from the ninth chapter of the First Epistle to the Corinthians. Then we said it all together, seventy unbroken voices: "I beat my body black and blue, and lead it about as a slave."

On another Sunday we were introduced to a distinguished visitor, a Jesuit, who spoke to us instead. This was Father Bernard Vaughn, and though we were mildly impressed and were ready to laugh at his jokes, we preferred (I think) the less flamboyant manner of the Headmaster. In spite of readings from von Hügel and digressions into the history of Port Royal and the Quietists, we enjoyed our weekly "Leander jaw." Though, now that I come to think of it, the approval was not unanimous. There was one boy, Tommy Walmsley, who used to make it his concern to obstruct every official function, whether it was the Headmaster's or anyone else's. Authority to him was a challenge; rules prompted him to heights of bravery in their destruction. Exactly what he did during the Headmaster's Sunday address I do not now remember, but I have a distinct picture of him (Eton suit and curly hair) standing up in about the fifth row to meet Dom Leander's stare. The culprit maintained complete silence, and all the Headmaster said, at intervals, was "Well, Wammy . . . well, Wammy." But after a minute or two of this, with the Headmaster's rosary twisting itself into knots in his hand, the boy broke down. Tommy Walmsley, whose soul had waxed fat for months on a diet of indiscipline, cried his eyes out and apologized. Nor did we, the spectators, look down on him for doing so.

Sometimes on his way up to supper in the monastery, Dom Leander would stop and speak to us outside the Junior School Dayroom. Not a man of small talk, he was often hard put to it to think of something to say. What usually happened in these casual encounters was that he would thump one on the chest a few times, and then observe through clenched teeth: "Life is very difficult." Since there was no obvious comment to make on this statement, one would either say "Yes, sir" or keep silent. "Very difficult," he would repeat, "isn't it? Isn't it? Isn't it? Would you agree to that? Can you subscribe to such a view?" And then he would turn away abruptly, and run stiffly on his toes towards the stone steps which led to the monastery cloister. This peculiar run of his with the feet turned slightly in and the short strides was seen every evening at the same time, and we used to wait for it. Always there would be the rosary twined round the fingers of the right hand, and if he did not interrupt his run to thump us with this rosaried fist he would be praying aloud as he passed. He must have been late every night of the week for the community supper. There was no mistaking it, even to us: the Headmaster was a very rare and special person.

v

Then Dom Gregory Quinlan died, and we had Dom Thomas Symons for French. But nobody could stand our class for long, and after a little while we were given M. Cartel to rule over us. If I say next to nothing about these two masters it is because they are both still teaching, and there must surely be such a thing as commonroom etiquette which demands silence in matters of this sort. All I am prepared to say is that from Dom Thomas's teaching I learned more about how French people *thought* than I had learned from his predecessors who had tried to teach me how French people spoke and wrote. While from M. Cartel I learned how lucky I was not to be learning English in a French school.

An incident which belongs to this transitional period in our Junior School French studies (though, as we have seen, it was all more or less transitional) was occasioned by a piece of unseen which we were translating in class. M. Cartel asked John Acton (the present Lord Acton and grandson of the historian) if he had ever heard of Charlemagne. "Yes, sir," was the reply, "relation of mine." This was greeted with the usual applause, but it was not until I was staying with the Actons years later that I discovered why the question had been answered in such a way. It was not a joke: it was demonstrably true.

Then something happened—I forget what—and M. Cartel handed us over to Mr. Wylie. With Mr. Wylie we had met our Waterloo: under him we finished our French in the Junior School, and to him again we came when we touched French later on at a higher level. He was one of the most conscientious men I have ever met, upright and fair and patient in the extreme. He was absolutely unsparing in his efforts to serve his subject, but he was at the same time—let it be admitted—uninspired. If it had not been for the respect which everyone felt for him, and for the perfect discipline which he maintained, I do not know that he would have been able to teach us much. But as it was, he taught us a great deal, and almost all of those who sat for exams did well. When a man has had the word "Thoroughness" engraved on the inside of his watch, you may expect the worst, and the only trouble about Mr. Wylie was that he would go over the same thing again and again until you would want to throw your head back and scream. One boy in fact, Louis Warren, did scream. He did precisely that: threw his head back and gave a yell as if in pain. Louis Warren was a sensitive boy with an original mind and a sense of humour. But it was not because he was original and funny that he screamed in Mr. Wylie's class: it was simply because he could not endure another minute.

In after years I met Mr. Wylie again, and more than ever I was able to appreciate his qualities. I admired his courtesy, his almost ceremonious formality, his clothes, his iron determination to see to a finish the thing in hand, and the courageous way in which he fought his increasing infirmities. I admired also his hitherto quite unsuspected sense of fun, and also his deep humility. But this was long afterwards, after he had retired from active life at Downside. We are moving ahead too fast, and must go back to investigate some other subjects in the same parallel.

With our German group we are once again in the world of high comedy. It is true that Herr Heronberger did not wear a red dressing-gown; nor did he, like the swordstick

man, look into the paper-cupboard before the class began
to see that there were no dark beauties spying on him from
the foolscap and chalk. But he belonged to the same tradition. In his inseparable velvet-collared blue greatcoat,
wearing always mittens and spats and muffler, Herr Heronberger looked like a drawing by Harry Rountree of an
owl. He spoke in a thin reedy voice like escaping gas,
and as one seldom heard what he said—even if one could
guess what language it was that he happened to be saying
it in—there was little chance of either keeping abreast of
the syllables or deriving much benefit in the way of pronunciation. For pupils this longsuffering man had before
him a shifting population numbering, according to what
counter-attractions there happened to be on any particular
day, from six to a dozen. I seem to recall a die-hard
nucleus, consisting of Harry Cryan, Alick Dru, the two
Sykes brothers,[1] the two Berington brothers, the two
Howard brothers and myself, which survived termly, and
even half-termly, changes in personnel. As in the French
form mentioned above masters came and went, so in
the German form it was the boys who came and went.
And I am not altogether surprised.

Herr Heronberger, like one or two others on the staff
at this time, had given up teaching some years before and
had returned to the rostrum only on account of the war
emergency and in order to fill a gap. How he escaped
being interned—or even being shot as a spy—I do not
know, for his nationality was unmistakable. The Heronbergers lived in rooms in Chilcompton from which they
emerged rarely into the light of day. It was alleged that,
apart from Herr Heronberger's sorties in the cause of our

[1] Christopher, the younger, introduced the names of several of our
Downside celebrities into one of his novels; both M. Cartel and Herr
Heronberger appear—but not, unfortunately, in character. About
Richard, the elder brother and present baronet, I hope to say something
later in these pages.

education, the couple sat behind drawn blinds all day in a temperature raised to blood-heat by a porcelain *Offen*, and that they drank beer at every meal from pictured tankards with lids. Certainly they moved, when at all, in great mystery, for one saw them together only on one day in the year—on the day of Prizegiving. On this annual occasion they would be seen advancing very slowly, and in all their finery, along the west drive from the direction of Chilcompton: she wearing a feather boa with velvet strings, he with festal tiepin and Wagnerian-looking rings. Below Frau Heronberger's purple toque (satin and velvet with aigrette erect) and above the feather boa, there would appear—as it were supporting the carefully dressed grey hair of the head—a horizontal sweep of blonde. (It was this golden tress which earned her the name of *die Lorelei*.) Her walk was ceremonial—for she raised her feet (button boots) delicately, as though treading on eiderdowns—and her complexion was of the palest wistaria. Seeing the two of them together, and lamenting the absence of a dachshund, one would marvel that a Somerset countryside should be the setting. At that time I had not yet been to Germany, but when in later years I visited Bonn and Heidelberg and the towns of the Rhine I could hardly believe that the places were new to me. I had been there before—in the Heronbergers. Especially did I feel this about Heidelbergian spring; because of the wistaria.

For geography, after the first fumbling about the earth's surface under the patient direction of Dom Paul, we were taken by Dom Roger Hudleston, author of several works of fiction and afterwards editor of Abbot Chapman's *Spiritual Letters*. In this we were well placed, for it seemed that most of the geographical discoveries, engineering enterprises and archæological ventures of modern times had been either initiated or integrally participated in by one or the other of his male relations. Eiffel Tower, Assuan

Dam, Forth Bridge: we had ringside seats. "Is it true, sir," asked John Phillips who stuttered, "that your uncle b-b-built the hanging gardens of babby-babby-Babylon, sir?"

My cousin, Christian van Zeller, who came to Downside in 1916 and who was three years my senior, said of Dom Roger that if only he prepared his classes and followed up his brilliant inspirations he would be far and away the ablest master at Downside. Whether or not this was true, it was a curious remark for a boy of thirteen to make. But then Christian was a curious boy. He deserves a paragraph to himself.

During the short time he was at school in England—he had been at St. Antony's, Eastbourne, before coming to Downside—he spent most of his time either reading or fighting. Possessed of a weak heart, and therefore too delicate to play games, do gym, go for runs, fence, bathe, he had more leisure than most of us in which to pursue his two main interests, so when his eyes were not closed as the result of combat he would be found poring over books in the library. He and I got on well, and the only thing I had against him was that his name on the lists caused me to be van Zeller Two. It was he who put me on to a number of authors who had escaped Mr. Carter, while I for my part introduced him to James Barrie, Kenneth Grahame, and Walter De la Mare. Particularly we shared an enthusiasm for Ian Hay, and on the occasions when I could persuade him to leave off fighting for a little while and come with me for a walk we used to recite whole passages of *A Knight on Wheels* and *The Safety Match* to each other from memory. In the holidays we went together to see *Tilly of Bloomsbury*, and afterwards wrote joint letters to Arthur Boucher and Ian Hay, saying how much we had enjoyed the adaptation. (I thought of this the other day when, as a guest at the Garrick Club, I sat next to the distinguished author of *The First Hundred Thousand*, *The Lighter Side of School Life*, *The Man's Man* and other fascinating books. I should have liked to ask whether he remembered receiving a letter from the cousins aged thirteen and ten.) Christian van Zeller left school early and died young. I suspect that he disobeyed his doctors' orders and had a few really good fights. I would willingly have remained van Zeller Two indefinitely.

There was also History Class. Most of the Junior School's history, and most of the Upper School's as well, was taught by Dom Lucius Graham. Dom Lucius has taken more classes at Downside than any other master, monk or layman, and is still adding to a record which surely nobody else will come within measurable distance of breaking. Whatever history knowledge I possess, I learned from him. And when today I am held up for a date or a fact, I either ask Father Lucius at tea or else borrow one of those glossy black books of notes with which every Gregorian for the past forty years is familiar.

This brings us from brain to muscle, for the only period in the timetable still to be accounted for is that which is allocated to physical training.[1] Gym was a particular feature of the Dom Leander régime, and no amount of ingenuity would enable those of us who belonged to the Phillips school (and who did not?) to substitute for it something else. So particular a feature was it that for a short time we had no less than three instructors directing it. And when I so much as record their names it will be clear at once that we are back again in the kingdom of the burlesque. Sergeants Popple, Willison, Bastable were all of them veterans of the South African War. Today I have sometimes to convince myself, by appealing to the authority of Father Lucius to whom Downside lore is a

[1] There was also Religious Instruction, but I am not proposing to comment on it.

living voice, that these three men really existed and were not merely the figments of my fiction-fed imagination. But always I am assured that not only did they exist but that they were frequently to be found in the same gymnasium, riding as it were the same box horse.

In 1914, that year of great changes, Sergeant Popple, who had helped with the school corps since its inception and who had done part-time service in the gymnasium, was seconded to the rifle-range where he presided with extreme danger to everyone within miles until he was too old to do anything else. (I am coming back to him in a minute.) The same year saw the arrival of Drill-Instructor Willison, but about this particular comedy figure history is not so clear: either he had been engaged to tide over the period of Popple's relaxing grip or he had come as personal friend, as *fidus Achates* in gymnastic matters, to Sergeant Bastable who was just then assuming complete control. Perhaps it was a little of both. But be this as it may, I know that it was under a triumvirate that my life as a physical trainee began.

The oldest was Popple, a wiry, root-like man, with thick grey hair which curled like my cousin Thérèsette's and with a face which, in the absence of teeth, folded up like a purse. He took us for shooting twice a week in the break. Nobody could have been more assiduous than he to preserve his range from accident, but not even the many red flags with which he decorated the confines of the Ballplace could prevent the marksmen on the mat from aiming wide of the target. Tommy Walmsley, I remember, on one occasion brought down a rook, and nearly always after shooting practice there would be groups of small boys digging out with pen-knives the lead which had lodged in the bark of the surrounding trees.

Sergeant Bastable, younger than Popple but far from spry, was tall, bald, walrus-moustached and better liked than the other man. There was something very winning about old Bastable with his boiled blue eyes and unashamed vest appearing on his rolled up sleeve, and though I was frequently reported by him I could not find it in my heart to bear a grudge. For one thing I sympathized with him for feeling the cold: he wore thick flannels, dark woollen socks, sweater and collar and tie, and in this costume he did his gym. I would have given much to be allowed to do the same. For us the dress was singlet and shorts.

Sergeant Willison was both men's junior by a number of years, and though I had less opportunity of observing him than I had in the case of the other two I received one quite clear impression of him—a little man in a brown suit (he made no concessions whatever to the accepted picture of the gymnast, even sticking to thick-soled boots where his two colleagues at least condescended to rubber shoes) popping up with startling suddenness here there and everywhere, and shouting over our heads "Am I right, Mr. Bastable?" To which Bastable, on his toes from the opposite side of the gym, would reply "Perfectly right, Mr. Willison." After a few words of command (or explanations or demonstrations) this jack-in-the-box performance would be repeated—both darting about until the courteous exchange rang out afresh. The couplet recalled the variety stage: the recurring catchword of a music-hall pair.

Each of these three men was a disciplinarian—not to say a martinet. Punctuality and silence were insisted on, though for gym offences we were punished with the tolley and not the cane: a distinction which is typical of Father Leander's mind. But even the tolley could hurt, and well I remember the ritual afterwards of being allowed by the Headmaster to put my stinging hands on the stone of his windowsill to cool. It was the only time when the rush of

HERR HERONBERGER

cold air from the open window was welcome to me. For obvious reasons the alleviation of the windowsill was confined to tolley punishments which were always on the hand.

The only person whom I remember to have circumvented the gym régime was a quiet unassuming boy called Andrew Wilson ("Willie Five," the youngest of a tribe) who successfully cut gym for over two years. The way he did it was this. When for medical reasons we were off gym, we had to present ourselves to the presiding instructor (or instructors), answer our names at the rollcall, and then take our places on a mat in the corner of the gym next to the hot-pipes. We did not have to change for this, and were allowed to bring non-work books to read during the forty minutes while our companions were doing "arms bend" and so on. Now after an experimental fortnight, Wilson, whose frail appearance was helped out by an expression of angelic innocence, decided that gym was not for him and that all he had to do was to sit on the mat and answer his name to the rollcall each day. For some reason, perhaps because he was a new boy and looked pathetic, his off-gym chit was not demanded, and in the course of his two years he read John Buchan's war books one after another as they came out. He used to join us in the changing room while we were flinging on our clothes before the bell went for the next class, and tell us how Richard Hannay was getting on. I forget how Willie Five was finally caught, but I know that he made a lot of money out of his achievement because all our speculations as to how long he would be able to keep it up were defeated. I am told that Willie Five, who is now a big business man in the Argentine, still looks delicate and innocent. That he was as strong as a horse when I knew him was proved by his knocking an older and bigger boy into pulp behind the Ballplace.

The accepted site for fighting was behind the Ballplace, a locality much frequented by my cousin Christian. In my first term I witnessed some magnificent fights there, but by the time I was half way up the school the custom seemed to have died out. On a summer evening in the early days it was like a scene out of *Rodney Stone*. Boys are extraordinarily true to type, especially in the primitive sports and pastimes, and I can hardly believe that in this sophisticated age they no longer take off their coats and use bare fists. Do they settle their disputes only in the regularized ring—or, worse still, by negotiation? Is there not a circle of noisy backers any more—shouting the odds and giving incoherent pieces of advice? If not, then again I am glad that I was born in time to crouch breathless among an admiring throng, and to have bloodstains pointed out to me which represented even more historic encounters than those which it had been my privilege to watch.

But to get back for a moment, to the gym. When the Inspectors—that august body of whom all school personnel live in dread—visited Downside, they were amazed at the level of smartness and general proficiency reached in the matter of drill, but were disappointed, apparently, at the neglect of apparatus. Popple was either on his range or dead by this time, and Willison had left us, so it was Bastable who had to meet the findings contained in the Inspectors' report. He met them as he had met the bullets on Majuba Hill. Alas, the fact that we were better than any other school at raising our heels and firming our hips made little difference: he had been slapped with a gym-shoe and he knew it. The personal reflexion he was big enough to take in his stride: it was the introduction of new method which he minded. The spring-board, the medicine ball, the weighted rope for round-the-clock jumping, were all to him concessions and not of the real thing. To Sergeant Bastable the only apparatus which was allowable was one or other of a short list: horse, wallbar, beam. Everything else was almost indecent. And even the beam, since the day when his teeth had slipped to the floor while he was demonstrating a particularly tricky exercise, was not much favoured. The Inspector's report meant (he told us) that before long there would be games in gym, and that the winners of the shield would be more often circus-tricksters than gymnasts. But the gift of prophecy is no consolation to a disillusioned man, and with the Inspector's report iron had entered into Mr. Bastable's soul. We knew that he would not be with us much longer.

When the day came for Sergeant Bastable's presentation and farewell speech, I was in the front row so I know all about it. He spoke shortly, and though the teeth were seen to slip for an instant every now and then they were gulped back into position without difficulty. Like a retiring religious leader he warned us about the abuses which were creeping in, and pronounced a doom upon the innovators. With a parting benediction, or something very like it, he sat down. The ovation which he received on this occasion was sincere and deserved: the school genuinely liked its Bastable—which is pronounced, incidentally, with the broad "a," *Barstable*, and not as Mr. Willison had done, giving it only a short flick, as in "elastic."

At Popple's presentation I was also present, but this was earlier and, though he too spoke, I do not remember the occasion. But in any case nobody could have followed a word, because even if the purse of his face opened wide enough, Popple was not golden tongued: sentences came out haltingly, and without ring or much meaning.

It is difficult in this less rigid age when gym is done out of doors, when acrobatics and round games are replacing the knees-bend of thirty years ago, to imagine the gym-

nasium as it was for us at Downside during the First
World War. I for one am glad to know, on the evidence
of the Inspectors' report, that such an advanced institution
as ours—and it was considered if anything *too* progressive
at that time—was at least in this behind the times. It is
comforting at this distance to reflect that, while the rest
of the world rolled on, we were kept strictly in line with
Kimberley and Omdurman. Perhaps this is why Father
Leander, an ardent progressive in other ways, made such
a feature of our already obsolete method: he disliked
circus-tricks. But whether he did or not, I know that when
I last had to sit through an inter-house gym competition
(which is the most boring thing in the world) I sighed for
the Bastable lily-neck sweater and pale green tie, for
the Popple mumble of disapproval, for the Willison boots.
"Am I right, Mr. Bastable? Am I right, Mr. Willison?"
Yes, of course you are—perfectly right, my dear sirs,
perfectly.

VI

During the winter of 1915, my second winter in England,
I got pneumonia, and though this was not of course as
bad as the chilblains of the year before, I was out of
school life for quite a time. Father Leander gave me the
Last Sacraments, and a notice was put on the board asking for prayers. Notices had a way of staying on the
Headmaster's board for a long time, and I was surprised to
find, when I returned to school after six months' absence,
that it had been taken down. Some of the notices stayed
up for so long that the typed lines faded completely,
and only the signature in ink remained. In a list of
school rules which we had sometimes to learn by heart as
a punishment, occurred a clause forbidding boys "to roll
or play in the long grass outside the Petre Library,"
but as the Petre Library then looked out onto the un-

grassed quadrangle—and had done so since living memory —the prohibition was presumed to belong to an earlier period. ("Of course this was all green fields when I arrived," Bernard Lane was heard to say when showing some visitors through a part of the building which had been standing for at least half a century.)

During the months when I was away in Ireland convalescing after pneumonia, I was supposed to be keeping up with my form subjects by private study. This was the time that I sat at the feet of the Miss Ford described in another book. It was now also that my aunt Yolande and I played our literary games, greatly to the development of my general culture.

In buses, tubes, and public gardens we elaborated the Carter practice of spotting characters in fiction, awarding marks for aptness and accuracy, imposing penalties for not knowing the references or for not being able to give a name to someone who suggested an obvious person to the mind of the other player. For instance "That soldier is somebody whom every schoolboy knows. Who is he?" If the other player answers promptly "Mulvaney" and is right, it is his turn to ask. If he says "I don't know, but I challenge you" and the other person has not got anyone particular in mind, he scores. It is thus to the advantage of the questioner to pick on some clear-cut character from some rather difficult author. We played this game a lot. In railway stations, during those war years, we found more Mulvaneys, Learoyds, and Ortherises than we needed, but there were still some A. J. Raffleses, Mr. Pollys, and young Lord Stranleighs about.

For a while the game was extended from authors to artists, and we kept our eyes open for Arthur Belcher charladies, Daumier lawyers, Bellini children, Memling nuns, Shepherdson Etonians, and so on. But this was not such a success because Yolande does not draw and I was more or less in the profession.

Indoors we played an even better game. One of us would have to read aloud from a book which was held under the table so that its cover could not be seen, and the other would have to guess the author. It would have to be a book which we had not read to each other before, so the game was one which depended entirely on the recognition of style. The only difficulty about playing it was that unless we were in a house with a good library we soon ran out of new books to experiment on. We found that Dickens could usually be recognized after about five lines. Chesterton next with perhaps eight, and then came a mixed bag consisting of George Birmingham, Conrad, Jeffrey Farnol, Bret Harte, A. E. W. Mason, and Robert Hichens. Vachell was for ever getting mixed up with E. F. Benson, but these two belonged to a somewhat later period.

As may be guessed, this was a phase of considerable literary interest. Yolande used to read to me for hours on end. I could never have enough of it, and she never appeared to mind. Indeed she assures me now that she enjoyed it. I came to know her techniques so well—and to know also, I hope, the style of the author whom she happened to be reading—that I could tell at once when she was skipping or soft-pedalling the text. Such liberties were heavily taxed. She herself cared so much more for style than for intricacy of plot that some of my favourite authors bored her, and I had to read about Sherlock Holmes and the Scarlet Pimpernel on my own. Though there were gaps in our joint interest, and I do not think that she ever went all the way with Wilson Five and me about Buchan's inspired war stories, Yolande certainly gave me an appreciation for the sheer music of words. And this was ample compensation. Our tastes today run almost parallel:

Maurice Baring, Osbert Sitwell, Harold Nicolson, Max Beerbohm. But this is to go on too far ahead, and also she reads more French than I do.

If it should be thought odd that a boy of eleven or so was absorbing a literature of such variety and quantity, it must be remembered that my aunt Yolande, who more than anyone was responsible for my reading, came out of a book-lined background. All her life she had been associated with letters. Her mother wrote books and plays, and contributed monthly articles to the social-cultural columns of *The New York Sun*.[1] Writers, musicians and actors were constantly coming to the van de Veldes' house. First at Upper Hamilton Terrace and then at Lancaster Gate my grandmother gave large parties to which the lions of the period came and at which other lions, engaged for the purpose, performed. Bret Harte, who came to live with the family for a time, brought in his train such well known figures as Oscar Wilde and the famous American editor, Arthur Brisbane. Brisbane is chiefly remembered by Yolande as having a magnificent profile and as having a great love, apparently, for salted almonds. Saying hardly a word to his neighbour he ate salted almonds right through a dinner at which Herbert von Bismarck (son of the Chancellor), the Duke of St. Albans, and the great J. L. Toole were present. Other visitors to my grandmother's house were Jerome K. Jerome (who was present at my parents' wedding and who was so shy that he had to be dragged away from his corner to shake hands with the bride and bridegroom), the Bertons (who were acting with Sara Bernhardt), W. R. H. Trowbridge, and the romantic composer, Tosti. The biggest party of all was given at Lancaster Gate, and for this the services of Maurice Farkoa were engaged.

[1] For this, at the editor's request, my grandmother resumed her title, signing the articles "Comtesse Hydeline."

Opening one onto another, the three drawingrooms with their Gobelin tapestries, Louis XIV furniture and heavy red damask curtains were filled with guests. But all this was before my time.

I have a letter from Bret Harte in Scotland to Yolande in London saying that "poor Monique, whom we have just driven over to see, has sustained a heavy cold through having unwisely sat too close to an open gooseberry tart." All except Yolande were in Scotland for the first night of *The Babes*. The Monique of this letter is my mother.

So if at the age of twelve I was seeing two plays a week, and at the age of sixteen reading a book a day, it was because plays and books were about the only things that people talked about at home. When my father was present it was different, because he talked mostly about sport, but my father was serving in the army during the years of which I write. Only once during the war did I see him on leave in England, and except for his telling me on this occasion that whenever I visited a bank I was to take off my hat—since it was not like visiting a shop but like calling on one's solicitor—I remember little of his time in England.[1]

VII

But to return to the break in my school career which was caused by my getting ill. I formed during that time a hero-worship affection for Rupert, the younger son of two of my mother's best friends, Lou and Dunstan Cham-

---

[1] My father was much given to enunciating rules of behaviour. Once I showed surprise at his pressing a glass of wine on a certain piano-tuner who used to come every now and then to the house in Alexandria. "You always give wine to piano-tuners," he explained, "just as they are getting ready to go. And you talk to them about pianos. They expect you to talk about pianos. But if really important people come to the house—prime ministers for instance—you give them sherry when they *arrive*. And you do not talk to them about politics. They dislike it and it confuses them."

berlain. Rupert Chamberlain had just left Harrow and was doing his training before going out to France. Young people, as Miss Tennyson Jesse says, "cannot exist for long in an emotional vacuum, and so have to attach themselves to someone or something": nobody more suitable could have come my way, and I attached myself accordingly. I had seen enough of the loud-voiced heroes who commanded the distant admiration of my contemporaries, and Rupert's quiet manner and slow movements claimed my allegiance absolutely. To me he stood as a symbol of chivalry, goodness, restraint. Whether in his urban clothes and hard hat or in the blue mess uniform which he wore in the evenings, Rupert had a hushing effect upon me that was all to the good. Having shown, after a year or so at school, a tendency to rowdiness, my one wish now was to be like Rupert in all things. Especially did I want to cultivate the same air of quiet distinction. But this refinement must have eluded me, for I was constantly being corrected for my heavy-footed behaviour and my laugh. When in London I spent a good deal of time at the Chamberlains' flat, and Rupert used to take me to theatres. One night at a dinner party, Rupert's father asked me what I proposed to do after leaving school. "Join the Scots Guards like Rupert," I answered at once. "You aren't the sort altogether," said Rupert in his smooth Brook Street voice which was always in a lower key than anyone else's and which was yet not in the least sepulchral, "they would say you talked too much."

A year or two later, also in London, I saw Rupert on his last leave. Leaning against a window-frame in the flat while the others were dressing for dinner, Rupert, who had dressed earlier on purpose, gave me advice about public school life and getting older generally. He was not in the smallest degree pompous, as so many would have been, and there was no false sentiment. The standard he demanded was high, but it was all perfectly sane and un-dramatic. He was playing with the tassel of a curtain as he spoke, and he kept slapping it across his knee. I could see the shape of his head and figure, dark against the evening light outside. It must have been in a summer holidays. I felt, as I suppose one must always feel on these occasions, that Rupert was going out to be killed. Presumably, though he was far too reticent about himself to say so, he felt this too or he would not have talked to me as he had. Anyway Rupert Chamberlain did not come back from France, and I mourned him. I am glad that my last memory of him should be so clear; and that my gratitude, as romantic now as it was then, should remain so unforced. I see still the polished buttons, the line of the collar against the neck, the broad red stripe from thigh to wellington, the rhythmic movement of the hand. I know that on that occasion anyway I did not talk too much.

Other heroes of this time there were, but none quite like Rupert. Various heads of the school I looked up to, waiting for the far off day when I too might be able to conduct a house corps practice in flannels, first fifteen blazer, old fashioned pumps. Such a day never dawned for me in actual fact, but in the meantime I was quite content to admire R. R. Stokes for whom it had. With personality head and shoulders above anyone else of his year, Dick Stokes seemed to me the embodiment of masculine perfection. Energy came out from him in waves as if he were an advertisement: he was electric, and you could not be in the school hall for two minutes without knowing it if he was there. If ever there was the all-round athlete and magazine-cover Head of the School it was he. What I liked particularly was to see him serve at Benediction after a spectacular performance on the rugger field or when he had made a rollicking fifty in record time against good club bowling. After he left he frequently came down to the school, and as he was not above associating with Father Austin's rabble of small boys there were noisy games of "stick hockey" on the old asphalt tennis courts. He and another big man, Willie Jeffries (a colonel and a D.S.O. in the Second War) once came off the field carrying between them the whole opposing side on their shoulders. We had tried sitting on our guests, but it was no use. Dick Stokes became a major in an absurdly short time, and also won a bar to his early M.C. That he should have become a Cabinet Minister later on must cause no surprise to those who were small boys when he played hockey with them on the asphalt tennis courts: nor can it surprise them to see that he still cannot be sat upon by his fellow players.

My return to school after that six months which is delaying the course of this record meant homesickness all over again, and I sobbed in the train from Waterloo to Templecombe. In the carriage was Father Aidan Trafford, who at that time had not yet taught me, and who from all accounts was an alarming person. But no amount of this kind of alarm could have stemmed my flow of tears, and I wept regardless. As it turned out of course, Father Aidan could not have been nicer—even when a cherished stick of mine which I had cut for myself from a hedge, which I had peeled and sandpapered and oiled and nourished in my bosom, fell out onto the line just outside Basingstoke and was lost beyond recovery.

But it was the summer term I was coming back to, so nothing could be too bad. In fact, it is difficult now to think of anything which could be so good. The whole of Downside life appears to me today, and even after a fashion seemed to me then, to converge as in the beam of a magnifying glass under the sun upon the brilliant glaring point of the summer term. Whichever way I hold the magnifying glass in my attempt to focus on the past, I come back every time, whether thinking of the Junior or Middle or Upper School, to the concentration of the heatwave Downside rather than to the more spread-out rugger and chilblain terms of winter.

To some boys cricket may be a bore. It was not a bore to me. True, it meant only the briefest periods at the wicket as against long hours of fielding, long hours of scoring, of lying in the sun talking and chewing grass. But it also meant not having a care in the world, not having to rush, not having to be brave as in rugger, not having to go for runs. On the Junior School cricket field I came across George Bellord, who among all my Downside contemporaries is the one I see most of now, and Jimmy Reynolds, who used to bowl with enormous solemnity and vigour. *Le style c'est l'homme* was very true of Jimmy at this period. As it was with his bowling, so it was also with his swimming: despite the polish and highly professional wrist-work, the ball never seemed to reach the end of the pitch and the swimmer never budged an inch. All this was taken very seriously, and not until George Bellord, Tristram Hillier and I broke down his earnestness did James Reynolds reveal himself as a person. Had we not providentially intervened, the converse of the tag would have been equally true—*l'homme c'est le style*.

The cricket routine for the Junior School was as follows. No sooner had Dom Austin given the signal for "game over" than players all over the expanse of grass who had been more or less idle for two hours would jump about and show surprising activity. The contrast would be most marked. Boys pulled up stumps, ripped off pads, dashed into one or other of the huts which acted as pavilions, threw down their impedimenta in a heap, and started running through the patchwork of sunshine and shadow down the Green Lane. This was called, and rightly, earning a bathe. At the bottom of the Green Lane there would be a delay for the slower runners while the faster ones pressed through the Five Pins. (The Five Pins was the name given to the three stakes which barred the way to bicycles.) Here the slower drew breath before the last lap across the lawn, their chests thumping and beads of sweat trickling down their cheeks from the bands of their white felt cricket hats. The dust of the Green Lane was like glucose, and it powdered not only the grass and hedges at the side of the road but one's chest and arms as well. Once through the gap onto the grass where the going was easier, one plunged down the slope under the Conker Tree to the Junior School Quadrangle. (The Quadrangle was the name given to the unenclosed space which stretched from its single side, the line of buildings, to the Ballplace.) Then there was a dash through the boot-hole to the wash-house to pick up one's towel, and out again from the almost blinding darkness of indoors to the almost blinding glare outside. The boot-hole, through which one scraped and squeaked on one's spiked cricket boots, it need scarcely be said, not a "hole" at all but more like an overflow dayroom.

As fixed as the stars in their courses were the rites preceding the Junior School bathe. On a certain tongue of grass shirts, socks, boots and blazers were left, and one hopped, barefoot and clad only in one's trousers and towel, across the intervening grit until another tongue of grass was reached. Here one either sank gasping to the ground and waited for Father Austin's arrival or else flicked one's neighbour with a towel. There was always a delay, and someone—usually a boy called Clarke whose mother was a militant suffragette—always said "I told you we needn't hurry." During the invariable wait, which was for Father Austin's permission to go up to the pond and partly for the Upper School to finish their bathe, the more vocal among the small boys would start up the cry "May we go *up*, sir?" There was a special notation for this chant, and "*up*ser" would be screamed in a high treble by everybody at once. At the first blast of Father Austin's whistle, a hundred and forty feet would patter like muffins in a great rush over the asphalt towards the Petre. Towels fluttered and billowed from shoulders, and everyone would be yelling. It never varied.

These were the days of open-air bathing. As soon as the covered pond was built the ceremonial was dropped, and few went near the Petre. When I first knew it, the Petre was hidden by a thicker forest than it is now, and there were cubicles with striped curtains for dressing in. When the partitions of these cubicles were knocked down (in 1915) the Gothic exterior of the original structure was preserved, and it still looks, as Monsignor Knox once observed, like a local Swiss railway station. For a long time I kept a piece of discarded curtain: I felt that it represented the passing of an epoch. In one of our many moves during the holidays I must have lost the strip of faded calico, because when I wanted to decorate my room with it later on I could not find it.

Occasionally we were allowed up to the pond in time to watch the last few minutes of the Upper School bathe. This was a treat because some of the trick diving was worth seeing. Particularly expert were Geoffrey Maclachlan and Wilfrid Turnbull, the latter leaping into the air from the top board with what appeared to be reckless abandon but which was in fact, as I knew from my training under Mr. Martin, consummate skill. Each year the swallow dive was won by Wilfrid Turnbull, and in 1917 the competition was held up for a quarter of an hour because a saw had to be sent for to remove an offending projection on the hand-rail of the top board. The hand-rail had never offended before, but Wilfrid Turnbull, then a most important person in the school, decided that it was putting him off, so while the fag was on his errand we stood about in the sun and marvelled at the magnificence of school prefects. And now when I look up at that truncated hand-rail, I recall the suspended competition and the yellow sawdust blowing down over the surface of the water . . . and if anybody happens to be with me I doubtless become a great bore about it.

Another 1917 memory (though this is keeping us a year ahead and will have to be corrected in a subsequent paragraph), and one which is again connected with the Petre and Wilfrid Turnbull, is the Life-Saving Test. Each July a man used to come out from Bath to judge whether or not those boys who were "taking" life-saving could be awarded a diploma. The whole thing lasted only one afternoon, and the signed certificates which one got for rescuing the two wastepaper baskets tied together were shown off with pride to those who did not "do" life-saving. Since the wastepaper baskets were packed with newspaper and dumb-bells, it was no easy matter to lift them from the bottom of the pond—though what relation they bore to the drowning body I do not know—and one swam to the side with bursting lungs. So perhaps, after all, the certificates were deserved. Anyway such was the procedure. The particular test of which I write, however, introduced variations.

The professional from Bath was due to start judging the life-savers, numbering about a dozen and including Lane and me, at two o'clock. There we were with our towels round us, sitting in the sun. As the man had not arrived by a quarter to three, Wilfrid Turnbull, who was in charge of the party, dressed and went to look for him. Some forty minutes later the two of them appeared round the bend of rocks and trees—Turnbull obviously labouring under a great strain and the life-saving instructor wearing a top hat, frock coat, and black gloves. He had just been to a funeral. Round his top hat was a broad band of crêpe. We all got up from the hot step on which we had been sitting, and bowed. Turnbull, reverently lowering the gentleman's bag which he had been carrying for him and which contained his bathing things, explained to us the reason for the delay and told us that in order to save time, since it was now getting late, our efforts in the water would be judged hastily from dry land. The judge produced a large book from his bag, put on a pair of spectacles, sat as far as he decently could from the edge of the bath, and we plunged in with our wastepaper baskets. It was the only year that I failed my test.

The reason to which I attributed my inability to rescue the 1917 dumb-bells from drowning was a whispered remark of Lane's. "He only wants a beard," said Lane as I was bending to dive, "and he would be one of President Kruger's staff." As I came up spluttering, I heard him add "or even Oom Paul himself."

The business of the afternoon was so soon dispatched that we pleaded for a demonstration from the judge before the party broke up. "Oh yes, sir, do . . . just a short exhibition, sir, it won't take a minute, sir . . . we had one last year, sir, and the year before . . . you look as if you could do it beautifully, sir." The poor man was most unwilling, but as we were almost taking his coat off for him by this time he allowed himself to be persuaded. But even now there were difficulties: he refused to undress in the open, and the cubicles had been done away with . . . he would have to be driven to the station because he had a train to catch, etc. etc. "That's all right, sir, we'll arrange everything," and we propelled him towards a sheltered recess behind the diving boards where we held up towels by way of a screen at the entrance. Modesty received its due, and after a little while our judge came

out in a sagging black bathing suit which reached below
the knee and which buttoned high on the chest against
the throat. He looked, with his heavy black moustache
drooping over the line of his mouth, very sad. But it was
too late to do anything about that now, and "come along,
sir," was the encouragement he received, "you will love
it, sir, once you are in." Walking firmly, but with his
eyes half closed against the sun, he reached the edge of
the bath. "Gentlemen," he said, "the *plonje*." Where-
upon he gripped his nose firmly with the right hand,
dropped into the water feet first, rose slowly to the surface,
and swam for the steps. There was a pause, and then
everybody politely clapped.

So ended, with water dripping from the black moustache, and the bathing suit flapping against his legs, the
instructor's visit to Downside in 1917. It marks, among
other things, the last time I ever saw crêpe round a top hat.

Further delights of the summer term included tennis,
haymaking, "party-days," watching First Eleven matches,
and going to bed later. Tennis was possible only on Sunday mornings and in the evenings—if one was lucky
enough to get a court. There is nothing to say about tennis,
except that though I tried valiantly to be good at it so
as to be able to keep up with Maurice Turnbull, who was
passing me on the ladder of seniority, I was very bad at it
and so ceased to compete.

Haymaking was war work, affecting only my own generation of Junior School boys. We must have made faulty
stacks, because it was only in 1915 and 1916 that our
services were needed. In 1915 I had measles and was thus
able to spend most of the quarantine period in the fields,
helping the German prisoners who had been lent from a
camp nearby. Knowing their language I was employed
as an interpreter, which suited me down to the ground.
Cider was provided for prisoners and measle cases alike,

the idea being that it prevented hay fever. It must have worked, for we stacked a lot of hay and there was not a sneeze from any of us.

Party-days were special occasions on which even the youngest of us were allowed out on bicycles, were allowed to eat as much as we liked, and were not bound to change into black regulation suits for supper. We made up our own parties, and, provided we had a master to take us, we were free for the whole day. This meant that for weeks beforehand there would be discussion of the relative merits of different foods, different masters, and different places to go to. It is proof of the law of distribution that not every party wanted the same master or the same place to go to. They all wanted much the same foods, but this did not matter because they could order their own from Bath. Party-days could be the greatest fun, even in the rain. It was my practice to send, in the continental manner, postcards from every village we visited, and while going through my mother's correspondence after her death I came upon some quite hideous views of the West Country. We in Somerset do not make the most of our Farrington Gurneys and our Temple Clouds. All that sort of thing is done better abroad.

Another notable summer activity was Upper School cricket: from a place apart we studied the leviathans at play. This was before the present pavilion commanded the field, and when even the field itself was smaller. Few smells are to me more emotionally gratifying than those of bat-oil, cut grass, and wet blanco. Few sounds so charged with nostalgic content as the swish of a ball along a net, the klonking of a giant roller on a pitch, and the double smack of caught slip.

During my first two summers at Downside I was able to see some famous cricketers: C. W. Wright, L. C. H. Palairet (who was considered the better bat of the two brothers, though R. C. N. lacked nothing in the way of grace), Lord Hawke, Audley Miller (the Wiltshire captain) and a number of others. We always hoped that C. B. Fry would be among the M.C.C. team one year, but I do not remember that he ever came. The most spectacular catch I ever saw on any ground was when Audley Miller, having hit two sixes into the sunken road and one over the Green Lane, sent up a ball into the sky which had time to summon people from inside the pavilion to watch its flight. It seemed to hang in the air and say "Now look at me." When Theo Turner, who like most of the home team was fielding on the boundary, was seen to edge along the line of the bank, it was realized by the spectators that it might not be a six after all. By the time Theo Turner had got into position under the ball most people had stood up to see what was going to happen, and the batsmen were not bothering to run. The ball must have swayed in the last dozen yards or so of its course because when Turner caught it he did so with his right hand extended at full arm's length. A great whack of applause greeted the feat, and the person who made most noise was Miller himself on the way back to the pavilion. He was delighted, and kept slapping his pads saying "Well I'm damned." This was in 1918.

Another triumph of Turner's, but in another field altogether and belonging to an earlier date, was when he was called out of the ranks at a General Inspection. Though I cannot claim to have witnessed the incident, there is good enough authority for its truth. Apparently the Brigadier who had been sent down by the War Office to inspect the O.T.C. (as it was then) had said in his concluding speech that all members of a school contingent should follow the course of the war. "You, for instance," he roared, "you with the bored expression. What do you know about the war? Come out here and tell the platoon where the line of fighting is in France at the present moment." Private Turner (who is now a K.C.) stepped forward smartly and recited a list of names, thirteen of them and each correctly pronounced. The Brigadier, unlike Miller, showed no delight at being caught.

During unusually hot weather it was the practice of masters to take their classes out onto the lawn, where, in the shade of a tree, the boys would study the habits of insect life while the master discoursed on French or whatever the subject might be. This pleasant custom was eventually abolished—some boys having decided to follow the class, with cigarettes, from the branches of a sycamore—but for a time even Mr. Wylie's clipped and cultured diction could be heard coming over the grass. Herr Heronberger too was prevailed upon, if a state of heatwave had definitely been declared, to take to the open. Blinking nervously at the brazen sky through his spectacles, he would wrap himself tightly in his blue overcoat, put up the velvet collar, draw woollen gloves over his rings, select a lozenge for his throat, and move imperially towards the stump of a certain tree which his class had prepared for him with a cushion. Here for forty minutes Herr Heronberger would expound huskily in his steam-kettle voice, and nobody would hear a word. "Let's go in," Richard Sykes would say at intervals, "I hate fresh air." For this period in the open, Richard would be lying flat on his back with a white hat over his face. If Herr Heronberger asked him a question, he pretended to be asleep and the matter would be dropped. "H'sh, sir, not so loud, sir," the others would say—of Heronberger's whisper—"or you'll wake him." The bees would buzz, an occasional petal would flutter to the ground, and in the far-off distance there would be the working of the mine.

In these all too brief interludes of extreme heat, not

only was the whistle for going to bed blown later but there were pyjama-bathes after prayers. These differed from the ordinary bathes in that they were conducted in complete silence. Also, of course, they were icy. One's body was still stinging when one got into bed. Pyjama-bathes were voluntary. And since it was considered soft to take a dressing-gown, the flock of boys running up to the Petre looked like a flower bed on the move.

VIII

The winter of 1916-17 was more severe than the one before, and I got ill again. This time I did not go home, but stopped on and on in the Old House while other occupants of the same room came and went. I did not mind this in the least; in fact I rather liked it. I read all Robert Hugh Benson's historical novels, and then started on the modern ones which I finished during the Christmas holidays. At one stage, when the large sickroom was full, I was deputed by my fellow patients to tell stories after cocoa and biscuits at night. It was generously supposed that I was making up the stories as I went along, whereas in fact I was telling the horror stories of Edgar Allan Poe. Fortunately no one had read Edgar Allan Poe, and more fortunately still the epidemic lasted only a week: had I relied upon my own imagination I must surely have been discovered.

A fleeting patient to the Old House at this time was Maurice Turnbull, whom more than anyone else in the school I was anxious to impress. Nearly two years my junior, Maurice was in everything else my senior, and though I finally managed to play in the First for rugger and cricket—without which I could not have belonged to his circle—I have no illusions about what he thought of my prowess. But here, in the Old House, I was (heaven forgive me the phrase) batting on my own wicket. I could draw, I could recite, I could tell—albeit other people's—stories. But even so I do not know that I made much impression on Maurice, and when I got back to school I went for long runs and played rugger as hard as I possibly could. In after years when games fell into perspective—even for Maurice Turnbull who played for Cambridge and then for England—we came to understand one another so well that there was no striving, on either side, to impress. Maurice Turnbull served my first Mass when I was ordained in 1930, and in 1939 he asked me to perform the ceremony at his wedding. When he was killed during the last months of the war I was in the middle of a letter to him. Had I foreseen all this, I should have spared him, and myself as well, a good deal of trouble in the early days.

The Old House was presided over by the Matron, Miss Poynter ("Maggie"), who combined strictness and humanity in exactly the right proportions for such a job as hers. When I was a new boy and homesick she used to invite me to her room while she was having breakfast; when I was more settled and throwing pillows about, she used to send me off to the Headmaster to be beaten. Her shrewdness in detecting false motives for seeking admission to the Old House was proverbial. And she was perfectly ready to take risks: she sent one boy back to school whose temperature registered a hundred and one—and rightly, for he had a method of his own by which he sent it up. Working with Maggie Poynter was Dr. Pollard, a ginger-moustached physician of the old school. As a young man he had ridden round his practice on a horse. "Keep away from doctors, my boy," he told me when I had broken my arm doing what was called a fish-dive in the gym, "unless you can't cure yourself." An unprofessional piece of advice which I have endeavoured to follow since. He grew strawberries in his garden at Midsomer Norton, and allowed me to exercise his pony.

On account of the frozen ground there were no games during the Lent term of 1917, which meant that boxing and skating supplied. The gym was in constant demand, and everyone was using everyone else's bicycle. For boxing, we of the Junior School had Dom Rupert Brace-Hall to teach us; for skating, as will be seen, we made our own arrangements.

Having watched some truly monumental fights between Upper School heavyweights, I threw myself with zest into ring business. Dom Rupert, who had boxed for Downside in the Public Schools Contest as a boy, fired my enthusiasm and I practised nightly. So did Jimmy Reynolds. But for one reason or another I did not keep it up. Whether I was discouraged by Jimmy's superior footwork—fortunately he seldom hit me with his glove— or whether I felt that in taking up boxing I was playing too much into my father's hands, I do not now remember. Certainly my father was very keen, and whatever my father was very keen about I showed a tendency to drop. How often am I not reminded of the landlady in one of Dame Ethel Smyth's operas—who confesses in song: "Suppose you mean to do a given thing, let someone come and say it should be done . . . and suddenly you'd rather die than do it." I fear my boxing may have been a case in point.

But Jimmy boxed on. Eyebrows meeting over a piercing stare of concentration, lips tight over clenched teeth, elbows sailing like the wings of a seagull, Jimmy boxed on. That he never did the least damage was sheer delight to George Bellord and me, but he was still, at this boxing period, filled with the seriousness of his every undertaking. At what precise moment it was that he saw the light I do not know, but we are considering here a time when he could still say, in a voice shaking with passion and with tears not far from those fine eyes, "No, no, it's simply not *true* that in the holidays I wear long pants."

When, quite early in the term, it was decided to flood the tennis-courts and have our skating outside our windows instead of having to go to Emborough for it, we all wrote home for skates—to take to Emborough. Emborough, or "Sir John's," is a large lake about four miles distant from the school, and if one possesses a bicycle one can skate there on a "short afternoon" and be back in time for class. But one never possesses a bicycle: one's own has always gone on ahead with someone else up.

In 1917, skaters who had not provided themselves with bicycles, were conveyed to and from Sir John's by horse brake. Mr. Fry's brakes were related, by not so many removes, to the open tumbrils of an earlier page in history. Lane and I used to play Tale-of-Two-Cities in them on the way to the station before going home. (It was hardly an appropriate moment, immediately before the holidays, but on the return journey some weeks later we were not in the mood for hilarious play. *The Tale of Two Cities*, incidentally, was the only one of Dickens's books which we did not like: "The girl ought never to have married that ass Darnay," said Lane, "it stays in your mind the whole time and spoils the whole thing.") For the skating journey we did not have to wear the kind of clothes which we wore for going home, and instead of the school cap or flat "boater" we either wore mufflers round our heads or else went bareheaded. It gives me a feeling of great and gratifying age when I remember the screech of the metal against the wheel of our tumbril as we slowed down on the hill at Naish's Cross and by the railway bridge—and then the jerk forward as the pressure was released.

One of the most satisfactory noises to hear for the first time is that made by several hundred people gliding swiftly on steel over the surface of frozen water. It is a more resonant roar than traffic in a city. Also more personal. If skates had tongues they could make a very frightening mob.

Small boys had to behave on the ice, or they were sat upon by big ones. Knowing less than nothing about skating, I received my tuition eagerly but in a hard school. It was clear to me on my first day of trial that if I was to enjoy myself and make any headway at all I should have to get a better pair of skates than those which I was using. John Phillips, who as may be judged from a previous reference had anticipated the Black Market by a matter of some twenty-five years, was emphatic when he gave me my pair of skates in exchange for a microscope that the old-fashioned strap-on kind were really better, anyway to begin on, than any other. Twenty minutes on the ice convinced me that he had lied.

At the suggestion of a well-informed boy (Harry Ellis, whom I later came to know and like) I abandoned my intention of searching out John to tell him what I thought of his skates, and instead was persuaded to visit a Mrs. Gamble whose grocery shop stood at the top of the hill. "Old mother Gumboil sells everything," I was told, "she'll have the latest thing in skates." Taking with me the strap-on pair in case I might be able to effect a part-exchange, since I had not been in the Junior School for nearly two and a half years for nothing, I went to call on Mrs. Gamble. Gamble seemed an improbable name to me—as improbable as Popple—and that I should be able to get skates off Mrs. Gamble seemed more improbable still. But within twenty minutes I was coming down the hill again with a perfect pair which shone in the wintry sunlight. How these modern-looking blades had come to be among the potted meat, button-hooks, balls of string, corsets, biscuit tins and dusty onions is still a mystery to me, but it did not surprise anyone at the time. To those who knew their Gumboil it was the obvious thing.

Today the little shop is, and perhaps was then though I did not notice it, a post office. In its dark interior, surrounded by every sort of household necessity, sat Mrs. Gamble. One thought at once of the shop and the knitting sheep in *Through the Looking-Glass*. Mrs. Gamble is now dead, but she must have been a personality in her time because her Dickensian name (becoming in Somersetshire "Muthur Gumble") was widely known in the district, and always associated with being able to give you anything you wanted over the counter at a moment's notice. "Run over to the Gumboil's and get a crane" was the sort of remark which was made.

Skating at Sir John's that year went on well into March. It became the routine thing, and it was difficult to remember when there had been regular games and no skating. Some people became very good at it, and there was ice hockey. Two Canadian boys, Michael and Alan Scott, dazzled everyone with their grace and swiftness. I, as became my years, contented myself with sailing in a gentlemanly manner wherever there was space enough to fall down comfortably without knocking into my elders. Jimmy Reynolds, perfectly turned out and with boots from Switzerland, was mostly interested in figure skating so I did not see much of him. Occasionally a crouched figure would flash past me which might or might not be my friend, but not until I heard the metallic crash a moment later would I know for certain.

On March 10th the ice broke and a boy fell in. For some days there had been ominous sounds of cracking, and then Walsh Two, in his brown knickerbocker suit with the pleats and belt, went through. I was not at that end of the lake at the time and so missed it, but Lane described the incident to me afterwards with a wealth of vivid detail. Apparently Walsh had had to bump his head three times on the other side of the ice before he found the hole and hoisted himself out of it. "Just like the sub-deacon banging at the door on Palm Sunday," said Lane.

This meant the finish of skating at Emborough for that season. But there were still the flooded tennis courts to fall back upon, and the Try Ponds on the far side of the Mile Road. The ice on the tennis courts was of poor quality, and only the keenest enthusiasts like Jimmy and myself were prepared to push off from the side and slither hopefully over the sugary surface. Jimmy's elder brother John, the present baronet and lately in command of an Irish Guards Battalion, having swept with a lofty state-liness over Emborough for six weeks, put his skates in a box and sent them to Prince's—where they would be overhauled and prepared for use in the Easter holidays. The frozen tennis courts were not for John.

But for a few more days the Try Ponds, much smaller and shallower than Emborough, could be relied upon to bear. So off we all went in our bizarre costumes to get the last inch out of our skating limit. Junior and Upper Schools had the ponds to themselves on alternate after-noons. A master was in charge of the younger party, and he was supposed to skate two or three times across the middle so as to assure himself that the ice was still safe. On March 17th, trying out the ice in this way, Dom Aidan fell in.

I know the date because it was the last entry in my diary, the diary which Mr. Carter had so much wanted me to keep, and thereafter until 1921 when I was sixteen I recorded, against my list of books and plays, only the date of the Armistice and the month of the Spanish Flu —both of which I might easily have left for other author-ities to commemorate.

That the diary should have ceased where it did at least shows the significance which I attached to the closing scene. There we were, skates strung together round our necks, waiting the permission to sit down on the frozen snow and make ready. Then the simultaneous whip-lash crack, splash, and white lines running out from the break in the middle. Then Dom Aidan walking calmly but dreadfully ashore: six foot three of him, with his wet skates slipping as he walked. There was not a sound from the spectators until (how do these things happen?) I laughed. I alone, nobody else. Father Aidan walked straight up to me and said with a voice like a pane of glass, "I should have thought you would have had more sense." Then we all went home again.

It was a short afternoon's outing, and as we took off our boots and sat about gossiping among the hockey-sticks in the boot-hole, I pondered Father Aidan's remark. So he thought I should have had more sense? I remember the way in which, when there was snow on the ground outside, the boot-hole would be lit by a reflected glare which was almost green. And I remember the way in which, when one was thinking deeply in the boot-hole, one held one's stockinged foot in a reflective hand and vaguely wondered whether it would be necessary to change. Father Aidan had been teaching me now for two terms, and his remark was puzzling. Puzzling because until that moment, sense had been the last thing he had seemed to expect from me. Well, there it was. I was expected to have sense. I was growing up.

IX

From now onwards, till I am in my seventeenth year and have taken up my diaries again, there will be fewer dates. So let me enlarge for a few pages on those two landmarks in time already mentioned. Armistice and Spanish Flu. On Armistice Day I was in bed with scarlet fever, and when Spanish Flu was raging I was in bed with Spanish Flu.

From the windows of the sanatorium it was possible to see the glow in the sky of a gigantic bonfire. It was also possible to hear the cheering, songs, firing of blanks. The noise of it all coming over the fields seemed to me, perhaps because I was the only case of scarlet fever, infinitely sad. I had got used to the war, and with the conservatism of youth was slightly apprehensive of a change. I was in the middle of a book by W. J. Locke which told of the war's beneficent effect upon an apparently spineless young man, and I felt that unless there was a war going on we would all be spineless young men. This was a not very original thought, but it moved me profoundly as I sat on the window seat in my rug and envied Rupert Chamberlain his chances and his escapes.

When I got back to the school I could see at once that we were living in a quite different Downside, a Downside which may or may not have existed before the war—arriving in September, 1914, I was too late to know—but which was already not the same place that I had known for four years. Long afterwards when I read in Shaw's *Major Barbara* the speech where Undershaft says that with every discovery there is always at first a sense of loss, my mind flew back to the 1918 discoveries of a new Downside and a new peace.

In the event, of course, the adjustments were effected automatically and it took no time at all to get used to the freedoms and returning luxuries. Soon we were looking back with indulgent smiles at the days when we had worn little round celluloid pictures of Kitchener in our buttonholes, when we had collected bits of shrapnel and the twisted sheets of aluminum which were supposed to have come from "strafed" zeppelins, when we had plastered the walls of our lockers with shiny reproductions torn from magazines devoted solely to the war, when we had kept our money in a hand-grenade. Gone was the hitherto ubiquitous German helmet, black with its metal eagle and spike, which is now a museum piece. Even more noticeable was the change when we went back for the holidays: everything which we had associated with the war seemed to have folded up and become as much part of the past as *The Four Feathers*. The shapeless blue suits of the wounded appeared to have walked away from the Park and Kensington Gardens, the Bairnsfather cartoons seem to have slipped off the glossy pages on the bookstalls, the posters which had pointed from the walls and hoardings were asking for something else. *The Bing Boys, The Maid of the Mountains, Chu Chin Chow* (which one had seen every holidays and had thought would go on for ever) were all so many wartime echoes—like the rumble of guns in France, the whispered rumours of spies, and the marching feet in Victoria Station. Nurse Cavell and Florence Nightingale were the same person. Little Willie was as old as Little Titch. Spy-fever had given place to jazz-fever which was worse, and religion, which had been resorted to as a last desperate hope, had grown cold again—as cold as the snow on the boots of the Russians who did not pass through the Midlands by night on the way to the Front. No wonder I had cried when I heard "Tipperary" coming through the sanatorium window; it was perhaps the most sensible thing to do.

But if the world outside sank back exhausted after the Armistice and listened to tight-waisted gentlemen playing an awful thing called a swannee whistle, we at Downside lost no time in catching up with the tide of civilization. Members of the staff who had been taken on because there had been no younger men gradually returned to their hydros and their clock golf. New and energetic masters were engaged. These did not all stay, and certainly I did not find them so easy to draw, but they stirred things up while they lasted. A raffish young man taught maths for a while, making jokes which we thought were in very poor taste, and there was a musician who was with us for about a week and whose earlier career was unfolded for us some months later by the cheaper press. In spite of these minor weaknesses, however, the studies as well as the games and corps made great strides after the war. So much so that it would be difficult for a Gregorian of the present generation who has risen on a curve which has been mounting since 1919 to visualise the rather seedy kind of tuition which we were receiving during the worst years of the war and which has been touched upon above. It is matter of congratulation that Downside, with conditions as they were at that time, did as well as it did. Dom Leander Ramsay, whose health broke up before the end of the war and who retired into the profundities of the monastery until the school saw him again when he became Abbot of Downside in 1922, was Headmaster at the most difficult time of any. So far as foundations go, there is no one to whom Gregorians owe more.

But I suppose what we, in 1918-19, appreciated most about the new era of peace and progress was that we were no longer getting that curious licorice substance which was designed to sweeten but instead turned one's porridge into a dark sticky morass that left a coat on the roof of one's mouth. And there were other changes as well. Mr. Fry's horsebrakes, our tumbrils, were being replaced by a number of primitive, tinny-looking, buses. Eton collars were going out. Stiff shirts were no longer obligatory on Sundays with regulation suits. Caps and straw hats were discarded absolutely, and everyone wore felt (hard or soft). But to go hatless, whether playing an away match or leaving at the end of a term, was still unthinkable. In the Junior School the smaller boys were beginning to wear shorts and jerseys while the rest kept to their striped trousers, black coats and waistcoats. By this time I was creeping up to the top of the Junior School, and I would have cheerfully died rather than take advantage of the innovations. For Jimmy and me it was a point of honour to retain the least detail of what we felt to be a departing convention, and we went on wearing hard-fronted and hard-cuffed shirts till the end of our school careers. May the day never dawn when the traditional black tie, starched white collar, city-man suit are sacrificed either to comfort, to prevailing fashion, or to some nonsense connected with social theory. Having survived two world wars and made no greater concession than that of reducing the four buttons on the coat to three, the costume as worn at Downside by boys between the ages of thirteen and eighteen has proved itself. Not suitable to the depths of the country? Nor is a policeman's helmet. Not economical? Nor is education. Not as becoming as an open neck shirt and corduroys? Nor is an umpire's coat or a professor's gown or a deacon's dalmatic. So Jimmy and I stuck to our waistcoats and boiled shirts. What happened to all the straw hats with their red and yellow ribands I do not know. Probably John Phillips bought them up and sold them ten years later in the colonies.

Not only in the matter of hats and methods of transport were there changes at Downside; there were changes also in the matter of schoolboy idiom. It may have been as much because we were growing up as because we were tired of wartime phraseology that we became scornful of "topping" and "old bean." Though some of us tended to become purists, banning the well tried "puny" and "putrid" and "ghastly" from our vocabularies, we were as loyal to our specifically Downside words as we were to our specifically Downside habits of dress. It would be tedious, particularly since this book is not for Gregorians only, to enumerate and account for these words of local interest, but in the

SGT. INSTRUCTOR BASTABLE

case of the term "tay" there is good reason for putting on record its origin and meaning.

"Tay" is a word which came in almost overnight, was used (and on occasion roared) for a dozen years, and then quite suddenly was dropped. The present generation has never heard of it, and unless mention is made of it here its very existence (let alone its derivation) will be lost to future historians. "A tay" means someone who is too forthcoming. It is not quite as strong as the modern "thruster," not quite as spiteful as "bummer up." For example a boy would be "taying" if he volunteered to give out programmes at a concert or run out with lemons on a plate at a match. In every generation there are born tays: boys who quite naturally assume jobs which other boys either do not want or do not want to be thought to want. As one went up the school it was easy enough to find the requisite number of tays to get those things done which one had no intention of doing oneself.

To perform an act of courtesy was often to "tay." Thus if a boy handed to the Captain of Rugger his sweater on coming away from the ground, there would be a murmur of "Tay." Once the Headmaster dropped his watch just before prayers in the Hall, and a boy (one of nature's tays, incidentally) picked it up: there was a rising whisper of "Tay." "Sounds a bit tayish to me," was the comment of a boy in history class on Walter Raleigh's chivalrous gesture with the cloak.

The derivation was simply this: a boy called George O'Callaghan used to cite the authority of a certain Lord Tatham for much that he did. George was one of those ingenuous people who are up and coming before they realise that they have started. From being called "My-friend-Lord-Tatham-says" he was shortened to "Tatham" and then to "Tay." George was the first, and most un-offending, tay.

As a pendant to the above I might add that I was recently on the telephone with a Downside contemporary of mine, and the subject under discussion was the progress of his daughter in a convent school at which I happened to be giving a retreat. I was explaining that the nuns liked the girl very much but that they considered her to be a little forward, a little premature, not quite subdued enough, for one of her standing in the school. "I see," came the cheerful voice over the telephone, "what you mean is she's a tay."

There are some words, words like "cad" and "chap," which are used in all schools and by all generations. These particular two are used by grown-ups as well, but always rather between mental inverted commas: they are words which belong primarily to the young, and the grown-up knows it. Also to the adult mind the terms have a limited meaning: a cad is a bounder, a chap is a male person. To a boy the word "cad" may apply to a woman, a liar, a brute, a bully; "chap" may mean almost anybody, and on occasion someone specific. "Give it to the chap"—the professional, the servant, the expert, the man at the wheel. "He's a chap"—a personality, a man to be reckoned with. The use of the word in a flattering sense was music to my ears on an occasion when I was witnessing, a few years ago, the performance of one of my own plays before a schoolboy audience. Between the acts a small boy in the row in front of me turned round and asked whether it was true that I had written the play. I admitted, coyly, that this was true. "Gosh, sir, did you really, sir?" came the gratifying appreciation, "because it's just as if it's by a chap."

Returning from the digression to the second of the two landmarks of 1918, there is little that need be told about the plague which was called Spanish Flu. As it so nearly coincided with the Armistice, and therefore covered part of the time that I was in the sanatorium with scarlet fever, my own part in the epidemic was negligible. Apart from nose-bleeding and sickness it seemed to me the same as any other kind of flu, but I had it so slightly that my own experience was nothing to judge by. It was only when I saw the suddenness and violence with which it brought down masters, monks, servants and other boys less fortunate than myself, that I recognised here an excuse for going to bed which was not likely to be forgotten. For a week everything was disorganised: nurses were unobtainable, extra help from the village had ceased, classes bore little relation to the timetable, and even the school bells (those last ditchers of Downside life) were unreliable.

Nearly all the dormitories were turned into wards, and the whole place smelled of disinfectant. The sick were helped by the not-so-sick, and the few stalwarts who remained impervious to the germ acted as porters and messengers in the school. I remember seeing Harry Ellis carrying a smaller boy on his back to the Old House. In fact the work done by the helpers, with even the most improbable boys reaching heights of unselfishness, so impressed the emergency medical staff that some of them wrote afterwards to congratulate the school on what they called its "field hospital spirit." In spite of this it was impossible to make all the beds and sweep all the floors. One exquisite and very good-looking boy, Bunny Blundell-Hawkes, confessed to me sadly that he had not had a bath for nine days, and that if his parents knew of this he would be taken away and sent to another school. Why he was unable to have a bath I cannot think, but there must have been some good reason because he was essentially the bathing kind. The remark struck me particularly because most of my friends would cheerfully have endured the hardship for even longer.

Then, when the horror stories were at their height, my

scarlet fever declared itself and I was isolated. But bad
as those weeks were with us, other places apparently fared
a great deal worse. An Old Boy told me that at Bushey
where he was doing his training only five of them remained
on their feet to do the hack work of the whole barracks,
and that because they drank nothing but champagne they
were able to survive the epidemic without having to take
so much as an aspirin. This and the cider cure for hay
fever may be reckoned among the most significant medical
discoveries of the century.

x

Of the following summer I remember little—except that
I went in several times to Bath and Taunton with Maurice
Turnbull to watch county cricket, and was very nearly
late for prep when I got back. Running all the way from
the station, with the afternoon's ginger beer still tingling
in one's nose, was again among the many things at which
Maurice was better than I.

But by this time, 1919, I was head boy in the Junior
School, and what I failed to achieve in impressing Maurice
Turnbull I at least in part made up for by wielding the
authority which was now mine. In short I was more objectionable at this stage than at any other. Perhaps this is why
I remember so little of 1919 and 1920: it is our tendency,
so psychologists tell us, to submerge into the unconscious
those phases of which the conscious does not wish to be
reminded.

After Christmas there was a return, but only for about
ten days, of last year's keen frost; and out we went with
our skates to that most blessed of all lakes, Sir John's.
By this time Jimmy and I were evidently considered
senior enough to be allowed the use of our own bicycles,
and each afternoon immediately after lunch we shot up
the monks' drive in our eagerness to lay a claim on what

we considered to be the best part of the ice. When we arrived we would always find that except for Dom Laurence Kynaston and Mr. Wylie, who had brought sandwiches and were making a day of it, the lake was ours. There was a certain sense of achievement about having come first, and there are few greater satisfactions than putting on one's skates and pushing off onto an enormous dance floor of grey glass. Both Jimmy and I had had lessons since the previous year, practising together at Prince's in Piccadilly (which was then an ice rink, and where we enjoyed the experience of being on the same floor as Admiral Lord Jellicoe, the Jutland victor), so we were able to keep upright and at the same time appreciate what was going on around us. Jimmy's appreciative faculties seem to have developed before mine —at least I was given to understand that they had—but certainly I date from these 1920 visits to Emborough the awakening of my first recognisably aesthetic responses. The pewter sky, the yellow and orange sunsets, the bare trees reddening behind the flames of an enormous bonfire . . . and then the ride back with the cold cracking one's face and the skating-stiffness pressing on one's shins.

This was the last winter that we skated at Sir John's: after that there must have been some mild Lent terms, because I do not remember going again until I had been some years a monk. As we were the first to get there, Jimmy and I were usually the last to leave. Even Dom Laurence and Mr. Wylie, who were indefatigable skaters, preferred their tea to skating in semi-darkness. Mr. Wylie had tutored a boy in Russia under the Czarist régime, and had there learned to move about the ice with a grace which surprised those who were familiar with his stiff puppet-like motions in the classroom. Unless spoken to, Mr. Wylie skated in complete silence: lips pressed together and a look of solemn absorption. On one of these last days at Sir John's I observed casually in passing him, "Le plaisir est comme la glace; n'appuyez pas—glissez toujours." He beamed with pleasure, a quick smile lighting up his pink face and numberless little lines appearing where one least expected, and answered without an instant's reflection: "Ho, ho, my dear fellow, you may be very good at bluffing, but I know where you got that from." He mentioned an author—I forget now who—and he was right: I had been reading in the library the night before and the phrase had suddenly come back. It was a tayish thing to say, and I deserved exposure. "Ho, ho, my dear fellow"—in accents which are still imitated today by middle-aged men at Downside dinners.

XI

The next term found me moved up to the Middle School. I should like to leave this chapter on the Junior School from the most characteristic place in the buildings allotted to our use—namely Father Austin's room. Certainly during the last two years of my time under his care I spent more recreation hours in the comfortable untidiness of my superior's study than anywhere else. While a crowd of boys between the ages of nine and thirteen talked, played games, put record after record on the gramophone, ran in and out, wrote lines and lay on the floor with books and papers, Father Austin contrived not only to correct exercises and type complicated letters to parents but also to remain sane.

I should like to say a good deal about Father Austin's handling of his Junior School, but I know that my glowing testimonial would be met by a letter from him of puzzled, slightly indignant, and entirely genuine repudiation. Rather than take any risk, therefore, I confine myself here to the briefest statement of impressions received under, though not directly connected with, his authority.

If the senior boys imbibed any sort of culture during their stay in the Junior School, and I would claim that they did, it was unconsciously given and unconsciously received. There were good books lying about and there were good records to play. It is something to go by that when we were given a free class at the end of the term, we asked Father Austin to read to us poems out of *Realms of Melody*. Indeed I discovered afterwards, when higher up in the school, that the level of taste, manners, and conversation was by no means as childish as I had supposed it to be at the time. It is a good thing when small boys take it for granted that they are small boys, and we of the Junior School were evidently more sophisticated than we realised. For humour, the standard of those days would be hard to beat, and I venture to think that the spirit of religion was not too bad either. Since none of the credit of this can go to the small boys themselves, it is presumably the tradition and the people at the top of things that are responsible.

If the Junior School left a lasting impression upon me, I cannot think that I left much impression upon it. Two major reforms, however, I may claim to have had a hand in. The first was when Alick Dru and I, both of us new boys, succeeded in having tea and milk put on the table separately instead of already mixed. "Our parents aren't paying large sums to have us brought up in a canteen," said Alick in his most blistering voice, and we pushed the measure through in the teeth of opposition from the housekeeper. The second was when, in my time as head boy, I broke the pyjama coat convention. I cannot now remember whether wearing it inside or outside the pyjama trousers spelled the shibboleth, but whichever it was I reversed the practice. Why I should want to do this I do not know. And that is the sum of my influence during the four and a half years of my stay in the Junior School.

Reluctantly I left the congenial climate of Father Austin's room—with its noise, its laughter, its battered furniture and its never opened windows. That I should ever again come under an authority and discipline which were vested in so informal a figure seemed unlikely. The whistle swinging from the pocket, the fountain pen wrapped in adhesive plaster, the spectacles held together with string and sealing wax stood for me as symbols—symbols of the best that an understanding education can give to a junior boy.

III: Middle School

THE MIDDLE SCHOOL, under Dom Anselm Rutherford (later Headmaster and now Prior of Downside), was a recent introduction. Designed to sort out newcomers to the Upper School and to delay the supposed rigours of fagging, it corresponded more or less to the present Junior House. Its members enjoyed certain freedoms which obtained neither above nor below. But it was a shifting business, and nobody stayed in it longer than three terms at the most. For games and corps it merged with the Upper School; for everything connected with religion it was on its own; for classes it was divided—the backward members working with the Junior School. I, for maths, worked with the Junior School.

Up till now I had belonged to three quite separate circles of friends, feeling equally at home in each. There had been the earnest, there had been the frivolous, and there had been the athletic—to this last I was indebted more to Maurice Turnbull for my position than to any athletic powers of my own. George Bellord and Jimmy had gone into the Upper School before me, Tristram Hillier was either with them or with his parents abroad taking a term or two off, Bernard Lane had suddenly and irrevocably attached himself to a set with which I had nothing in common, Maurice was left behind in the Junior School to win their matches for them. I found myself therefore with people whom I had known only slightly before, and to whom there is no reason to believe that I was welcome. As it turned out, the two terms that

I spent in the Middle School were as agreeable as any I spent at Downside.

We numbered about forty, and were housed in two dormitories which shared the same bathroom and linen-rooms. From the Top Dormitory down to the Museum Dormitory ran a narrow and very steep staircase . . . so that in battle the defender of the Top was in a strong position, and any attacking force from the Museum would have to go round by the changing-room below and strike upwards from another direction. This same narrow staircase branched off at two levels: the one leading into a disused organ loft overlooking the onetime chapel (and the Museum Dormitory), the other ending up in the bathroom. Thus it was possible for someone who was looking for a bath to find himself suddenly in what appeared to be a church.

The Museum, this one-time chapel,[1] was the dormitory in which I was lodged, and with me were collected some fifteen boys who might almost have been chosen for their similarity of outlook. They were boys who were not athletic and who did not figure prominently in the social life of the school, but who, under a cover of superficial and misleading seriousness, tapped a vein of humour the existence of which—at all events in those particular subjects—I had not hitherto suspected. These solemn, industrious, well-mannered boys used to get a lot of quiet fun out of burning each other's pyjamas in the middle of the dormitory before the master in charge appeared, in tying their blue enamel jugs to the wires which hung from the Gothic windows and swinging great fans of water along the walls, in playing "curlers" with their basins along the

[1] And also one-time refuge of stuffed animals. Between the periods of being chapel and dormitory, the name of the place was justified by glass cases which ran down the centre and which contained pottery, coins and arrow-heads. Gregorians of my generation still call it the Museum, though few of us have ever seen it as such.

two strips of linoleum which ran in parallel lines along the ends of the beds.

A game which went down well was one which we called the "holy fire" game. It was invented by a boy named Gordon Mitchell, whose heavy, sad, phylacterial face both belied his true temper and admirably suited him to the role of high priest. It was played like this. On the way to the dormitory from the Assembly, where we had prayers each evening with the whole school, the players gathered in the Middle School dayroom, twisted one or two daily papers into a torch, lit it, and bore it flaming through the corridors to the cries of "Make way, make way for the holy fire." The brand, carried either by Gordon Mitchell or by his deacon (another unsmiling and respectable boy, Tom Berington), was raced up the wooden stairs and met at the top by a boy holding a virgin taper. By the time the taper was alight and the torch stamped out on the stone threshold of the Museum, each boy was by the side of his bed waiting for the next rubric in the ritual. The object of the game was to keep the flame alive—somehow, anyhow, at whatever cost. Until the master in charge had come down from Compline in the Abbey this was easy enough: one simply handed the taper to one's neighbour and, waiting one's turn in the next round, got on with one's undressing. But once under the eye of authority the passing from hand to hand called for adroitness and despatch. Those whose task was the trickiest were the ones who occupied beds at the end of the dormitory, because this meant crossing over; but even for the rest it was not easy when the taper was burning low. If the holy fire was still alight when the wax stem was too small to hold, the flame had to be transferred to whatever else one was able to find which could burn. To allow the holy fire to go out unnecessarily— indeed to allow it to go out at all, short of being left with hands injured for life and a burnt-out clothes-locker—was the greatest disgrace, and I remember seeing one of our company emerging from under a bed with a blazing celluloid soap-container at the end of a pair of nail-scissors. The smoke and smell on this occasion was terrific.

There was supposed to be the strictest silence in the dormitory, but in our time this rule must have been imperfectly observed. The monk who presided, a young father too kindhearted for the burden, slept in a sort of pen at the bottom of the nave. His walls were of wood, but he had no roof. And so, like us, he gazed up at the Gothic vaulting as he lay in bed. My bed was in the sanctuary, and since the original decoration of the chapel had never been altered I had above me a canopy of blue—a rich ultramarine diapered with little gold stars. "It's so nice to go to sleep in church and not feel guilty," said James Murray whose bed was next to mine. "I hate waking up under those stars," said Richard Sykes, "I feel I'm in a field."

Fifteen years later I was given the job of restoring the Museum Dormitory to its original status as a chapel, and it went to my heart to have the blue and the stars painted over.

Another dormitory diversion was the nightly duty of gargling. Experiments in hygiene never lasted for long at Downside, but there must have been one going on that summer because spoonfuls of white powder were dealt out each evening after our washing—which we did off a long counter running the length of the central aisle—and we gargled to whatever tunes we fancied. Our prophylactic orchestra was conducted with a toothbrush from the organ loft and we always ended with the School Song and God Save the King.

Richard Sykes not only had his own special chant when gargling, based upon Dom Roger Hudleston's rendering of a Lamentation, but he had also his own special gargle.

A pink pill, dissolved in a tumbler of water, probably made a good gargle. A dozen pink pills in a basin was much more effective, and into this crimson sea Richard would press his quite enormous sponge. He would then hold the dripping sponge aloft and cry "Behold the head of Holofernes." One day he threw the head of Holofernes high against the wall over the master's cubicle, and the red stain remained for many years. Since there was no roof to the cubicle the damage done by the sponge, which was larger than a football (and when filled with water, heavier) was considerable. Today when I see pictures in the *Tatler* of Sir Richard Sykes at a race meeting or at Sledmere I think of the drooping expression and tired eyes of the boy in the Museum dormitory. "Holoferneeees"—said with the mouth dropping to sepulchral depth.

The Museum was the only dormitory in my experience where an attempt was made on the part of the wilder spirits to interest the rest in the project of a "midnight feast." Happily the idea fell through. I think that we probably shrank from being identified with the typical English schoolboy. Those who tried to promote the venture, volunteering to keep awake in relays, were quietly discouraged. "I detest school food at any time," Willie Berington (Tom's brother) told me, "but to eat it cold after it has been smuggled into the dormitory in towels would be more than I could stand."

On the days that we got our clean washing we threw our dirty washing over the rail into the organ loft, from which I suppose someone must have collected it next morning.

II

That summer was memorable for other things besides our gentle bedtime frolics. For instance it was the time of great bets in the Upper School. The phase lasted for perhaps a

month and whether large sums of money changed hands
or not I was too junior to know: all I know is that there
were some noteworthy manifestations of it. I was lucky
enough to witness Miles Koe riding off the top board into
the bathing pond on a bicycle. I saw Gregory Littledale
walking up to supper in a dinner jacket and tennis shoes.
I saw some spectacular roof-climbing and some competition
eating. What I did not see but was told about afterwards
was the flight of the peacock from the top of the Roberts'
tower during a ceremonial parade of the corps. The bird,
no mean weight, had been carried up under a cover of
mackintoshes during luncheon, and having made its historic
contribution to the story of winged power was rewarded
with a pork pie and a glass of brandy. I am told that the
landing was particularly effective, the great bird perching
itself, after its flapping and croaking passage through the
air, in contented silence on the metal bar which ran along
the top of the stop-netting of the tennis courts.

An achievement of a similar kind, but one which belongs
to a somewhat later period, was when the kangaroo was
brought into a certain master's class and made to sit in the
back row wearing a school blazer. The kangaroo, incidentally, was a present to the school from Sir Mark
Sheldon, and it lived in the greatest luxury somewhere in
the neighbourhood of the stables. There was an idea at one
time that it might make a suitable mascot for the Contingent, but the problem of keeping in step proved insuper-
able. Occasionally it would stray onto the railway line, and
kindhearted engine drivers would get down and shoo it
away. Once it stopped the Pines (Bath-Bournemouth) Express. The Sheldon kangaroo resembling myself in this
respect, felt the cold a good deal, and during winter its
room was heated by a stove. The poor beast nearly met its
end prematurely when it fell through a glass skylight into

one of the monastery cloisters. Abbot Chapman (then Prior) happened to be saying his rosary in the cloister at the time, and had the kangaroo fallen on his (Abbot Chapman's) head instead of merely glancing off his shoulder he too might have suffered serious injury. "I have never in my whole life been covered in so much kangaroo blood" was Abbot Chapman's comment afterwards.

A head mounted on mahogany and hanging in the Sheldon Pavilion recalls a host of incidents connected with our Australian visitor. If those glass eyes are unable to focus on scrub and bush, at least the national game is reflected in their retinae. And no need now, at the drawing of a season's stumps, to bring along the kindly stove.

For me the greatest excitement of that summer term was my uncle Marcel's visit. He came unexpectedly while I was playing tennis, and took me out to tea in Bath just as I was without waiting for me to change or get permission. He was in terrific form, having come straight from Cheltenham where he had had a run of good luck backing all the winners. He must have left my aunt May somewhere because I remember that he came alone. Stepping out of the big hired Daimler in his light suit with the rose in his buttonhole, he looked little older than the prefects who were playing in the next court to me. From his neck hung the longest pair of fieldglasses I have ever seen: out of their pale leather case they looked like bottles of hock. He stopped for two nights in Bath, and each night we had a box at the touring company operas of *Faust* and (strange contrast) *Madame Butterfly*. I and a party of my new Middle School friends were picked up after class, taken off in the car to dinner at the Pump Room, brought back again after the final curtain. Marcel's only regret was that we had not a free afternoon as well as these two free evenings: he wanted to have a picnic so that we might open the case of champagne which he had brought with him. Though my uncle was seldom opulent he was always magnificent, and I wondered all during his stay what my Middle School friends were making of him. Probably they thought him too magnificent.

In the holidays I had found that from the cheaper seats to which my finances obliged me when visiting the theatre on my own I could never properly see the stage. Rather than borrow from my aunts the ridiculous little opera glasses which might have been reels of cotton encased in mother of pearl I got into the habit of taking with me my father's telescope. I had not thought of this at all as being an affectation; it had seemed the obvious thing to do. Marcel for some reason thought it very funny, and told me that in future whenever I went to the theatre—and particularly if I were occupying a box—I was to continue to take with me the telescope. "Even in the front row of the dress circle you can kneel on one knee and rest your telescope on the velvet edge." It was this posture in the box which had appealed to him.

On the third and last morning of his visit, Marcel came out from Bath in time to see me during the eleven o'clock "half." It was a grilling hot day, and I was taking part in a Band practice outside the Gym. While I was blowing myself purple into a bugle and longing for the practice to end so that I might have more time with him, Marcel was leaning in a characteristically wilting attitude against the mudguard of the car, and looking at us through his eyeglass. When the Band was dismissed before the bell for class, he said as I came up to him, "You know, this is all absurdly pleasant; but I suppose you hate it, don't you? One always does until afterwards. And then it's too late."

Having handed me a princely tip, he got in and I asked him where he was going to lunch on the way to London. "I expect my friend the shuvver and I shall have a little picnic somewhere"—and he raised his eyes to the roof of the car on the top of which, discreetly covered by a waterproof sheet, could be seen among the luggage the harder outline of a wooden case. I remember how the brilliant sunshine glanced off the car as it slid away down the drive and out under the trees by the school gates.

I was to see a lot of Marcel during the holidays which followed. It was then, while staying with my aunt Rita at Broadstairs, that Marcel and I had a kipper high tea with the proprietor of a pierrot troupe in his van behind the stage. Whether or not I took the telescope to open air performances I cannot now remember.

III

It has been stated above that the Middle School curriculum was so planned as to allow boys who were below standard to do some of their subjects with the upper forms of the Junior School, and that this closely affected me. For mathematics I was still firmly in a class which was short of everything in that subject beyond the stage of long division. Faced with Dom Aidan's algebra, geometry, logs and fractions, we of that link-class felt that it was a far cry now to Mr. Campbell's comfortable multiplications and subtractions. We were in a world which seemed to have no message for us: between us and the theorem there was a great gulf fixed. Three days in the week, the days on which our maths class covered two periods and so lasted for an hour and a half, were dreaded so fervently that they cast a shadow over the other four. I found myself wishing that I had spent less time with Mr. Carter on reading English and more in preparing for the incomprehensibilities of Euclid.

But if maths were a trial to me, I must have been just as much of a trial to my maths master. For two years I was taught by Dom Aidan, who had no doubts about my idiocy, and during all that time I never rose above the lowest place in the form. Unequivocally bottom for the first year, I was joined in a ding-dong competition for this unenviable position during the second year by John Pollington.[1] My views and abilities in every branch of this subject were identically Polly's. In exams we used to get sixes and nines, that sort of thing, and seldom reached double figures out of the possible hundred marks. Towards the end of our time in this class, Father Aidan, realising that we were doing our best, wrote us off as incapables, and conditions became much happier. Among other things he made me draw a series of Polly caricatures which I believe he still possesses.

One small incident connected with these maths classes remains to this day as a monument to that element of mystery in a material world which neither reason nor science can explain. A black shoe, several sizes smaller than anything which could have been worn by a member of the class, appeared quite suddenly one day on Father Aidan's desk in the middle of a demonstration at the blackboard. Investigation, even when carried out among ourselves afterwards, failed to reveal the hand that had put it there. It had not been thrown, or we would have heard the noise; it had not been there all along, or we would have seen it. Nor was it ever subsequently claimed. "Obviously fourth dimension," concluded Dom Aidan, and lobbed the shoe at Pollington's head. Then we went on with the class.

Despite all the earlier tribulation, I was quite sorry to leave Form IV. 2. B. when the time came. And I suspect that Pollington was too. When together we left the Middle School we came under Mr. Lush for maths, but this is to take the present chronicle into 1921, so Mr. Lush will be reserved for a later chapter.

[1] Then Viscount John Wentworth Savile Pollington, now the Earl of Mexborough.

IV

During the summer holidays of 1920, a full seven weeks because the Middle School did not go to camp with the rest of the Corps, I went on several visits—apart from the one to Broadstairs where my aunt had taken Dickens's house for the summer. (She said she would never again rent the house of a celebrity who was dead, because people were constantly coming to the door and asking if we served teas.) Among the friends whom I stayed with was the Spensly family who had a house at Great Missenden.

Old Mrs. Spensly was a friend of my grandmother's, the next generation were friends of my aunts and mother, and there was a boy, Simon Staughton, who was a friend of mine. The Spenslys were very kind to me during my parents' absence abroad, and I used to be invited each summer for as long as I cared to stay. It was a delightful house, large and with considerable grounds, in what to me is still the pleasantest part of the home counties. Simon was a year older than I, and at Eton. Though we argued interminably—mostly about how ridiculous each other's school was—we got on very well. The Spenslys were not Catholics, so on Sundays I went into Aylesbury for Mass. If my aunt Yolande was a guest at the same time, we used to go together; but I far preferred it when I had to go alone. I felt reliant—the Catholic carrying the Pax of Rome through the lanes of Buckinghamshire.

The year's difference in age between Simon and me amounted in some ways to a greater gap than that which had separated me from Rupert. I looked upon Simon as the man of the world, and felt very young and inexperienced beside him. Perhaps religion had something to do with it: Rupert Chamberlain had been a Catholic. One day Simon and I argued religion for the whole of a morning, and it required the healing touch of Ethel, Simon's aunt, to bring us to speaking terms again in time for tea: we had spent the afternoon at opposite ends of the garden, each scowling in a hammock.

On days that we were not violently quarrelling, Simon and I used to go out on bicycles immediately after luncheon and smoke vile cigarettes on a neighbouring moor. We also used to visit an inn which was sufficiently remote to be safe, and drink port. Ruby port in the afternoon. I was now fifteen, so there was presumably no great danger to my soul in smoking cheap cigarettes and drinking port on a bicycle ride, but unaccountably my conscience rebelled against the practice and gave me no peace. Not having the courage to tell my sophisticated friend that I thought we were doing wrong, I used every effort to avoid these excursions after lunch. I even asked the priest about it when I next went to confession in Aylesbury, and I suppose I must have made out a case against myself because the priest, assuming from my account that I was turning the quiet countryside into a playground for Bacchus, urged me to put a stop to such wild ways. Still ashamed of giving my real reasons, I told Simon that I could no longer drink port with him in the afternoon because it gave me gout. "It's in the family," I said, "my father gets it whenever he drinks port." Rightly incredulous, Simon said that this was nonsense and that one could *see* gout—not like a headache or feeling sick. And here, at long last, my chilblains came in useful. Even in summer my fingers were red and swollen, so all I had to do was to show Simon my hands. I even volunteered, so pleased was I at having found a way out, to take off my socks and show him my feet. But Simon was convinced. Was also, I think, a little envious. Not even at Eton did boys of fifteen suffer from the gout. Downside's stock, by that curious logic with which boys reason, accordingly rose. And for my part I was pleased to find that there were some things which Simon did not know—one of them being what a gouty finger looked like.

One summer day when I was at Havenfields with the Spenslys, whether it was these particular holidays or the year before, the whole party drove over to Howard Spensly's house, Westoning Manor, for luncheon. The house is in Bedfordshire, of which county Howard Spensly was High Sheriff, and when its owner died it was offered to the nation. The lunch was in keeping with the grandeur of the place, and while our elders were grappling with their livers over coffee and old brandy, Simon and I were sent off to amuse ourselves on the lake. Belonging to a school with fine rowing traditions, Simon pulled out manfully from the boat-house while I lolled in the stern. Soon tiring, however, and feeling that sleep alone could do justice to his uncle's lunch, Simon shipped his oars and asked me (like the good fellow he knew me to be) to hand him the cushions I was sitting on. The upshot was that Simon did not get his sleep, and I fell into the pond. The water was not deep and I was only up to my waist, but the question which worried us was how to appear in the drawing-room in two hours' time. Simon's ingenuity was always better than mine, and at his suggestion the trousers were rinsed out under the pump in the stables stretched on a sunny but unobserved patch of grass, and pressed by the heavy roller from the tennis courts. When I finally presented myself for tea, there was not a raised eyebrow. Simon, and the hot sun, had found a way. "I am afraid it must have been rather boring for you in your shirt and waistcoat," said Simon when we got home and reviewed the day, "but really there was no option." There was nobody who could put things right after a row more gracefully than Simon Staughton.

To illustrate how Simon and I seem to have been by nature destined to continue our differences into the ripe old

age and in spite of ourselves, I cite the following sequel
which belongs to the present time. When not long ago I
wrote a novel called *The End* I did so under the name of
Hugh Venning, and before the book had been out a month
I received a letter forwarded from the publishers beginning
"Dear Mr. Venning, I have read your book with interest,
but not, I am afraid, with any sympathy. If you will forgive me I will put before you the points with which I feel
myself in violent disagreement." Then followed a list of
quotations, objections, arguments. The letter was of course
from Simon who had no idea that I was Hugh Venning,
and who had not written to me for years. It is as if there
were a magnet working between us in reverse. Simon
has himself produced a novel since the day when he so
violently objected to mine, and I am not at all surprised
at the combative sentiments which its perusal has aroused
in me. I consider *Prince Lucifer* a most disgraceful book. So
there we stand, great bargepole friends.

V

Returning after the holidays I brought my brother with
me. The five years between us made it impossible for either
his circle to include me or mine to include him, and it was
not until very much later in life that he caught up with my
friends and I caught down with his. The only new boy of
my brother's age who came that September whom I can
remember with any distinctness is Billy Morrison who was
a prisoner in the Second War and who is now a Dominican.
If I were asked to give the name of the most typical
Downside boy, I would give his. He had not only the
jargon, the walk, the appreciations of the essential Gregorian, but he had also the deeper qualities which I like to
think are associated with the concept.

As the Michaelmas term drew towards its close, the
Museum dormitory became uncomfortably cold. The com-

bination of a lofty Gothic ceiling, antiquated hot-pipes, and a window-space which might have suited a church but which did not suit a place to sleep in made undressing a chilly business. On nights when it was particularly cold I used to take a book down to the linen room, which was beautifully heated, and read myself to sleep among the blankets and woollen underclothes. It was as well that others did not feel the cold to the same extent or I should not have had such a range of warm shelves to choose from. In this flannel atmosphere I read *The Beloved Vagabond*, *David Blaise*, *The Hill*, and a strange book called *When Satan Ruled* which brought about in me a religious revival. Thereafter for the rest of the term, and indeed for a good part of the Christmas holidays, I read nothing but spiritual literature.

It was as well that this spiritual revival came when it did because it drove me into the sphere of Dom Anselm's influence. As Middle School Master, Dom Anselm could hardly have been bettered, and though he was over me for only a short time his effect was such that whenever I was in difficulties higher up the school it was to him that I applied for extrication. His sermons in the Lady Chapel after Vespers were so exceptional that it was by no means uncommon to find Middle School boys stopping on in the Abbey for as long as half an hour afterwards. Nor was it uncommon for Upper School boys to absent themselves from their own sodalities in order to listen to ours. I can think of few higher compliments than these.

IV: Fag Year

I

IN THE SUCCESSIVE STAGES of my school career I seem
always to have been moved up at the wrong times. I have
never accordingly been able to hail a fellow Gregorian as
belonging to "my year," because except for the Junior
School period I belonged always to odd bits of any given
year. This had advantages and disadvantages, but mostly
disadvantages. Landing in the Upper School after Christmas meant that I was a fag proper for three terms—and a
fag liable for five.

Fagging as done at Downside in those days was not
unduly arduous, and I understand that it is now less arduous still. Provided one had a fag master who was
moderately reasonable, one could not complain that there
was never time to wash or do up one's shoe laces. Fags
nevertheless tended not to wash or do up their shoe laces.
Indeed it was my experience that there was less regard for
the refinements of life, intellectual as well as physical in
the lower part of the Upper School than among the smaller
boys. As a fag I read fewer serious books of fiction than
at any other time, and in conversation there appeared to
be a ban upon anything remotely cultural. Nor, among the
lower forms at any rate, did one find much inspiration.
The impulse was not cultural but examinational, and I came
to loathe all authors whose books figured in the syllabus.
I have never quite got over the dislike which I felt at that
time for Shakespeare and Chaucer. Thank heavens they
did not try to teach us Shaw or Tchekov. The fault was

clearly mine, for if I had possessed any true appreciation I would not have been put off by textbooks and footnotes, but I remember now the feeling of bubbling hostility which Shakespearian lecturers and reciters used to rouse in me. Even the touring company which visited the school each year and gave us (if fine) open air performances of *Macbeth, Midsummer Night's Dream* and several others, provided me with nothing more than a few additional faces to caricature and endless material for irreverent wit.

A bucolic phase which confines itself to a department of life, to termtime or to a particular subject, need not matter to a boy; but when an aggressive philistinism is carried into the holidays and extended to the social as well as to the finer arts, there is likely to be a total eclipse. In my own case had it not been for Father Bede Jarrett who came to give the school retreat at the end of that Lent term I tremble to think how long the eclipse might have lasted. Elsewhere I have written of Father Bede and of the rescuing powers which were peculiarly his own, so I will say no more here than that he shook me to bits during Holy Week and reassembled me in (I hope) a more satis-factory combination during the years of our friendship which followed. The spiritual reading which had begun in the linen-room the term before may have had something to do with it, but the 1921 retreat was the occasion of my really having to face the possibility of a religious vocation.

My first fag-master was the Head of the School, Morgan Duncan, whom I already knew because we had both been guests of the Reynolds's the year before at Dove Park. (This had been during the Strike, when there was a certain amount of disorder in Liverpool and when volunteers were driving trams, buses and local trains. Jimmy, who took the emergency much to heart, met me at Lime Street with the words: "I am glad you are wearing a bowler hat: strikers have to hit twice if you are wearing a bowler, and they don't usually bother after the first.") The Head of the School was also Head of the House which I was in (Caverel), so I had more to do than most of the other fags. He was Drum Major as well, which meant my cleaning a good deal of brass and white buckskin. On cold days when we happened to be standing easy on parade and Morgan Duncan clapped his gauntlets together, sending off a cloud of white into the air, I felt a great glow of pride at the handiwork which was mine. No manservant is a hero to his master, so I had to be a hero to myself.

Coming into the Upper School should have meant picking up the relationships which my Museum interlude had interrupted, but Hillier was in Roberts and Jimmy was in Barlow, and though George Bellord was in my own House I was a long way below him on the list. My Middle School friends seem to have reverted to the status which relatively they had occupied in the Junior School, and somehow I was now without the key to their society. In fact this would have been a gloomy chapter in my rough schoolboy story had not Dom Rupert suspected my loneliness and invited me down to his room in a Junior School dormitory where each evening I was able to associate again with Maurice Turnbull. These after-prayers parties of biscuits and boiling lemonade were a delight which more than compensated for the boredoms of the rest of the day. They were a post-graduate course of the Junior School, which I felt I ought never to have left. In fact I feel I ought to be in it still.

Another outlet during my fag terms was the firm friendship, which I had formed long ago but only now was coming to lean upon, with an elderly spinster who had a house in the village. Miss Symes was a dear, holy, ineffectual, literary and artistic wraith whom we loved but made fun of. "We" here amounted to half a dozen boys who ate her excellent teas and were perfectly at home in her company. We seldom went together to see her, but as on most free afternoons we drifted down there on our own we came to know each other fairly well and to regard ourselves as the old lady's champions. If she happened to be out, we would walk in, read her books, make tea, wash up, leave a note saying "Thanks for lovely cake," and go back to school. Arthur Woods, Alick Dru, Napper Dean Paul—boys whom I had lost sight of completely during the last two years—were always to be found at Miss Symes's, and I imagine that they too were taking their time in the business of settling down to Upper School life.

Miss Symes had a triangular face which rocked unsteadily over an absurdly thin neck. "Let me, Miss Symes," Arthur would say if she bent down suddenly to pick up a fallen scone from under the piano, "or your head will roll off . . . and we don't want *that*, you know." She was also very short-sighted, almost blind later on, and would peer at you through half-closed lids calling you by another boy's name but probably meaning you nevertheless. She wore no make-up, but on each cheek was a spot of bright red. "Galloping, my dear," Alick explained each time we came away from her teas, "absolutely galloping." On the upper side of the triangle, hair grew in dry straight wisps, and these were parted in the middle. Miss Symes did a lot of gardening, and her hands were hard and strong. "Like shaking hands with a wicket-keeper," said Napper, who had never been near a wicket-keeper in his life.

Particularly helpful to me in my newly discovered religious interest was Miss Symes's library of spiritual books, She was herself a Franciscan Tertiary, and had read every page of the literature which crammed her shelves to bursting. From the moment when I confided to her the secret of my wanting to become a monk there began one of those complicated exchanges of trust which leave the parties —or at all events this is how the present one left me—in a state of uncomfortable hypocrisy. But the fact that she knew, and that nobody else did, kept me up to the mark and I read the books which she lent me.

Miss Symes loved concerts as much as she loved pictures and poetry and nature. So we, her cavaliers, used to tug her up to the school whenever there was music, and tug her down again afterwards. She could never have seen her way otherwise. The escort was always provided with something unexpectedly delicious in the way of a supper, but I do not think that this was really the motive of our friendly action. We were genuinely fond of our Symes. "Damn it, she's an institution," said Alick once, "and what's more we've made her one."

A year or two later my brother took to visiting Miss Symes, and much the same sort of group was formed all over again. I hardly ever met him there, because for one thing his timetable was quite different from mine and for another it would not have been easy at that age to overcome the termtime barriers, but it pleased me and my own contemporaries to know that the Symes, an affectionate though undemonstrative soul, was not being left without a band of youthful swains.

II

By the time the summer term came round, Morgan Duncan had left and I was someone else's fag. This time it was Kevin Turnbull, Maurice's eldest brother and again Head of the House. He gave me no trouble except on one occasion when he saw me throw his corps uniform from the top of the iron staircase outside the Caverel block of buildings onto the tennis courts below. Such had always been my practice on Fridays when there was little time between corps and class, and on this one occasion my fag master happened to have come down before me and was having his teeth seen to in the surgery at the opposite side of the Quad. At least the incident seems to show that I was getting used to life in the Upper School, and even beginning to show something of the old technique which the Lane-Phillips-Kilkelly tradition had imparted to me in the Junior School. A Kilkelly triumph which occurs to me as I write is the ten minutes' interruption which he effected in the Servants' and Village Ball. The Ball took place in the Gym, and Kilkelly, mounted on the roof of a passage which runs alongside, threw a handful of lighted squibs and catherine wheels through an upper window onto the dance floor. The result was judged by all, even by Kilkelly immediately afterwards, to be well worth the consequences—which were severe.

A personality whom I had come across a good deal earlier on, but who developed to his full stature in the Upper School, was Jack Carroll. He, like Pollington and me, was maths-logged for a long time, and we seemed to move up the school by the same slow degrees, sharing the same punishments, until we finally left at the end of the same term. Jack was very lordly, and never came in time for anything. Most of his classic observations began with the somewhat Edwardian opening: "But my dear feller, I thought . . ." Once he came on parade very late, and was shouted at by the Commanding Officer, an able and human soldier called Major Colley. "Not late, sir, surely," said Jack, "just neatly punctual, I should say." "*Late*, man, ten minutes late by Greenwich time." "At Downside, sir," said Lance Corporal Carroll, "we do not keep Greenwich time: we have our own."

Jack turned up one year for the annual House photograph wearing an auburn wig which had been used for *The Merchant of Venice*. "But my dear feller, I thought it might be a slight variation: all you fellers look so dashed smooth and glossy." It was at the corps camp that Jack appeared, when he was in time to appear at all, to advantage. His smartness was proverbial, and nobody could understand how anyone who took so little trouble could achieve such excellent results.

Our first camp was at Mytchett in Surrey. Thereafter we were allocated either to Tidworth Park or Tidworth Pennings each year. As our entry on every occasion was conducted in a downpour, and as at each of the three camps the food and the smell and even the features of the landscape seemed to be identical, I tend to telescope my military experience—placing it at Mytchworth Parkings.

A canal formed one side of the camp bounds, and here, when the parades were over and we had washed the grease from our supper plates, we spent the evenings. There were boats and we could bathe. One of the qualities of Mytchworth was that when we were not baling rain water out of our tents we were being baked in a heat-wave. Each year, after the annual cloudburst which had us splashing about the lines and going to sleep in that atmosphere which it is the prerogative of damp khaki to produce, there would be a tropical sun to take the skin off our faces and drive us to the canteen for ever larger and larger iced drinks. Discovering that it was cooler to wear pyjamas than anything else under one's uniform, I wore a pair which were so often thrown into the canal by my fastidious friends that I had to take a taxi into Aldershot on the only free afternoon to buy another pair. It was as well that I did, for the original pair (which were of black silk with orange facings) were ceremonially burned on the last night—together with some of the more permanent fittings of Mytchworth Camp. The year following I again wore pyjamas under the uniform, but either they must have been of a less ambitious design or else I must have provided myself with a more frequent change, because I do not remember seeing them going up in flames at the end of the lines.

On the Sunday that we were at camp we had Mass in

the open, attended by the Catholics from the other schools at Mytchworth and celebrated by Dom Ambrose Agius who also preached. At the last camp which I went to (in 1923) I was again keeping a diary, so a description of the Sunday Parade will be reserved till we come to it in the present chronicle. Dom Ambrose said Mass every day during the week in the recreation tent, but his congregation was not large: sleep, it must be remembered, was at a premium during those well-filled days at Mytchworth.

III

From camp we used to go back to Downside for one night before making for our holiday destinations. The idea was that we should return our equipment to store, get ourselves clean of the Surrey mud, and appear at home as civilians rather than as battle-stained irregulars. One year I had to go straight from camp to Southampton so as to be in time to catch a boat to Egypt,[1] and not only did I narrowly escape a military punishment for failing to salute an officer in the street but I had the greatest difficulty in shaking off a young woman who introduced herself as preferring the army to the navy any day.

The first week of the summer holidays I spent with the Gubbins family, who used sometimes to have me to stay

---

[1] It was during this holiday in Egypt that I had occasion to share a room with my father for one night while accompanying him on patrol. Though he was probably as surprised at my evening devotions as I was at his morning exercises, the thing which remains most clearly in my mind about the excursion is the surprise which I felt at remarking the narrowness of his feet in comparison with the width of his shoes. We had often swum in the sea together, but I had apparently never noticed my father's feet. Next day when we were lunching in the open I mentioned this matter of his feet, and asked why, since his shoes were always made for him, he did not insist upon getting a better fit. "Because I like doing this," he said, drumming his fingers on the napkin which lay, stiff and folded, across his knee, "with my toes." He then extended a leg, and, sure enough, under the thin leather of his riding boot I could discern a distinct ripple.

either in London or in the country. This time they had rented a very lovely Elizabethan house, Kentwell Hall, in Suffolk.[1] I was beginning to take an interest in architecture, and I can look back to my Kentwell visit as an aesthetic delight which had all the joy of a first discovery. The house is E-shaped, the three sides flanking a courtyard which looks down a drive a mile long. It is the complete dream mansion of the boy who has read his *Chums* and *B.O.P.* It has its moat, its ghost, its secret hiding places, its suits of armour. I was there only during the summer, but I imagine that it was at Christmas that the house really spread itself: its panelled walls seemed to be asking for the squeak and scratch of holly, its great Tudor hearths were aching for the splutter of logs.

So keen were the members of the family on tennis that even before breakfast one would hear the *ping-phut* and "I couldn't see but I think out" of an earnest single. The two sons, Richard and Roderick, were possessed of an energy which defied competition, and while they were

[1] "Kentwell Hall, Melford, stands a little to the north of the church in a well wooded park. It was formerly, and for many ages, the seat of the Cloptons, a family who took their name from a village in this county . . . Sir Thomas [de Clopton] acquired the manor of Kentwell by marriage with Catherine, daughter and heiress of William Mylde . . . the descendants continued to reside at Kentwell until the decease of Sir William Clopton Knt., who by Anne his first wife, daughter of Sir Thomas Barnardiston of Clare, left a daughter and sole heir, Anne, the wife of Sir Symonds D'Ewes, who inherited the same in her right; whose only surviving child, Sissilia, married Sir Thomas Darcy Bt. of St. Osith in Essex. She deceased in 1661, and left no surviving issue . . . Sir Thomas Robinson, early in the last century, sold the estate to John Moore . . . it was purchased by Robert Hart Logan Esq. who was High Sheriff of this county in 1828 and elected representative in Parliament for the Western Division of the same county in 1837. He deceased April 13, 1838, and this estate was soon afterwards purchased by the trustees of the present proprietor, Edward Sarkie Bence Esq., then a minor, who now resides there." *Page's supplement* (1844) *to Kirby's Suffolk Traveller* p. 950. See also Kelly's *Directory of Suffolk* and Coppinger's *Manors of Suffolk*, Vol. I, pp. 148-57. And, for more readable matter, *In Constable's Country*, pp. 153-6, by H. W. Tompkins.

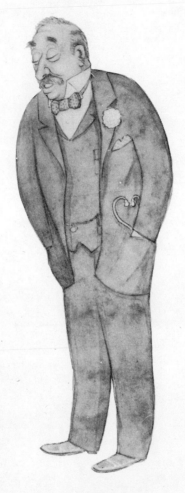

Dr. Pollard

riding round the park after innumerable sets of tennis and perhaps a round or two of golf, I would sit in a shaded corner of the courtyard and try to draw the wing opposite. But I have always found it harder to get likenesses of houses than likenesses of people, and I doubt if any of the many owners of Kentwell would have recognised the house from my pictures. When one has drawn a house (or for that matter a face) one goes on feeling a certain friendliness towards it for ever, and I know that even if I had not spent a lyrical week there but only managed to do half a dozen very bad drawings of it I would, if Kentwell Hall were thrown open to the public, go back as often as possible . . . and weep into the tray which is held for the cards of callers by the mailed but hollow figure who stands sentry in the hall.

On the 15th of August, after assisting at the laying of the foundation stone of Blackfriars, Oxford, I went off with Father Bede Jarrett, the founder of Blackfriars, and Leonard Parker, then an undergraduate in his first year, to Brittany and Normandy. We were away for about three weeks, spending most of the time in a château which had recently been restored by an American painter who was painting a portrait of Father Bede. There was bathing, boating, and a lot more tennis. Leonard and I, despite the undergraduate-fag discrepancy, got on well and told each other all our secrets. When the holiday was over and we were back in England we still got on well. But we regretted having told each other all our secrets.

IV

I got back to Downside with my drawing book stuffed with pictures of Brittany (the Kentwell series I had destroyed), and with the fixed determination to devote myself seriously for the next few years to the cause of art. But I had reckoned without Maurice Turnbull who, like Eurydice coming

up from the shades, now joined me in the higher heavens—
in Caverel as a fag. This meant my plunging myself furi-
ously once more into athleticism so as to be able to hold my
own. If only it had been tennis and not rugger I might,
after all that pre-breakfast practice in Suffolk followed by
hours of it in Brittany, have returned a few serves and so
justified my existence. But not even the brothers Richard
and Roderick had introduced rugby football to Melford,
and I was still in the kick-and-chase-it class. So Eurydice
melted into thin air again for the time being, and as there
were more of Aristaeus on the horizon than there was ever
likely to be of Orpheus I gave up not only athletic ambi-
tion but "art and friendship and all that nonsense," and
concentrated instead upon getting as much amusement as I
could out of my classes. In this I was helped by having
Mr. Moorat and Mr. Lush to teach me.

I had now been six years at Downside and had never yet
sat at the feet of Mr. Lush. The defect was remedied, and
here I was learning maths together with such familiar associates in this study as Carroll, Hillier, Pollington and
others. Mr. Lush is as much a legend in the story of
mathematics at Downside as is Mr. Wylie in the story of
French. Both men were imitated with ruthless inaccuracy
by young and old, but where most boys found Mr. Wylie's
French class a great burden, all found Mr. Lush's maths
a delight. This is the place to mention a feature of Upper
School life, the "Lush Roar."

The origin of the Lush Roar is wrapped in obscurity,
and probably dates back to long before the First World
War. It was certainly being observed when I arrived in
1914. From time to time, when they tended to obtrude,
Lush Roars were put down by higher authority, but sooner
or later they would begin again and all would be well.
The procedure was as follows. Mr. Lush would pause in
whatever demonstration he was engaged upon at the black-

board, turn round, toss the chalk from one hand to the other a few times, put on a particular expression which one learned to recognise after a while but which might have been mistaken by a newcomer as heralding a sneeze, and make a very weak joke. Then the back row of the class would begin a subdued groaning noise, hardly above a whisper at first and all on one note, which would be then taken up, row after row, until the whole of the form was gently humming. Growing in volume and rising in key, this buzz would swell to a great sustained bellow, accompanied, on a really good day, by the thumping of desks and the rattling of foot-rests. Then, at a signal from an approved source at the back, the roar would quite suddenly cease and all would be quiet. Mr. Lush, meanwhile, would be standing with a smile of assumed bewilderment, shocked concern, studied irresponsibility for as long as it lasted and then would go on as if nothing had happened. One hand raised in mute protest, chalk between finger and thumb, was all that could be brought to stem the violence of the Roar when once the flood of it had reached full spate.

Now there was this about the Lush Roar, that as years wore on it came to be governed by certain fixed sanctions. For example it was not a practice which might be extended to the classes of other masters. Nor might the Roar be initiated in any given class by a younger boy: only the back benchers were permitted to decide upon both its suitability in a particular case and the moment of its starting. Lastly, if the number of Roars per term tended to exceed what tradition had assigned—there were seldom more than three in even the noisiest forms—senior boys from other classes would see to it that the Lush Roar did not become cheapened. The whole thing was admirably controlled, and such warnings from one class to another (since a Lush Roar was not a thing which could easily be kept secret) were by no means uncommon.

Mr. Lush, as may be judged, was the most good natured of men. He was also a remarkably able master. Had I been at all potential material he would undoubtedly have got me through my exams, but as it was I can testify only to the first of these two points—namely that he was the most good natured of men—and claim for him that he was without exception the best liked of the lay masters who were at Downside in my time.

Perhaps because he was accustomed to dealing with formulae and thinking in terms of definition, his humour tended to become stylised. There was a stereotyped joke which was characteristically his, and though never repeated in the same form was recognisable at once as of the genus. The traditional opening included first the name of the boy whom he was addressing and then the words "I understand that you." Thus one would get: "Hillier . . . er . . . Hillier . . . I understand that you are a painter. Now my bathroom needs a new coat." Inherited from the formal, and quite unfunny, joke, would be the formal way in which Mr. Lush was mimicked and drawn. In imitation the voice was a stereotyped voice bearing little relation to the original; the delineated outline, perfected by Hillier, was an abstraction rather than a likeness. Both accent and caricature were recognised immediately: one was the quintessence of Lush in sound, the other the abstract impression on paper.

The Hillier formula, doing scant justice to Mr. Lush's honest features, decorated every page of our mathematical textbooks. Particularly in our volume of Mair were represented the familiar poise of the head, the greying hair parted in the middle, the dark moustache, the half-closed eyes and inevitable cigarette. (Mair is one of those authorities who propose conundrums of a kind which are presumably dear to the mathematical heart. Thus when Mair asks his readers how long they think it would take two taps running at a certain pressure to fill a bath of a given cubic capacity if every so often a body of stipulated displacement were inserted into the water while at the same time a faulty waste-pipe was releasing a stated percentage, the only answer which he is likely to receive from the particular readers whom we are considering will be a picture of a bath surrounded by innumerable Mr. Lushes either letting out the water or getting into it, turning on the taps or trying to turn them off.)

The form decided one day to make a presentation to Mr. Lush, so a Hillier-van Zeller landscape was commissioned. The picture was requested to be bad, and bad it was—bad beyond belief. The occasion was taken in good part by Mr. Lush, but the artists responsible felt so guilty afterwards that they embarked upon a private painting venture and made presentations of their own. Mr. Lush was delighted with this sequel, treasuring the two canvases for years, and proudly exhibiting them when we came back as Old Boys.

For the last class at the end of term Mr. Lush was in the habit of talking to us about the great men of mathematics, geometry and so on. If we had two periods running and there was time over, he would bring in a structure of his own, the "pin-head camera," the subtleties of which he would then explain to us. From this there resulted a fine Hillier series entitled "Geometrical Photography down the Ages, by W.R.L.," depicting Pythagoras, Archimedes, Avagadro, Lobachevski, Saccheri, Felix Klein and a man whose name appeared to be Lar Plarz: these eminent authorities were shown clasping enormous pin-head cameras, and either running over hill and dale in pursuit of an escaping triangle or else making a cabinet portrait of a posing rhombus family. The "R" in the never to be forgotten W.R.L. was taken to stand for Roigbiv. William Roigbiv Lush.

Mr. Lush was never late, and never missed a class: illness could raise no claim against his regularity. When towards the end of his career he was invited by the Head-master to the Downside Dinner at the Savoy he first of all refused. When pressed for a reason he admitted that he could not be sure of getting back in time for the first period next morning. A notice went up to say that the class was cancelled, and Mr. Lush went to the dinner.

At about the same time, that is to say about twenty years after Mr. Lush had first tried to teach me mathematics, I was one day taking some parents past the Science Wing and up towards the cricket field when I heard a low burble of sound coming through the open window of a classroom: the sound gathered, and in a moment I knew it to be a Roar. I stopped dead in my conducted tour, the years falling from me, and I knew that the spirit yet lived and that the world had not grown cold.

When Mr. Lush ceased teaching at Downside my place was in the monastery and I was unable to attend his fare-well. However, the speech was reported to me almost ver-batim immediately afterwards, and it appears that this is what happened. Wedged firmly into a well-prepared and well-delivered survey were one or two not bad jokes which were received with gracious, but subdued, applause: the school was, as befitted the occasion, on its best behaviour. Then, after one or two more jokes, the truth began to dawn, and the whisper went round: "He wants a Roar . . . the old man is expecting a Lush Roar." So when he said: "I understand that you Downside boys are getting quite a name among the connoisseurs for copying old masters" there was the drone, at first, as of a distant squadron of aeroplanes . . . louder, louder . . . until the Roar burst with a violence of which we older Gregorians would have been proud. In the Assembly Hall there were no desks to thump or foot-rests to rattle, so it all had to be done by the human voice. Nevertheless it must have been terrific, and my informant tells me that though he saw boys of eighteen bellowing themselves hoarse with tears in their eyes, Mr. Lush himself remained perfectly calm. The hand raised in gentle unexpecting protest, the look of bemused non-comprehension. "Eh? Eh? I don't follow. Well, now let's get on."

v

Almost as memorable in his way—and especially to those who did mathematics higher up in the school—was Captain Le Seur. For years he had run the Corps, and was now, at the time of which I write, the doyen of the Common Room. What he was like as a master I do not know. I never reached the level at which he taught. I knew him, however, in private life, and was always in admiration of his benignity. Captain Le Seur, "the By" as he was called, exuded a kindliness which was often severely taxed by the unscrupulous. So characteristic were his walk, his expressions, his way of holding himself, that mention must be made of them. Head always on one side, a shoulder raised, an arm pressed against the body, knees slightly bent and left foot turned slightly inwards, the By must have taught at Downside for upwards of twenty years. In face and figure he remained the same from the time that he came until his death at the end of the Second War. His white hair and moustache looked all the whiter for the khaki of his complexion, the black of his eyebrows all the more severe for the gentleness of his expression. But perhaps the most memorable thing about the By was his habit of saying "will you" at the end of his sentences. It was not a question or an invitation. Nor did it imply a command. It simply took the place of, or possibly emphasised, the full stop. "There'll be no parade today, d'you see; it's just raining, will you." Or again: "I've heard from the

War Office, will you. Camp this year will be in Yorkshire." Finally there was the noise made by the By which denoted the enjoyment of something funny. It was not quite a laugh and not quite a chuckle; it came from the back of the throat, in short, staccato bursts. The jokes which were thus applauded had this about them—that they were never seen by anyone else. There must have been some strange secret humour attaching to certain situations or combinations of words which evoked this response, because often one would find Captain Le Seur with tears of laughter rolling down his brown cheeks while all around him would be blank and puzzled faces.

After his retirement, Captain Le Seur lived on for some years in his house in the village, coming up to the school whenever an excuse presented itself. No guest could have been more welcome. Everyone knew that he loved the place with every inch of his warm nature, and we delighted in the belief (verified, we were told, on numberless occasions) that on Tuesdays and Fridays he still cleaned his buttons and Sam Brown.

The pride of Le Seur's life was his son Jock, who was so much senior to me in the school that I scarcely knew him but whom I remember as resembling in many ways his father. Jock became a regular soldier and was killed at Dunkirk. To those who knew the By, Jock's death marked the only real change in the father's life.

VI

Mr. Moorat was a Modern Languages master, an Old Boy, a man of considerable charm and eccentricity. Knowing seventeen languages fluently, he had been an Intelligence Officer in the First War and had done a good deal of travelling. He always claimed that he was by nature a seaman, and that it was only by accident that he was a schoolmaster. He ran his class as if it were a ship's company, employing the idiom of the sea wherever possible and dealing out punishments with a salt water taste to them. What with the yard arm and the rope's end, one felt, sitting in Mr. Moorat's Fifth Form French, that it only wanted a wave to break over the desk and one would be in the middle of a Conrad story. Yet anything less like a sailor in appearance than Mr. Moorat, with diamond ring and pearl tiepin and peculiar walk, would be hard to imagine. True he wore a beard—his colleague in the Modern Language faculty, M. Cartel, also wore a beard, so we were not badly off at that time for men who looked every inch their parts—but it was a scholastic and not a naval beard. He spoke in a high-pitched voice, almost falsetto when excited, and his arched eyebrows gave the impression that he was in a constant state of surprise. Like so many of our masters, Mr. Moorat was, from the draw-ing point of view, a gift.

Also like so many of our masters, particularly Modern Language masters, he had his own system of marking. It involved the use of coloured chalks, and by the time one got back one's prose the paper resembled the back of an elaborate piece of needlework. M. Cartel's corrections were just as confusing: he wrote the number of mistakes and not the number of marks at the end of each line—so that the worse one's exercise, the better at first sight did it appear to be. Herr Heronberger used to put, foreign fashion, a varying number of exclamation marks according to how angry one's mistakes made him feel—suggesting to the English mind that it was all a huge joke.

During the holidays Mr. Moorat, whenever he could afford it, went on mysterious cruises in the Baltic and Mediterranean and elswhere, returning with strange and unlikely tales of his life afloat. His quite phenomenal knowledge of languages made adventure more accessible to him than to most men, so possibly some of the stories were true. Possessing the freedom of so many tongues, he spoke with a certain pedantry in his own. It was as if he were making a translation of a carefully phrased memorandum, and in order to keep his conversation light and flexible—for he was aware of the tendency to stiffen—he used to introduce the idiomatic, and even the slangy. But it was always the slang of an earlier generation. "Oh dear me," he observed to me sadly one morning, "I have had such a wigging from the Head. By Jingo, I feel so distressed. He levelled the charge that I had failed to secure pass degrees for my candidates in the School Certificate, and when I told him that one boy had passed in Spanish he retorted that this was not surprising since the boy could speak no English and was straight from Majorca. What I need now is a pint of bubbly to keep my pecker up." In the Common Room he cast himself for the role of what I believe is now called a "greeny," and some of the stories which he told against himself were very amusing. But he was not by nature a dupe, and very shrewd were his judgments of boys.

Once when we were feeling our way heavily through a piece of French prose, Mr. Moorat asked the class what "tadorne" was. Nobody knew. I put up my hand and said, "I'm pretty sure, sir, it's a sheldrake." I do not know now what a sheldrake is, but the word was written in the margin by some previous owner of the book, and I acquired a reputation with Mr. Moorat for a more than casual acquaintance with the language. Often in after years, sometimes when we were teaching different subjects to the same set of boys, Mr. Moorat would remind me of the much higher standard which had obtained in the early twenties. "There's nobody *now*," he would say in his high voice while his eyebrows mounted higher and higher up his forehead, "who can tell me in this class what the French is for sheldrake." Then he would add, with a beaming smile, "I've never *met* such a lot of jugginses."

In addition to his nautical interests, Mr. Moorat had what might almost be described as a passion for ties and pipes and keeping his shoes from turning up at the toe. He took me to see his ties and pipes, which were certainly very numerous, in his house on the corner of the village street. He also told me on one occasion that he endeavoured always to walk in such a way that his toes maintained a constant downward pressure, and that when he took off his shoes at night he was careful to insert the shoe-tree into the one even before he had started unlacing the other. So eager was he to forestall any sort of curling up.

During most of the time that he was teaching at Downside, Mr. Moorat was a widower, and when his young wife died, leaving five children, he seemed for some years to be quite unable to look after either his family or himself. The combination of absentmindedness, generosity, dislike of accounts and any sort of business method, made running a house more difficult than it need have been. Nor was his the kind of house which ran itself.

If people can be house-proud to a fault, they can also err in being house-humble: Mr. Moorat, though heaven knows he had every reason to, decried his property. When, during the Second War, he was taken to hospital for his last illness, it was discovered that he had not bothered to black out a single window. After dark he must have sat behind a screen with a candle or a torch. If one had asked him why he had not taken the necessary steps, he would have said, as he said about many things, "I am not a practical man, and I always leave these things to more competent people." It was certainly true that he was unpractical: he could not cut a loaf of bread or sharpen a pencil properly. "How clever," he would say in genuine admiration, "I have never been able to tie a parcel." How the

"Skipper," as he liked to call himself, would have managed had he been given any responsibility on his mysterious cruises one trembles to think. His characteristic "I never thought of that" was as sincere as were his fits of absent-mindedness. His abstraction was such that he would suddenly break off in the middle of a sentence, either his own or someone else's, and say something which showed that he must have been thinking of matters quite different. This was all the more confusing because of his look of rapt attention. It was in fact a look of absorbed and profound inattention. He once observed to a fellow master who was discoursing heavily and without pause on the subject of rising school fees, "It's such a mistake their printing photographs now in *The Times* newspaper." I have heard him while teaching French break off without so much as a comma or a drop of the voice, and say: "I wonder if angels ever sit down spiritually . . . they should, you know, if they have spiritual bodies." And then go straight on with the French without further reference to angels.

The duplicated noun, as in "*Times* newspaper," was a familiar device of his, and not, I think, an affectation. To speak of port wine, the railway train, the polka dance, and even the Bible book was part of the archaic mode which had to be balanced by all sorts of horrors like "ripping," and "half a jiffy."

His house, though he despised it and asked few people (apart from myself and at the most two others) to cross the threshold, was a reflexion of himself. It was full of humour as well as of litter. Good and bad taste, classics and detective stories, fresh air and froust were represented in equal proportions. Nearly everything showed signs of its owner's impress—mostly in the form of clumsy mending. Sticking plaster, that refuge of the amateur mender, was well to the fore, and the nearer one got to the kitchen departments the more one wondered how it was that Mr. Moorat had survived so long.

The pantry was suffering from the damp when I first saw it, and by the time I left school a fungus of sorts was spreading in rich profusion from wall to wall. There was a theory in the school that Mr. Moorat was being driven from room to room by a vast spreading vegetable culture which, as if in a Wellsian fantasy, was gradually over-powering him. It was alleged that already (in 1922) the way upstairs was barred by cactus, and that lizards nested under the carpets. I believe it is true that there were ferns in the sink, and that a stuffed stork peered frostily at one through the bathroom door, but this need not betoken neglect so much as a fondness for nature. "He may be keen on nature, but nature can't be very keen on him," said a clever little boy who afterwards became Headmaster of Downside, "because although the house is called The Rookery, even the rooks won't go near it." Nicholas Passmore was junior to me in the school, and I only wish that I had possessed enough foresight to cultivate the acquaintance of so unusual a youth.

Mr. Moorat (resembling Herr Heronberger, Sergeant Bastable and myself in this respect) possessed the sala-mandrine quality of being able to breathe freely in conditions of great heat. Mentally and physically he expanded when the temperature reached the eighties. While his fellow masters were being reduced to silence in the Common Room, Mr. Moorat, a silk handkerchief tucked into his collar as if he were about to play the violin, would scintillate. "Moo, for heaven's sake, keep quiet," said one dripping master, "not only do you look like a Turkish Bath advertisement but you make us feel like Esquimaux who have found themselves in the middle of the Sahara and forgotten to change."

Mr. Moorat was never fully appreciated. This was

partly because he wore his great talents and abilities with
such a supine unconcern that it was not always easy to see
them. It was also partly because his particular kind of wit
and learning goes for little in a modern society. Progressive civilisations have no particular use for their Mr.
Moorats. But if generosity, unfailing good spirits, de-
tachment from worldly things, and a religious sense quite
above the ordinary are qualities still to be valued at their
Christian worth, Mr. Moorat, though he left next to
nothing in the way of money, has certainly done his share
in handing on the things that are worth while.

A club to which I belonged while attending Mr. Lush's
and Mr. Moorat's classes was one which was founded by
a subtle heckler, Aidan L. B. Philip. It was called the
H.S.P.C.M. and was very select. Its members numbered
half a dozen and all were officials of the society. Finan-
cially it was kept afloat by an elaborate system of fines.
The initials stood for Humane Society for the Prevention
of Cruelty to Masters. So frequent were the occasions of
being fined that it became an expensive club to belong
to, and few of its members were equal to the burdens.
The proceeds of the fines were intended to provide a
dinner per term, to which the hardest hit master should
be invited, but though I can remember the dinners I
cannot remember that we ever invited a master. Perhaps
the funds did not run to this. Or perhaps we forgot.

A master who was well enough able to defend himself
without the assistance of our society was Mr. Cunningham, who taught Latin and Greek. He also took a Colts
game, coaching for years in rugger and cricket. A smiling
disciplinarian, Mr. Cunningham demanded a high standard in the classroom and on the field: in the classroom he
used a ruler with devastating accuracy, at scrum practice
he applied the lash of the spoken word. Correction,
therefore, was always received in the same place. In

order to meet the requirements of scholarship I bought for myself one holidays a copy of Dryden's translation of the *Aeneid*. As I had looked for nothing more than a crib, I was delighted to find myself caught up in the poetry and the plot of Aeneas' affairs. How far Dryden helped in the actual translation of what was set by Mr. Cunningham I do not know, but he gave me the interest necessary to suggest that there was industry behind my bland attention. An additional spur was provided by the fact that Jimmy Reynolds and I had a list of contemporaries to whom Virgil's characters applied.

Mr. Cunningham had a schoolmasterish way of saying things which, though not archaic in the manner of Mr. Moorat, was curiously stilted coming from one who was so obviously a man of the world. The periods rolled off the tongue, modulated, ordered, thoroughly in keeping, every part of speech correctly placed. "Be Latin never so dead as a language, Reynolds, it acquires, under your handling of its subtleties, a new and even starker mortality." And another one: "To give us 'dyed the shocked grasses with their sacrificial blood,' van Zeller, for the poet's homely *cum virtute in acie ceciderunt* is rather sugaring the cake, is it not? Fulsome, van Zeller, a little fulsome I think."

The Dryden experiment proving so fruitful, I tried Pope with his *Odyssey*. And with equal success. So should these lines reach the retired eye of Mr. Cunningham, they must bear witness with gratitude to the literary adventures which his classes inspired me to embark upon. I have him to thank for teaching me Latin and Greek: the Classics I taught myself—out of translations.

At about this time the series of fleeting drawing masters tended to stiffen, and a truly delightful Dutchman named Mr. Goosens looked like becoming a permanency. He differed from his predecessors in being able not only to draw but to teach drawing. All of us who took the subject became deeply attached to this quiet humble man, and we made no attempt to play the fool with him. It would have been grossly unfair to have turned his art lessons into a riot, because he was a sitting bird and was simply asking to be shot at by the heartless. Like Mr. Moorat he was vague almost to the point of vacancy and was profoundly religious. He never knew the date unless it was a feast day of the Church. He never kept accounts and had no idea how much money he had on him or in the bank. Often he would have to borrow from us—having missed his trains and buses—in order to get home. He would then not remember how much he owed us, and would put a heap of silver on the desk at the next class saying, "You take . . . you know . . . English money to me is muddle." Mr. Goosens was the most open-handed of men. Once when he had an exhibition of pictures in London, he gave away the canvases which he saw being admired, saying, "You like it? But how nice of you. I make the present." His childlike pleasure at finding his pictures appreciated was only equalled by the pleasure which he found in giving them away. He exhibited in Bath too, but he never made any money.

Mr. Goosens was the kind of man who could have got on only if he had been married or if he had belonged to a religious order. As a bachelor living in the world he lacked organisation, and so to a certain extent dissipated his energies. As an artist he was not so much of the first rank that he could afford to paint in the way he liked, and as a man of God he was blocked by being unable to follow his spiritual inclination. In my last year at school, when I had a room of my own to paint in, I came to know Mr. Goosens very well indeed. We talked endlessly about painting and religion—mostly about religion. In later years, when I had become a monk and when he was still wondering whether he was too old to be one, we used to go for walks in the monastery grounds after he had finished his painting classes in the school. For these walks he was invariably late. Indeed the only thing he was ever in time for was the daily Mass in St. John's, Bath.

Our art classes used to take place in a somewhat remote room behind the gym. The roof leaked, and in bad weather we used to paint under umbrellas. The period was supposed to last an hour, but three of us stopped on after the others had dispersed; Woods, Hillier and I would sometimes work from luncheon till evening classes without even a break for tea. Woods and Hillier sang while they painted, and it was all very jolly indeed. Mr. Goosens never sang, but he would wave a brush like a baton, beaming through his spectacles and obviously enjoying himself enormously. Often we would discover at about six o'clock that he had not had any lunch, and someone would jump onto a bicycle and go out in search of something to eat. When we had rooms in the attics later on, Arthur Woods and I used to keep a store of bananas for Mr. Goosens. For a time we pretended we preferred painting still life to figures and landscapes, and in this way we usually managed to share a meal of salad and fruit with Mr. Goosens when there was no longer any light to paint by. Arthur knew exactly how to handle Mr. Goosens, lending him raincoat and goloshes without the least suggestion of patronage, buying him cheroots almost without his knowing it, and even telling him how to manage the rebellious elements in his larger classes.

Mr. Goosens had a particular objection to mixing certain combinations of colours, and when pressed would say, "Ah, it will go all *black*." The final word would be spat out with the utmost venom, and Mr. Goosens' homely Dutch features would seem suddenly to take fire. We of the painting group adopted the phrase as a sort of slogan, and once in a Religious Doctrine Examination the answer given by Arthur Woods to the question, "How is the soul affected by mortal sin?" was the familiar "Ah, it will go all *black*."

Schoolboy howlers can become tedious beyond endurance, but an answer to an examination question which is worth recording here—and which incidentally is not a schoolboy howler—is one which was given by either Richard or Christopher Sykes to a question in a General Paper which ran, "Mention the discovery which you consider to be the most significant to man since the invention of printing, and give an explanation of your choice." The answer was stated briefly at the top of the page by the languid examinee thus: "The deck chair. But of course one can't *explain* it exactly."

Mr. Goosens had patent methods of his own for preserving the freshness of colours, for "fixing" charcoal and pastel drawings, for cleaning badly varnished oil paintings. He was full of tricks, and I learned more from him than from my father who was the better painter. The trouble about Mr. Goosens was that he had learned and taught too much. Making use of too many styles, he never fully developed his own. This was a pity because he was not without originality. He certainly had a genius for bringing to the surface the latent originality in others. Perhaps it was that he was too selfless to settle.

Unconventional, Bohemian even, Mr. Goosens steered a wavering course on the choppy waters of his profession. But if as an artist he never quite knew where his next meal was coming from, as a near-saint he never quite cared. The course of sanctity was not so uncertain—at all events to those who looked on from the outside—and I for one must record the debt I owe to that rare being in a world composed of exhibitionist artists and self-consciously devout, the simple soul. How few there are who can be simple without being imbecile, spiritual without being soulful.

VII

It must have been about now that electric light was installed in the place of the original gas. I do not know why this should have seemed such an important change, but it did. The shower of soft white gas mantle which fell like snow every time one's aim went wrong was now to cease. The hiss and flicker would no longer make themselves felt when one's attention was released from whatever one was doing. And there would be no smell. Jimmy and I, conservative in our waistcoats and stiff shirts, used to go up to the gasometers behind the stables and sniff nostalgically at their metal surfaces.

The improvement was most to be noticed in the Abbey, but this was not until somewhat later. The changes in the Abbey during the early twenties were watched with the greatest interest by the school, and by none more closely than by ourselves. We who had (I hope not too obviously or arrogantly) set ourselves up as the arbiters of taste were as ready to discuss a new line of Eric Gill's lettering or a Comper window as we were to offer our opinion on an Old Boy's suit of clothes. Great, consequently, was our enthusiasm when we heard that Sir Giles Scott's plans for the completion of the nave had been passed by the chapter, and that the work was being put in hand straight away. Still greater was our enthusiasm when we found that the preparations involved ropes, pulleys, and scaffold-poles among the back benches where we sat. During Vespers we played, I regret to say, a game which we called "Galley-slaves," rowing to the rhythm of the chant. The illusion was helped by the overhead gallery which was reserved for visitors and which we called the "poop."

The straining ropes, the creaking planks and poles, the religious darkness of the scene created admirably the hold of a Spanish galleon, and when Claude Marcel was sent up each Sunday with the collection-bag we always asked him how many doubloons and pieces of eight he had managed to take off the grandees and señoritas on the poop.

One señorita who used to come each year to visit her brother—and when he left, to visit his younger friends —was Moosie Haydon. On Easter Sunday, 1922, whether by accident or intent, she dropped her white kid glove over the rail of the poop, and it fell neatly across the top of my head. I and the rest of the crew in the hold affected to disapprove strongly of this piece of forwardness, and she admits now that she should have been more careful. Her visits were much looked forward to. She has not been to Downside for years, but this may be because the gallery has been removed and there is today a wide space over which visitors, if so inclined, would have to throw their gloves. Moosie's brother, Charles, became a regular soldier when he left school, joining the Irish Guards and winning distinction after distinction during the Second War. The respect which I now feel for this Brigadier and D.S.O. is the same in kind as that which I felt for the School Prefect and Colour in both First Eleven and First Fifteen.

Controversy is never far from the question of religious services in schools, and we are always being told that boys cannot pray for longer than ten minutes at a time. To judge from the letters which are written to the Press, it might be thought that boys were of so nervous a disposition that the effort to follow a liturgical Office must induce a breakdown and consequent reaction against all things religious. Possibly such letters are from ladies whose experience is limited to discussions with a recalcitrant great-nephew. Possibly they refer to schools, if any of the kind exist, where ceremonies are protracted beyond all reason and where the boys' free time is encroached upon. There may be many explanations. All I can say is that we never seemed to feel the services to be unendurable. It must be difficult for those in authority to strike the balance in this matter of church attendance, but I do not think that the Downside of the twenties can be fairly charged with ramming too much religion down the boys' throats. We certainly spent more time in the Abbey then than the present generation does now, but I do not remember more than a purely routine resentment. The present system, too, seems to me admirably sensible and adapted to the altered conditions of the time. Particularly the present-day emphasis on voluntary attendance at some of the non-essential devotions appears to be rewarding.

Whatever the merits of succeeding trends, there is nothing in the complaint against the older observance that it divorced public worship from any sort of personal devotion. Where the Liturgy is properly explained and taken part in by the boys—as it is and always has been at Downside—there is nothing impersonal or remote about going to church unless the individual makes it so. Looking back, I can see a truly remarkable and genuine piety in the most unlikely subjects, and this would surely have been impossible if the tradition had been unsuitable to the general level of Downside boy. Ceremonies, Gregorian Chant, retreats and sermons were all taken for granted and accepted as a familiar part of one's life. Like the rest of life, they contained elements grave and gay. Worship of God would be a creamy affair if it were all entertainment, and I can well recall what discomforts, boredoms, struggles against distraction and sleep may be necessary to redeem the service of God from the too-easy.

Among the flood of churchtime memories which press

upon me I recollect especially an occasion when we were
bidden by the Head of the School in the middle of a
psalm at Vespers to sing up. A boy called Esgar Guest,
having hitherto remained deaf to such appeals and maintained a tomb-like silence throughout all church services
without distinction, opened wide his mouth and gave quite
astonishing weight to the words *ab auditione non timebit*
which by a happy chance we had just at that moment
reached. So terrific was the noise which escaped from the
lips of this evidently voice-shy boy that the rest of us
turned speechless to look at him, and the psalmody col-
lapsed. The monks, taken equally unawares, failed to
take up the next verse and could be seen bending forward
in their stalls, looking with puzzled expressions on their
faces in the direction of the nave, clearly wondering
whence such a force of sound had come. In a moment or
two the psalm was taken up again, and all was well. It
was the kind of situation which in later years David
Langdon would have delighted to draw: every head in
the great church turned in the one direction, and then,
with a sense of order suddenly restored, turned swiftly
back to the business in hand. Some said afterwards that
the candles on the High Altar were seen to sway in their
sockets and that the flames bent back from the wick as
if wincing from the impact of a power. One boy declared
that the windows in St. Placid's chapel were shaken so
violently that a piece of stained glass fell to the floor.[1]
Certainly this little incident must have caught the fancy
of the school, for it was frequently cited in after years as
a location-point in time. "Would that be before or after
Guest sang at Vespers?"—in much the same way that

[1] Though not vouching for the truth of either of these statements, I
must record the fact that a section of glass, three inches by two, had to
be replaced shortly after the events described. Visitors to St. Placid's
chapel may see for themselves.

school history at Ladycross is divided between what happened before or after Mrs. Boden slipped in the custard.

If Esgar Guest was discouraged by the authorities from ever repeating his experiment in prompt obedience, we, less laudable in our response, were always being urged to take a more active part in sacred song. An unusual line was taken on this matter by the Sykes brothers, who sat immediately in front of me and whose activities I was accordingly able to observe. Why they should have been placed beside one another I do not know, for there was a year or two between them and Christopher ought properly to have occupied a row further forward, but I remember particularly that they shared the same Vespers book and also the same views about the chant. While the rest of us were singing in the Roman manner, the Sykeses held out with the classical pronunciation. Thus to our soft "g" and "r" they would come with the hardest of the hard, and as we were making the first syllable of "saeculi" rhyme with "cake" they would make it rhyme with "bike." The "Regina Coeli" gave them plenty of scope.

Our training in congregational singing was entrusted to Dom Thomas Symons, and many must have been the agonies which he suffered. The half-hour singing practices in the Abbey on Saturday afternoons were dreaded even by the unmusical, but in retrospect I would not have missed them for anything. Dom Thomas had, and has still, a lightness of touch which makes even the plainest of Plain Chant lively. It was perhaps my admiration for his patience in conducting the singing practices, and the zest which he brought to the subject, that drew me to frequent his room in the school. It was a musician's room, stacked high with scores and always ringing with piano play, and had it not been a painter's room as well I might always have felt that I had no business there. Alick Dru and Napper Dean Paul had the freedom of it, and soon I found that I was again part of the circle which had revolved round the musico-artistic personality of Miss Symes a year or so before. Such, I discovered, was the way of it at Downside: one was for ever impinging upon societies which had seemed to melt, for ever overlapping outside one's sphere and arriving at a sense of security and companionship to which one felt one had no right.

Dom Thomas's room, in spite of the view from the window which looked onto the roofs of temporary bungalows, spelled another of my returns to the pursuit of things beautiful and cultural. Here, watched from the peeling yellow walls by faces painted by Dom Thomas's father and brother, I read all the poetry I could lay hands on. My book list shows the ill-assorted names of Browning, Matthew Arnold, Omar Khayyam, de la Mare, Swinburne, Chesterton and Francis Thompson. What is more I seem to have had views on all of them, and since I had never read a line of criticism in my life I can only suppose that the views reflected genuine impressions. Poetry was a discovery, because my aunt Yolande was sadly short of verse, and until I had tasted its flavour with the cribs which I had bought in the holidays my mind was amply satisfied with prose. There followed (of course) the inevitable phase of writing dismally incompetent poems in rhyme and the kind of free verse which is so manifestly forced as to destroy the least sense of freedom. These poems I read to my friends, who were kindness itself but who did not implore me to compose any more. It is astonishing to reflect that for ten years I must have kept up the practice of writing poetry, and never for a moment did I impress anyone with the slightest sense of my worth as a poet. When working in an office in Liverpool I used occasionally to have my poems accepted by a paper which I think was called the

Evening Echo, but not even these literary triumphs were able to blind me to the unconcern with which the North of England and the Midlands were taking me. "But my dear feller," Jack Carroll consoled me, "all these poet fellers have to *start,* I mean." Nobody could have been more patient with my poetry than Jack. Jimmy Reynolds, whose mother wrote real poetry, knew it to be mud. To show my work to Alick, whose wit was inclined to be both challenging and astringent, I never dared. ("He will never do anything after he's left this place," said Alick of a certain rather dashing Head of the School about whom the prophets were promising great things; "you can see by the way he stamps a letter that he's a nonentity; by the way he looks at his watch; by the way he *shaves.*")

Also in Father Thomas's room I read *The Garden of Allah,* which I saw later on as a play with Godfrey Tearle in the part of the Trappist. I still think that this is a good romantic story. But this may be because I have never been a Trappist. Father Thomas never seemed to read any of the books which lay about his room, and yet whenever a book was mentioned he was able to quote whole passages from it. What impressed me still more was his ability to speak in the manner of any author you cared to mention—straight off at a moment's notice. Had he set his mind to it he could have written parodies as various as Max Beerbohm's and J. C. Squire's. One day, if I ever catch him with a book in his hand, I shall try and persuade him to do this. At the moment all his great creative energy is going into painting—he has even suspended his *magnum opus* on Lanfranc and the *carta charitatis* which monastic historians have been waiting for—and he is producing water colours so fast that while one is drying two more are being roughed out. Dom Thomas told me once that at home as a boy he had had little opportunity for painting because his brothers and sisters took up so much room, and spent so much time, with their acting and dancing and playing musical instruments. "We all recited our own compositions, but there was always so much noise going on that I doubt if anyone heard them." So there is evidently a price to pay for belonging to a talented family. "Who tidied up?" I, with my feeling for order, asked. "Nobody," was the brief but gratified reply.

Another room which offered shelter to the garrulous was Dom Raymund Webster's. Here in an atmosphere far removed from Dom Thomas's Chelsea overlooking the bungalow roofs, James Murray, Ambrose Dasent, James Cuming and I were accustomed to gather and discuss with our host, who took part in the conversation without looking up from his book, such diverse subjects as sailing, the recent war (in which Dom Raymund had been a chaplain), Scotland (three of our number were Scotsmen), tobacco, monasticism (about which, like Dom Thomas, our host was an authority), golf, Harrow (where Dom Raymund had been at school), the best sort of diet for keeping fit, and the folly of futurist painting. Always the talk seemed to come round in the end to the discussion of pipes. During the holidays we had taken up smoking, and though I secretly hated the practice I can recall to this day the peculiar thrill of taking my precious Dunhill from its grey leather glove, and polishing it against my nose. Though we were not at the age when we could smoke at school, there was nothing against our talking about it. Though we were not allowed to keep our pipes at school, there was nothing to prevent our sending for catalogues and samples of pipe-polish. There was a certain lemon-coloured cream which one rubbed into the bowl and which was supposed to preserve the patina. It smelled of almonds and camembert, and was very expensive.

The pipe craze lasted a long time, involving ceaseless argument, many anxieties and envies, much correspondence. The literature had to be studied, each new model had to be considered, every cleaner and scraper and filter had to be tested. This was at the time when the rough-surfaced briar was coming in, and we of Dom Raymund's room were in two minds as to its suitability. Was it a passing fashion? Might it not be designed by unscrupulous pipemakers to conceal possible flaws? Were not the straight-grained Barlings to be preferred before the black but comely stipple of newer firms? These were only some of the problems which were debated by the four of our symposium while the fifth was reading his history of Camaldoli or following the course of the *Amaryllis* in her cruise round the world. The general picture was nearer to *Stalky and Co.* than anything I experienced at Down-side. Four boys aged fifteen sitting on a window ledge overlooking the quadrangle, a pipe mania, endless talk and planning, an Old Harrovian master, digestive biscuits, books, books, books, and never long enough to enjoy it to the full because of the bell for evening Assembly, which meant clattering down the stone stairs of the Turret Tower from the Lower Gallery.

VIII

The holidays at this period, in the absence of the diary which will be coming back in a year or so, assume an uncertain sequence. There were visits to Ireland to my aunt Rita's; there were longer periods in London, at either my aunt Berthe's or the Chamberlain's or the Gubbins's. One incident sticks in my memory connected with an Easter holidays at the van de Velde stronghold in Lower Belgrave Street. I was trying to write a play about Rasputin and Czarist Russia, and so was more than normally distracted in mind. The work required such concentration that for whole days at a time I hardly knew where I was, and it was only with effort that I could have said which had been the previous meal; the day of the week, like the hour of the day, meant nothing to me. I was feeding in the Palace at St. Petersburg, I was driving in a droski through the snow. During this phase of abstraction I was taken by some people to see *Mary Rose* (with Fay Compton and Robert Lorraine in the leading parts—though I noticed nothing of their acting on this occasion, and had to go again later with my aunt Yolande to see a performance which I would not have missed for anything), and half-way through the first act I awoke to the feeling that I had left the bath taps running and forgotten to have my bath. At the fall of the curtain for the interval, I sped from the theatre (presumably clasping my telescope) and drove up to my aunt's house in an anxious taxi—expecting to see a crowd looking up at the rising line of water against the glass of the windows, expecting to see water spurting from the sides of the front door and down the steps onto the pavement. It was reassuring to find the house looking the same as usual, and still more reassuring, as I ran up the stairs three at a time, to hear the sound of song coming from the place of my quest. The parlourmaid, Ivy, had found the bath full of hot water, and, as none of the family was in, had decided not to waste it. So after shouting at her through the keyhole and binding her to secrecy, I went back to *Mary Rose* with a light heart.

Twenty-five years later—not that this has any direct bearing upon the above—I found myself travelling in the same compartment with Mr. Ernest Thesiger who had taken the part of the crofter's son in *Mary Rose*. It was during the Hitler War and we were sharing the same packet of sandwiches. I told him that the last time I had seen him at a picnic luncheon was when he was doing a temporary ghillie job between the terms of a Scottish university. The reference delighted him, and the rest of the journey could not have been more enjoyable. So it was as well that I went more than once to see *Mary Rose* —or I might have got a Scots crofter mixed up with a Russian moujik.

Another occasion on which the throes of composition disrupted the normal processes was when I was staying with some people in Bryanston Square. I had had a bath and was in my pyjamas kneeling against the bed and reciting my evening prayers, when the son of the house came into the room and said that they were waiting dinner for me downstairs. I had been praying into the dress trousers which, together with the other garments of accepted evening wear, had been laid out for me to change into.

But this, and some of what has gone before, belongs to a slightly later period than that which is covered by my time as a fag. The next chapter is therefore somewhat overdue.

V: Privilege Period

AFTER VISITING Messrs. Dunhill's in the holidays, and so satisfying my devotion under the direction of the umpire-coated acolytes who minister at that shrine, I came back to Downside one term to find that my passage through the school was once again departing from the strictly measured progression, and that I was enjoying the privileges of the Upper Fifth. There had probably been some mistake on the part of the secretary or clerk whose business it was to type out the lists. Without demur, however, I availed myself of the right to discard the narrow black tie in favour of the kind which fans out. Other freedoms which my new-found station afforded me were: going later to bed, coming into the refectory earlier for tea, free bounds and leaving my coat open. There may have been others but I have forgotten them, and lest such liberty should appear too staggering to the reader it must be added that even now, with emancipation sweetening life at almost every point of contact, there were certain staircases and doors that were denied me, and I might neither wear the collar of my blazer turned up nor allow the white of a handkerchief to appear above the line of the breast pocket. So I was virtually still in chains.

Moving up like this meant, again, the reviving of old contacts as well as the formation of new ones. There was not the same danger of being branded a thruster if one was seen talking to members of the Sixth, or even to Old Boys when they came down. George Bellord had a room by this time, and though he had jumped ahead since Junior School days I was able to see something of him and his friends. In this society the man of wit was Kevin Hayes, who was then the editor of the *Raven*[1] and who is now a judge; his comments on people and contemporary life at Downside were couched always in correct epigrammatic form and so were, if not always repeatable, at least memorable. Leonard Parker's visits from Oxford no longer embarrassed either of us, and the comfortable Brittany relationship of a year ago under the inspiration of Fr. Bede was saved from extinction. We began now to keep up a correspondence which, for me at any rate, proved highly satisfactory. He fed me with poetry, his own and other people's, while I supplied him with Downside news to which he attached great value and sentiment. We used to post to each other, backwards and forwards, the poems of Rupert Brooke with ever increasing pencilled notes in the margin. Under his and Kevin Hayes's tuition I learned more about twentieth-century poetry than I would have done in class, and very little time was wasted in reading rubbish. I knew a lot of Housman by heart, for he admirably suited what I (mistakenly) conceived to be my prevailing mood.

Also at this time I read all the poetical works of Shelley, Keats and Oscar Wilde. How I missed Byron I cannot imagine, but I know that it was not until many years later that I discovered him. It was a discovery worth waiting for, and I read for five or six hours while sitting on the side of my bed undressing.

Invited to Oxford by Leonard, I came to find something in that city which I had never met before and which I have never enjoyed anywhere else. I was sixteen, I did not belong, I was not at my ease. But it was a magic place for me, a city of enchantment. When I go back

[1] The School Magazine.

there now I marvel at what it was that held me. Which shows how great is the gulf which separates youth from middle age. I ought to know but I do not. Oxford now is to me like any other town with a tradition and a singular, though overlaid, beauty. This is not because it has put on flesh, has lost its elegance, has hidden itself in a mess of cut-price stores, traffic lights, and pretentious villas. It is because human nature stiffens and the eye takes on a different focus. Anyway, Oxford saw me a good deal during the next three years, for I was allowed by my aunts (and my parents when they were in England) much freedom of movement. Not always did it see me to good advantage. My guide to the city of dreams was Compton Mackenzie's *Sinister Street*, which we were all reading eagerly at Downside, and my lodging (if I happened to be in funds) the Clarendon. When in low pocket I slept behind the bar of a friendly public house, the landlord taking me for older than I was. Sometimes I managed to be the guest of a college—as when Leonard persuaded the authorities that I would not disgrace Trinity—and later on I took to sleeping on sofas. I shall have a further word to say about Oxford when I come to my final school year and a Commem Week visit. As yet, at the time reached in the present chronicle, the question of belonging to the University had not arisen.

Among the new friends which my unearned promotion in the school gained for me was Thomas St A. Ronald, now a producer at the B.B.C. There was never a more generous or good-natured boy than Tom Ronald. His un-failing good spirits put the rest of us to shame: moodiness was the prevailing flaw in most of my contemporaries, but in Tom the spirit of gloom was never for a moment detected. Indeed there were some among us who felt that a little depression, a minor tragedy or two in his life, might be a good thing. He conveyed, despite the opposition

W. R. LUSH, ESQ.
From a drawing by Tristram Hillier

which he found in certain temperaments, a spirit of gaiety. The more he sensed an opposition the more was he gay, and inevitably one capitulated before the onslaught. His strong suit clearly lay, even at that early age, in the direction of the entertainment world. Apparently impervious to criticism, he got up revues, pantomimes, sing-songs, and to him rather than to the officials of the Dramatic Society went the credit of discovering talent in the school. As impresario he launched the most unlikely people, including myself, upon the stormy waters of show business, so it seems that nothing could be more apt than his subsequent choice of profession.

Nor was Tom Ronald's ability confined to showmanship: his own acting was as polished and professional as anything that has been seen upon the Downside stage. Mrs. Charles Brookfield, writing dramatic criticism for *The Raven*, singled out Tom's performance in H. J. Byron's play *Our Boys*, prophesying a dazzling future to this "dramatic aspirant who played his part with humour and a true sense of character." This was when Tom was only thirteen. Four years later, as Shylock, he showed what he could do with Shakespeare, and already Mrs. Brookfield's forecast was justified.

Apart from Shakespearean plays (in which I took only the smallest parts, and no especial interest) and straightforward drawing-room comedies (in which I usually managed to be given good parts, and for which I slaved with genuine devotion), the histrionic faculty at Downside was responsible for producing over a course of years a series of more or less informal entertainments ranging from the old-fashioned troupe-party to the classical one-act play by such authors as Synge, W. W. Jacobs and Lord Dunsany. In 1918 a variety programme was represented under the beach-and-pierrot title of *The April Fools*. Topical allusions abounded, and the production was probably rather appalling, but I can remember every song, every costume, every hasty improvisation. Though still in the Junior School I had been asked to help with the posters and scenery, so perhaps this, together with my first experience of back-stage and grease-paint life, had something to do with the sharpness of my recollections. A boy who possessed the name of Lovell Vyvyan Payne-Payne (which might have come out of a Saki story) gave a delightful rendering of a danseuse who stabs herself after killing the man she loves. He must have been a versatile performer because he also sang two hit songs of the day, and changed his costume four times during the evening. In the audience was his sister, Zoë, and the attention of the school was divided between the two members of that good-looking family. Zoë swept the school like a prairie fire, and many were the hearts that throbbed despairingly during the Easter holidays of 1918. No other visitor has ever done quite such a Zuleika Dobson.

Acting became so popular that House Concerts gave place to House Plays, and each year the rivalry between the Houses in this matter of putting on something original and breath-taking was keen. The strain of keeping up secret rehearsals, of pretending that nothing had been decided upon and that we would probably just fall back upon a few Old English Folk Songs and a flute solo, of finding material which would lend itself to topical references, was considerable. Since the Caverel Play always came last in the season, and since Tom Ronald and I were usually made responsible for it, we were able to present parodies of the House Plays that had gone before. There was only a week's interval between the Roberts' Play and our own, so it was not always easy to get out our script, cast the parts, learn the lines, take each of the players individually through the text, practise—when the performance required, as it did one year, a *corps de ballet*

—the steps, procure the clothes, paint the posters, design and make the scenery, print the programmes . . . in time. Tom has doubtless done a lot of this kind of thing since, and even I have had some slight repetition of it, but neither of us has at the same time been working for an exam and playing regular games. Surely no *crises de théâtre,* even at the B.B.C., can have been more exciting than those which sent up the temperature of a musical piece called *The Magic Gym Shoe* which we produced together in 1922. For this the score was composed by a Mr. Vernon Griffiths, who worked on our script for two nights without going to bed at all. What has become of this prompt musician I do not know, but for willingness and skill he certainly surpassed himself on this occasion, and the audience found it hard to believe that our operetta was not a professional skeleton dressed up.

In those days the Downside stage was lit by gas, and after one had been on the boards for twenty minutes the grease-paint was running down one's face. All one could see of the audience was a shimmering neutral-coloured haze, which seemed to have depth but no substance, and which hung uncertainly over a line of dancing, glaring, yellow fire.

In the April issue of the 1923 *Raven* there appeared an article on "The Downside Stage" which reflected—as well it might since it was the work of at least six of us—our views. In the main it was a plea for a more ambitious policy in the choosing of plays. It urged the performance of Shaw, Pinero, Galsworthy and J. M. Barrie. "Unfortunately the success and failure of the types of plays produced in London are mirrored at Downside. Farce used to be the most popular until recently, when it was superseded by musical comedy. Over seventy-five per cent of the Downside performances have been comedies in one form or another. Comedies in themselves are very excellent, provided that they sparkle and are well acted, but not all of them have very much dramatic value." The article goes on to say, with some pomposity, that "really good drama is one of the finest forms of education . . . the stage loses some of its glamour if looked upon as a means of education, but this cold fact could be subtly concealed." The truth is that the Dramatic Society felt envious, and rightly, of the more sophisticated line taken by its sister association, the Literary Society. While our neighbours in the book-enfolded respectability of the Petre Library read their parts from Elizabethan tragedy and Restoration Comedy, we of the Dramatic Society became increasingly conscious of our waning culture. In *The Raven* we read about how well *The Critic, She Stoops to Conquer, The Tempest, Strife*, passages from the *Inferno, The Ring and the Book, Iphigenia in Tauris* were received by a select audience. The notices about our own activities were no less glowing but they were certainly not so considered. And what we wanted was to be taken seriously. It was not enough to get all the laughs; we wanted the kind of awed homage which in the holidays we saw going to Ibsen and Tchekov. We were as Noel Cowards sighing after the T. S. Eliots.

I like to persuade myself that the article in the 1923 *Raven* gave impetus to the demand which in later years was satisfied by *Saint Joan, John Bull's Other Island, A Saint in a Hurry*, and, in the year of writing, *Murder in the Cathedral*.

II

One way by which, so far as I was concerned, this cultural resurgence expressed itself was in the efforts made by its promoters to educate the unenlightened. Priggishly we set about proclaiming the muse to which we happened to be devoted: ardently we wooed our proselytes. Thus it was that staying back a few days after the end of term I made friends with, and tried to "improve," a certain philistine whom for the space of about a year I was to see a good deal of—both at school and during the holidays. We were both either convalescing from something or else waiting for a boat, and since there was nobody else in the great shell of the empty school we were much in each other's company. Such friendships ripen quickly, and as a rule are just as quick to fade. Taken out of their ordinary setting they are felt to be more significant than they are, and put back in their setting afterwards they are seen in retrospect at less than their real value. But this particular one, as far as it went, was a success.

The two of us were the same age, we were even in the same house and form, but we had never noticed each other before. We were certainly not affinities, and I doubt if we were sufficiently opposite to be complements of one another, but we managed somehow to get on. I admired his generosity, impulsiveness, reckless stupidity; he for his part accepted me as an adviser of wide experience and mature judgement. Though I felt keenly the absurdity of the role for which I was cast, I played it for all I was worth—well knowing that none of my other contemporaries was ever likely to view me as a figure of sober wisdom. So did he, this boy, live up to his part, which was a lot more genuine than mine. Folly never came more naturally, or so gracefully, to anyone.

Ruthlessly I would tell my new friend where I thought he was wrong: meekly he would listen, plead, make excuses, give in, thank me almost with tears in his eyes —and then go off and do the same silly thing again. I still pray for him today, because I feel conscious—more conscious now than I did then—of the responsibility which I owed him, and believe that I could have used my influence to better advantage.

Here is an incident which will illustrate the nature of our relationship. By way of refining the quality of his mind I took this fellow schoolboy to the Tate. It was during the summer holidays, and while we were walking back along the Embankment discussing the pictures we had seen, I glanced down at the pavement and said (in a kind but disapproving voice): "Your shoes are too pale for the Tate, and I am not sure that you should wear brown shoes in London anyway. Also they are too pointed: they look bounderish." To which he replied at once: "I don't like them either," and, taking them off, threw them over the parapet into the river.

Hair-trigger personalities of this sort are an invariable source of delight, and if it were only a question of coming home in a taxi with people in their socks I would ask for more of them in my quiet life, but this particular friend tended sometimes to become an embarrassment—not to say an anxiety. As for example when I took him to Lower Belgrave Street, and showed him to the family. The mistake was mine rather than his, for I should have apprehended the lack of mutual understanding. He began badly by drinking a little too much at dinner and talking too loudly. My aunt Berthe, the most charitable of women, took an instant dislike to him, and my father was mollified in his opinion only when he heard (from me, half-way through the meal as I saw that things were going wrong) that he had boxed for Downside. My father called him "Pritchard" throughout the evening—though this was not the boy's name nor anything like it, for his was a French name. After dinner our guest did something which would probably never have been noticed by any family but ours: he put a used match back in the box. After politely lighting my mother's cigarette for her, the youth was probably too shy to look for an ashtray. The box was the obvious place . . . the action a commendable piece of tidiness. But I hoped nevertheless that the movement had escaped attention: I knew that with my particular family it would damn him out of hand. That it had not escaped attention I discovered for certain a few weeks later when the boy's name came up in the conversation, and when my mother, who normally liked my friends, said: "That's the one, isn't it, with the Y.M.C.A. tricks?" I knew at once to what she was referring.

With my mother first impressions counted for everything. No one could redeem himself if things went wrong at the introduction. In fact with her it was sometimes a preconception, and not a live impression at all, which coloured her settled opinion—whether of a person, a book, a country, or a situation. As an instance of this there was the case of a family which came to live in England after a period abroad in one of the colonies, and who built for themselves a home which for our present purposes we will call Kraal House. The name given to the house, though nothing like the "Kraal," bore a close relation to the colony from which the family in question had returned. Several members of this family were great friends of ours, but it so happened that my mother never chanced to visit Kraal House . . . and so in actual fact knew nothing whatever about the place except its name. Yet whenever the family or the house was mentioned by any of us, my mother would say inevitably: "I cannot understand them building that perfectly dreadful house . . . how they can live in it I simply don't know." Useless for us to tell her that it was a delightful house and not a bit what she imagined. "They have got plenty of money," she would insist, "so there's no earthly reason why they should build in that funny way."

The words "funny" and "dreadful" figured frequently in my mother's speech. Not only, as here ("I must say it's very funny of them . . . I hope they'll never ask me to that dreadful place"), but often in connections where the adjectives were more loosely applied. "When refusing an invitation, dear, always think of some nice excuse: then the people don't think it's so funny." "That dreadful man over there who looks hot . . . no, I don't know who he is, but I'm sure he must be dreadful, quite quite dreadful." "You said you would telephone to them, dear, and you didn't: I'm afraid they thought it was very funny." But to get back to the house which we have been considering, the Kraal, the response could be counted upon so invariably that my brother and I used to work round to the subject for the sheer pleasure of hearing the familiar phrases repeated. "I couldn't bear it for one minute myself." Thus the idea that a photograph of this agreeable house should be shown to my mother was sternly rejected. I doubt if even then, with the architecture staring her in the face, there would have been any change. A perfectly dreadful house it had been since it had appeared on the writing paper, and a perfectly dreadful house it must remain.

In this digression about my mother we have strayed some way from my friend with the brown shoes and the over-anxious clothes. To resume. My attempt to deflect from the tendency to be flamboyant, and instead to raise the cultural level, led to my drawing up a list of books to be read and plays to be seen. After outlining a course of Thomas Hardy, Galsworthy, and (more or less as a concession) Hugh Walpole, I took my friend to see Viola Tree in *Secrets*, Mrs. Patrick Campbell in *The Thirteenth Chair*, Robert Lorraine in *The Happy Ending*, Marie Löhr and Godfrey Tearle in *The Laughing Lady*, and Arthur Boucher in *The Risk*. But it was no good. Books he found hard to finish; the theatre, unless the play was a musical one, he found dull. So to musical comedy we went. Nor, to be truthful, did this process of coming down from the heights distress me. Perhaps, after a good whack of the National Gallery and the Tate, I was glad of the excuse to relax. W. H. Berry at the Adelphi, Wilkie Bard at the Coliseum, Laurie de Freece at the Gaiety and Harry Weldon at the Victoria Palace held us spellbound across the footlights. Best of all was Robert Hale, father of Binnie and Sonnie, with his references to Downside when he knew we were in the audience.

In those days it was possible to get for five shillings what was called a "Rover" ticket, which entitled the holder to a seat in any part of the house which he happened to find free. One "roved" during the first act, and settled during the second. Sometimes a late-comer would turn one out, and if the run were popular one might have to stand at the back of the house all the evening, but on the whole the system was well worth resorting to, and we saw a number of musical productions in this way. Somehow it was not very generally appreciated as a practice, but those who made use of it were so assiduous in exploiting their discovery that we came to know our fellow rovers quite well by sight as we went from place to place. I am told that the arrangement has now been dropped, and that even the lightest musical playgoing is today severely sedentary instead of, as formerly, peripatetic.

Since "shows" (though I never allowed the use of this word, nor do I now accept readily the phrase "going to a show") were not put down on my list of plays seen between the years 1914-24, I can be less accurate about the lighter side of our theatre-going at this period, but I distinctly remember that my new friend was enthusiastic about one of the musical productions which George Grossmith and Leslie Henson made successful at the Winter Garden Theatre. Insisting that we should go to it again and again, he turned up one night with a box of chocolates so vast that I could hardly bear the tension of nursing it on my knee during the opening scenes while he wrestled with the composition of a note to Miss Heather Thatcher. The boxes of chocolates on sale within the theatre were not, he told me, sumptuous enough . . . and would I mind interviewing the competent authorities and seeing to its delivery? It was typical that I should be assumed to know the approach—just as typical as that I should be called upon to approve, and if need be to amend, the text of his letter to Miss Thatcher. It so happened that I was acquainted with the porter at the Winter Garden stage door—my uncle Marcel had introduced me—and was therefore able to discharge myself of the mission without delay. There must have been a more than usual number of intervals during that musical piece, because messages came and went between the porter and myself for the rest of the performance. Anyway, the upshot was that the sumptuous box found its way back to my lap, and with it arrived a polite and grateful letter in the third person (is it one of the functions of a dresser, perhaps, to transcribe such documents?) explaining that Miss Thatcher was not in the habit of receiving gifts from strangers. My friend was crestfallen at the turn things had taken, and I am afraid I did not help matters by the somewhat unfeeling I-told-you-so attitude which I adopted. Since his appetite was spoiled, I made, during the time that remained to us, inroads into the upper layers of the box of chocolates, and I hope that my munching prevented me from saying that I had disapproved all along of his conduct.

Another incident in connection with this boy which I recall very clearly was at Downside during Dom Hugh Connolly's Scripture Class. Both master and pupil were on this occasion at their most characteristic: Dom Hugh, blinking, uncomprehending, trying to be helpful; my friend sublimely indifferent to the claims of scholarship. Despite his great learning, and even fame in his particular field, Father Hugh was singularly inarticulate on the platform, and after interminable parentheses, qualifications, hesitancies, highly involved sentences begun and left in mid air and then returned to without a recognisable connecting link, he wound up with a forlorn conclusion which trailed away into something like this: "Well, are you sure that's clear, then, about the Agapé? Because if you don't it's important. I mean it's important to ask, because if you don't understand what St. Paul meant, and what *I* meant when I was telling you, you will never understand how the people whom St. Paul was writing to understood why he, St. Paul, thought it was so important. I hope I am making myself quite clear?" My friend looked up from a gramophone catalogue which he chanced to be studying, and said—to nobody in particular and in a nice friendly voice—"Oh, bloody lucid." What poor shrinking Father Hugh, unused to the idiom of this world, made of the comment I cannot imagine. I hope he was not greatly shocked; though I fear he must have been.

The two of us were well enough suited during the sixteen and seventeen period, but ours was not a friendship destined to last for ever. At Downside our respective circles were too far apart, at home our families were never likely to meet. (His parents lived permanently abroad, sending him money at regular intervals which he would spend in the first two days.) My friends considered him to be vulgar, his friends thought me dull and strict. But I liked him, and would like him again if ever he turned up. After leaving school he drifted from job to job, from colony to colony. The last I heard of him was that he was selling drinks behind a bar in Sydney. An Old Gregorian, doing a zigzag tour round the world, came across him quite by chance in his bar, and generously offered to pay his passage back to England and put him on his feet again. My friend accepted the offer eagerly at first, but came next day to say that he had decided to stop on as he was. It is a pathetic story, but quite in character. I can follow the change in mood as clearly as I can see the change of expression on his pretty, rather than handsome, face. The truth of it was that he had never learned to keep at bay people whom in his heart he despised. It is the price which the goodnatured all too often have to pay. I asked the generous Old Gregorian, when he came back from his journey round the world, if there had been the same quick bubbling laugh, the same dog-like melancholy in the eyes. Yes, apparently both had been evident in the Australian public house. And the other day, seeing Miss Heather Thatcher's name upon a poster, I remembered with startling suddenness the figure at my side in the dress circle . . . his fingers playing with the flimsy little metal tongs which only the richest boxes of chocolates provide. Vivid too is the figure upon the stage, seen in the round frame of the telescope, with her cap of white fur and muff to match. "She may look pleased enough —even through that thing," says the rather depressed voice in the semi-darkness, "but I bet she's in the hell of a rage inside." It would be gratifying to hear that voice again. The estrangement of friends is the soul of tragedy.

As if in compensation for the relative fruitlessness of this relationship there came the bettering of conditions between Maurice Turnbull and myself. The unsatisfactory nature of things which had prevailed for years was altered in a single day, when Maurice happened at one and the same time to develop a high temperature, to play a shocking game of rugger, and to find himself badly let down by someone in whom he had apparently placed confidence. The occasion was the Clifton match; the place therefore Bristol. After the game, which we lost, a lachrymose scrum half and future double blue presented himself and suggested that we might leave the team to look after itself and have a quiet meal somewhere. This was so unusual a request, and one which was not likely ever to be repeated, that I jumped at it, and for the rest of that day Maurice leaned heavily on my moral support—until I saw him safely into the Old House with flu, and myself went off to face the consequences of cutting the Clifton high tea and returning independently by car. There is no joy like that of being heavily leant upon in the hour of crisis, and from this incident I learned the truth that for so long as people are elated and all is going well they seek out the friends whom they think they like, and that when life suddenly goes flat on them they turn to those whom in fact they actually do like. It was a most encouraging discovery to make, and thereafter all was serene between Maurice Turnbull and myself.

The Clifton match that year is further memorable because of the parrot. Pat Ward, an Old Boy who had come back to Downside on a visit of indefinite duration and unprecise purpose, bought this disagreeable bird in Bristol and presented it to the school. As the purchase was made before the match, and as the parrot threw in its lot wholeheartedly with the cheering touch-line crowd, the introduction to Downside life was as complete as any vociferous bird could wish. The donor, an altogether delightful person but apt to be airy when it came to practical affairs, omitted to provide himself with information relating to the rearing of parrots, and for about ten days everything connected with the colourful pet's diet, tastes, washing arrangements, and of course actual housing—for Pat Ward had forgotten to ask about a cage—was news. But the bird was robust, surviving all experiments, and lived on and on until one could hardly imagine a time when the parrot was not. Its screams, for all day long it appeared to be struggling (unsuccessfully) with violent passion, became part of the orchestration of Downside life. One would hear it while on parade— since the words of command and the confused cries of the roll-call goaded it to a peculiar frenzy—and while doing gym. Living in a wired-off corner outside the surgery, the poor bird was so placed that many corridors converged upon its retreat. Perhaps it was this lack of privacy which poisoned its mind against the human race, for every time one went by (it might be to have one's Virol in the surgery after supper, to speak to the C.S.M. in the armoury, to visit the barber's shop, to call upon a friend in the Old House, to take one's clothes to be pressed at the tailor's) there would be such an angry flurry of feathers and shaking of wire that one wondered how the feral constitution could stand it. The choleric eye, the ready claw, the hate in every line of its body, and above all the piercing yells which came from its beautiful yellow throat were evidence enough to show that parrots were not intended by nature to dwell as domestic playthings among men. When Pat Ward in due course went away, the light seemed to fade from the bird's plumage. There was no one now who cared to take it up to house matches or out for a drive in Mr. Fry's Ford. Without its original owner to feed it on expensive foods sent out from Bath or London, the unhappy beast had to rub along on what by contrast it must have judged to be a very plebeian regime of birdseed and digestive biscuit. True, it would often feed upon the hard white surface of those cascaras which came in such a steady supply from the surgery immediately opposite, but no decent bird can take its little luxuries from so bold a dish. In the end, screeching to the last at the merest draught or the noisy closing of a door, the parrot fell upon its back and died. Ten years, almost to a day, it had lived among us—and we were told that it was sixty years old when Pat had bought it. Small pieces of enamelled sugar were discovered on the floor of the cage, and probably if a vet had prized open those iron jaws he would have found upon the hard black leather of the creature's tongue a substance, as black and hard as the tongue itself and tasting somewhat of licorice laced with bitter aloes, which might have been traced to the medical cupboards over the way.

III

Resembling in some respects the subject of the preceding lines was Mr. Thomas, who kept the school shop. Explosions here, at the south end of the Assembly Hall, were as frequent as those outside the surgery. And with all the same justification. Possessing a heart of the purest gold, and with a reputation for every domestic virtue, Mr. Thomas was so sorely tried in the conducting of his office that a superficial observer might have judged him to be a highly irascible man. And his appearance would have added to this misconception, for not only did his eyes bulge towards you when he leaned over the counter (gripping its edge in an effort to control his irritation) but his moustache bristled and his heavy dark eyebrows were set in a permanent lowering frown. Small blue veins stood out at the temples, and on occasions his neck pressed so tight against his spotless starched collar that you felt it could only be a matter of moments before something or other would give. I remember that the hair stood almost upright on the backs of his hands, and that the skin here was often wet with the restraint which he exercised. The suggestion was that of an arrested landslide or of a suppressed volcano. Sometimes of course—how could it not?—the land slid, the volcano erupted. And then . . .

Mr. Thomas retired from the shop in 1922, and was greatly missed. It happened that his retirement came at a time when it was felt that farewell presentations were proving too much of a drain upon our resources, and that they had better be discontinued. Accordingly the word went round instructing that no collection was to be made for Mr. Thomas. In the event no collection *was* made, but somehow the money came in, and Mr. Thomas received privately from those whose frivolous requests had tormented him for years a tribute which must have left him in no doubt as to the appreciation which they really felt for him.

When you come out of the school shop and turn right, you pass through two rows of lockers (without locks) and come to one of those rooms which at Downside change their use from year to year. When I first came to the school it was called the Star Chamber, though what went on there I could never exactly define. Bernard Lane specified it as "a place where you waited about and got hit." For a time it became a ping-pong room, and then it was used as a kind of lounge for Old Boys and important visiting teams. Someone presented a billiard table, and the Star Chamber (the name forgotten by this time, and used only by people like Jimmy Reynolds and me) became a billiard room. But it was a billiard room for only a short while, because in the next reshuffle the existing Masters' Common Room became a classroom and the green table gave place to uncomfortable furniture. During the Second World War it became, since it was considered one of the safest places in the house, a bunker with two rows of beds one on top of the other. Now it is the Masters' Common Room again, and perhaps in twenty years' time it will get back to being a place where you wait about and get hit. If it does, I hope someone will, in a flash of originality, call it the Star Chamber.

Had you, in the early twenties, looked towards your left and not towards the Star Chamber, you would have seen, in a recessed window facing out onto the Quad, a complicated piece of mechanism which Phil Dorté (now a Director of Television at the B.B.C.) would have told you was the finest amateur wireless in the country. The second of these adjectives nobody would have questioned;

it was the first which was open to doubt. Phil Dorté was Vice-President of the Wireless Society, and it was he who had, together with Kenneth Lindsay and Denis Hanley (later a Member of Parliament), presented the loud-speaker which, in the words of the *Raven* report, was to "give to everyone a chance of benefiting by the 'broad-casting,' a scheme which entails the publication by Wire-less Telephony of all the latest news as well as numerous concerts by the musical 'stars' of the day." This was in 1922. The transmission set, and all the apparatus of the Wireless Society, occupied another part of the building (though I never discovered where this was), and it was only for the benefit of the unmechanical public that the loudspeaker, with a lot of mysterious connections and ma-terial at the back of it, was installed where it was. For oc-casions like the Varsity Rugger or the Boat Race the school used to be invited beforehand to "listen in." We all came, and it was great fun, but we hardly ever heard anything. I remember on one night when Joe Beckett was fighting for the Heavyweight Championship of the World, the Headmaster said that there must be a lot of sparrows in the Albert Hall because he could distinctly hear the chir-ruping. In fact the Wireless Society was for a long time the greatest source of humour to the Headmaster, whose flexible mind and wide vision were just what was wanted to encourage enterprise in the school. After being Head-master for many years, Father Sigebert[1] became Prior of Worth and then Abbot of Downside. His services to Down-side, both at the time of which I write and later, deserve a separate and more serious book than this. Until such a book is written, and I should be the last person qualified for such a task, the references to his name must necessarily remain piecemeal and deficient.

Proceed along the Dayroom Corridor in a southerly

[1] Brother of Father Aidan Trafford, mentioned earlier in this book.

direction and you pass what was then the Studyroom and is now the Smythe Dayroom. As a Studyroom it was a place of glacial chill, and even now a long dormant chilblain will start to my fingers as I pass its doors. Hurrying on, we come to what is now a lectureroom and was then the Petre Library. Here we are warm again, for one side of it gets the sun. It was in this place of lethal silence, surrounded on every side by books, that almost legendary figures of the past have—some to satisfy a wager, others from spontaneous whim—shaved, slept the night, changed into uniform and back, and smoked cigars. All these various things have been done, it should be noted, if not under the eye of authority at least while the eye of authority roamed. Somehow the Petre Library lent itself to fancy and caprice, because eventually an official was employed for no other function than to preserve order. Here this salaried official sat the livelong day, at a desk raised upon a platform, and when he was not glaring at the readers and writers in front of him, he stared through a large magnifying glass at (it was said) a completely blank sheet of paper. But these developments were not until much later, and when the Petre Library had moved up onto the first floor. Each of the changes of place (the Library had been in the older part of the building for many years—as already stated on an earlier page—and was transferred while I was still in the Junior School to the south-west corner of the New Buildings; the next move was after I left, and must have been in about 1925) favoured the lawless, because what one room lacked in the way of cover the other made up for with either an open fire or an electric fan. At one time the grate in the Petre Library had to be re-stocked with pokers and tongs every term, and fire-brushes were estimated to last about a week. The electric fan was so often found choked with tinned spaghetti that it was finally removed and placed over the buttery door in the monks' refectory.

Leaving behind you the room which was in my time the Library, you pass on your right the Barlow Dayroom— where a boy whose name I forget kept, hanging upside down in his locker, a sad little family of bats which used sometimes to be hunted in the evenings to the destruction of almost everything in the Dayroom except a bat—and so reach the then Prefects' Room.[1] Now the reason why I have ventured to take the reader on a conducted tour round the ground floor is not because I expect to rouse interest in the architectural layout of the school but in order to make intelligible a story about the Prefects' Room. Geography is always a more or less well-paid servant of biography and narrative, and unless there is here some slight understanding of Downside's plan it may be difficult to see how the secret telephone connecting the Prefects' Room and the Studyroom traced its course. The line was designed for the use of House Prefects and for nobody else. The wires, threading the Petre Library and Barlow Dayroom, ran behind the panelling and appeared at intervals above the grating of a radiator. Wherever a wire appeared it was discreetly hidden by a blotter, or, if on a vertical plane, by a picture. The idea was that the prefect taking prep in the Studyroom should be able to warn his fellow prefects in the Prefects' Room of the Headmaster's approach. The Prefects' Room was, in the days before all of them had studies of their own, the place in which House Prefects worked as well as recreated. In this room were desks as well as armchairs, textbooks as well as novels and magazines. The telephone was, accordingly, a great help.

Inevitably, of course, the fatal thing happened. The prefect in the Studyroom, calling the prefects in the Prefects' Room, duly gave the alarm. "Headmaster in the offing," he warned his friends, "but I don't know where. Last seen on the Sixth Form stairs. I'll send out a scout

[1] It is today an extra library.

and ring you when I hear he's coming." "Don't bother," came Father Trafford's familiar voice over the wire, "he's come." And that was the end of the D.T.C.

As may be guessed from the above story, Dom Sigebert Trafford had a way of being ubiquitous. If one strayed ever so narrowly from the lines laid down, he was there in the margin. Whether he was on the cricket field watching a match or in his photograph-lined room dictating letters, his authority and personality penetrated to every classroom, every dormitory, every dayroom, every study, every cupboard, every locker. Living and working in the school, he was far from being the figurehead headmaster which is often associated with the traditional public school. He was the nerve centre, the focus point. "Don't bother—he's come" might be taken as more than a casual witticism spoken into a mouthpiece: it is a pretty fair commentary on much connected with Dom Sigebert's long term of office.

Among his other many gifts he possessed that of ready improvisation. Once when he was giving a dinner to the First Fifteen in the Pump Room Hotel on the way back from a match I happened to be washing my hands at the basin next to his, when on his other side, busily turning on taps and fussing about with nail-brushes, was a high ecclesiastic of the Anglican Church.[1] It must have been a day when there had been some sort of congress or chapter in Bath, because the hotel was crowded with clergy who were waiting, as we were, for extra tables to be prepared in the dining-room. "Well, Canon," said the dignitary through the steam to Father Trafford, "I see you haven't brought along the old arch-deacon this time . . . how is he these days?" "Oh, getting along, you know, getting along," came the Headmaster's immediate reply, "of course not as young as he used to be, and we all thought that what

[1] I should add that I was present at this dinner as special correspondent to the *Raven*, and not as a member of the victorious team.

with his chest and these fogs it might be wiser not to risk it. I'll tell him you asked." When Father Trafford was in this mood anything might happen.

As a further instance of this enviable facility the incident is worth recording of Senator Gogarty's telephone call from Dublin during an epidemic of mumps in the school. This was during my last year, when it was one of my privileges as a school prefect to spend the evenings in the Headmaster's room. The call came through at about ten, and I, in the absence of Father Trafford who had just left us to see about something in another part of the school, answered it. Whether because my fellow prefects were making a noise, or because the long-distance line was indistinct, or because I was more than unusually stupid with the telephone, my answers to the Senator's questions regarding his son Oliver's condition were unhelpful. My confusion was relieved—and none too soon—by the Headmaster returning to his room and taking the receiver from my grasp. After scarcely an instant's pause his long-distance voice was heard shouting into the mouthpiece to Dublin: "Half-witted, I'm afraid, and I'm having to advertise for another. No, no, not a secretary, fortunately—just an office-boy. And I would never have kept him on for as long as this if it hadn't been for the very sad background. Now, about Oliver's mumps . . ." I told this story later on to my father, who for some reason did not think it was at all funny.

Knowing as we did the Headmaster's unfailing readiness to meet any situation we delighted greatly in the disparaging references which he sometimes made to himself—as when he claimed for instance that he was quite out of touch with the school. "On the rare occasions that I leave my room during study times," he said to us one evening at public Assembly, "I am sometimes puzzled to see boys not in their classrooms. Of course I am far too shy to ask them why they are wandering about in this way" (loud cheers) "but I must warn you all that in future I mean to screw up my courage . . . even perhaps to the extent of going straight up to them *and asking their names*." Since the Headmaster was known to carry in his head the Christian name of every boy in the school—together with each one's medical record, home address, preparatory school history, place in form and marks awarded at previous examinations—the roars which greeted this announcement can be imagined. If an intimate knowledge of the subjects under your care is the first requisite of a good superior, then Father Trafford can have nothing to reproach himself with. "Well, how are you celebrating today?" one would hear on one's way up to luncheon. "Today, sir?" one would repeat, respectful but blank. "Isn't it your birthday, boy?" "Oh, I see . . . today . . . Oh, yes, sir."

IV

In the Easter holidays of 1922 I went to Ireland to my aunt Rita's. One day on the way back from Mass, my aunt challenged me to race her up the drive to the house. Taking off her heavy teddy-bear fur coat, which she left at the lodge, she started to run at a surprising speed—high heels scattering the gravel, and a string of pearls bouncing on her back behind her—until I finally overtook her within a few yards of the front door.

My aunt gave a dance for me on my birthday, and since a number of Downside friends happened to be in Ireland that holidays there was no dearth of young men. Nor were the Jesuit schools badly represented at this dance, and I was told afterwards that feeling ran high among the convent school partners as to the merits of the Benedictine training and tradition when compared with those of the Society.

Among the Gregorian visitors to Ireland was James Mathew, whom, though a few years my senior, I had come to know fairly well at Downside, in London, and in my visits to Oxford. This interlude in Ireland sealed the relationship, and from then onwards we met frequently. The most recent of our meetings was a week ago,[1] so I can count his as one of the more lasting of my Downside influences. The stories which could be told about James would fill volumes, but since I feel that he would be the last person to approve of such a recital I shall confine myself to the briefest account of a prize-fight which he and I attended in a music-hall in Cork at the time of which I write.

I forget what the purse for the big fight amounted to, but it was a considerable one for those days, and the event proved a box-office draw. For days beforehand the population of Southern Ireland was being advised by rival representatives in the press as to the outcome of the issue, and every porter, every hairdresser, every policeman, postman, outside-car driver would be only too eager to impart information. So when James and I took our seats close to the ring we knew that we were in for an interesting evening. The early bouts were dull, everyone waiting for the heavy stuff. The noise was deafening—both between the rounds and during them—and after each decision was reached a number of supporters would have to be forcibly removed. Then, at last, came the event which had fired the sporting imagination, and two tremendous men were on the boards. Packie Mahony, well over thirty years and the veteran of a thousand frays, was clearly the favourite; Jimmy O'Dwyer (or it may have been O'Flynn), a finer figure and giving away years as well as weight, suffered the disadvantage of being a member of the British Army. The anti-British element in the house was distinctly noticeable, and my heart went out to Jimmy O'Dwyer (or it may have been Jimmy O'Flynn).

While Jimmy in his corner was pawing the resin on the

[1] July 1950.

floor, Packie displayed to the crowd his belt with the many trophies. The noise was so great, men shouting out the odds as well as applauding their choice, that Packie's speech was lost to us: his lips moved but that was all we had of it. Round Packie's ankles was tied a rosary—the kind of rosary, with beads of pink glass, which would have been more suitable to a housemaid than a prize-fighter—and both men were lavishly tattooed. The gong sounded, and the fighters lumbered into each other for the first round. Round after round followed. Sweat streamed, blood stained the floor, smoke went up into the dome and one's eyes smarted, one's head ached, one's skin tingled. How long the contest lasted I do not now remember, but it must have gone on for some time because the crowd became restive in its demand for a decision, and even Packie's popularity was not proof against invective. At last, when I for one was so tired of it that I neither knew nor cared who was winning, the referee made a mistake and so drew the whole volume of hostility upon himself. And that was the end of it: the audience rushed the ring, the judge and timekeeper disappeared in a flurry of tumbled bodies and furniture, the gong rang in futile protest, everybody hit everybody else, and people threw sticks at the electric light bulbs. "I don't think there's much point in stopping on," said James when he could make himself heard, "shall we go?" As I was not particularly keen to stay, we left—by a side door. A few minutes later we were walking under the stars by the quiet waters of the Lee. "The Irish seldom make good boxers," said James, "because they are much too used to fighting. With us it is something more artistic than a bad habit from the cradle upwards." This remark has stayed in my mind, and I have often wondered whether it was not perhaps true that our fellow ticket-holders of a few moments back, who were even now tearing up the stalls from the floor of the theatre and rending them apart in strong square hands, would never perfect a science which to them was not scientific but instinctive and endemic.

My father was delighted when he heard of our excursion into the boxing world; my mother on the other hand was not. "It is from me that you get your liking for pugilists," my father said to me the following year when we were going regularly to The Ring in Blackfriars, and since it was then that I was struggling to get his permission to become a monk he added rather sadly: "though where you get all this priest business, I can't think . . . you certainly don't inherit it from me." Years later I reminded him of this, and he seemed amused. "As the result of having your idols in different camps," he said, "you will find by the time you're forty that you can preach like Packie Mahony and box like Father Bede Jarrett."

v

Returning from the Easter holidays was not, with the prospect of the summer term, the dreary business which it tended to be at other seasons. The summer term that year was three months of blissful weather, rain falling only on the few days when it seemed absolutely imperative that it should hold off. An interesting experiment would be to go through the back numbers of the *Raven*, and see how many times the phrase "it was unfortunately wet again for Longleat this year" occurs.

The Longleat holiday, intended originally for choristers and those who had passed the previous year's public examinations, came in time to be the reward also of sacristy servers, members of the corps band, blowers of the organ bellows, and performers of one or two less formal offices. It was alleged that at its numerical peak period, the Longleat holiday was extended to the boys who held the coats of the boys who moved the cricket screens when the boys whose duty it was to do this were occupied elsewhere. But this must have been a gross exaggeration because it was not impossible for a boy to complete his school career without ever having gone to Longleat. For my part I took care to see that I was well insured in this matter, entitling myself to the annual holiday on two or more counts: the band, the sacristy, and even an occasional exam proved the validity of my application, so for four years I enjoyed the singular delights of what was traditionally the most looked-forward-to event in the school year.

The grounds of Longleat House, seat of the Marquis of Bath, were put at our disposal on the first Tuesday of each June, and with this generous permission went the use of the lake, the boats, the boat-house, and the Gothic pavilion. Those of us who came looking more or less presentable were sometimes fortunate enough to be shown over part of the house, with its interesting collection of pictures, and those who were fond of horses were taken round the stables. Since pictures, horses, and perhaps above all the Thynne state coach (with its draped box seat and silver arms and lamps) interested me profoundly I made a point of appearing respectable—one year bringing a change of clothes in a kit-bag for that purpose. The walk from the lake to the house was a long one, particularly in the rain, and most boys found that their aesthetic longings were amply satisfied by the sight of the rhododendrons on a part of the estate called Heaven's Gate which was not so far. Even with the rain slapping down upon their olive-coloured leaves, the great bushes which stretched with pink and purple blooms the whole length of Heaven's Gate looked magnificent: in sunshine, with steam rising from the wet and close-cropped grass ride which ran between them for a mile or more, they were not of this world at all.

In 1921, Jimmy Reynolds, who always did the walk with me through Heaven's Gate to the house, lost his pipe in the bracken on the way down from the wood to the ornamental garden. On the return journey we searched for it, in the pouring rain, for an hour. In 1922, and again in 1923, we renewed our search. My protests were of no avail whatever. "I am sure it was just about *here*," and, soaking wet each year, we would swish through the bracken yet again. Three or four summers ago I was once more at Longleat with a party of boys: instinctively on the way down from the woods to the ornamental garden I found myself peering through the dripping fronds in search of Jimmy's pipe. It might have been the same sodden trouser legs flapping against my ankles as those which had flapped in 1921, 1922, 1923. "I'm not sure that we oughtn't to take off our shoes for this," Jimmy had said, I remembered, in 1922, "in case we tread on it by mistake." But on this point, I recollected, I had remained firm.

Though a holiday, Longleat was no rest. The order of the day was as follows. Up at 5.30; Mass, celebrated by the Headmaster and served by the Head of the School, at 6.0 in the Crypt (the monks were still in choir at the morning office at this time, and it was vaguely gratifying as one hurried into church at this unusual hour to know that they had been there long before we had been called, and that they would be there again tomorrow and the next day and the day after that, while we would be sleeping); start from the Quad in buses at 7.0; 7.30 halt at Frome for coffee and the morning paper with yesterday's cricket scores; arrival at the lake somewhere about 9.0, followed by breakfast in the open air. Even if the rain was bouncing off our plates and the marmalade was awash, we always breakfasted, seated at trestle tables, in the open. But it was seldom as wet as this for a meal, because normally the Longleat rain admitted of clear intervals, and the business of eating was so spaced out as to avoid the more persistent downpours. On the occasions when the sun shone the whole day through, and there must have been some such, the

meals seemed to be going on most of the time. For breakfast there were always unlimited bacon and eggs, fried
by the two or three men-servants who had come in advance the night before and who had mounted their grill
on little pillars of bricks, and for luncheon there was
every kind of salad, trifle and fruit. One boy, whose name
I well remember but will not in these discreet annals dis-
close, having taken four fried eggs did the elephant trick
with the fifth. When we had helped with the washing up
we were free to bathe, row, fish, walk, play games (bridge
and ping-pong in the Gothic pavilion if too wet for outdoor
sport) or smoke and go to sleep.

While one boatload, evidently enjoying supernatural
protection, made its tour of the lake, another party would
form on the shore to take its turn in inviting discomfort
and disaster. Those who were here for the first time were
urged to row out to the island to inspect the banana tree
which grew there. This particular trip, I am ashamed to
say, I never made, fearing always lest the banana tree—
like the lily pond at the bottom of Charles Lamb's garden
—might not be there when I arrived to see it.

There was one Longleat which started off in such wintry
weather that for the early part of the day we ran about
and played "touch rugger" for the sheer sake of getting
warm. Sleety rain beat upon the water, and not even the
hardiest bathed. Then suddenly the sun shone out, and
in ten minutes we were smelling of warm mackintoshes.
A van came out from Bath with ices in the afternoon:
it was almost more welcome than the steaming urns of
coffee a few hours before. Someone boringly expressed a
theory that the sudden changes of temperature were due
to the particular formation of the Longleat estate: hills and
valleys, woods and lake. He was thrown into the water.

After an early supper there would be a final bathe, and
then seventeen miles of singing—assisted, if not led, by

Dom Lucius—on the way back. The School Song began at the lodge gates, everyone standing up in the bus and falling over at the corner by the Old House. In those days the buses were open to the sky—and if it rained it rained, because people could not be bothered with the tiresome business of the canvas hood. Before the days of motor transport, the Longleat holiday possessed variations on the theme known to us who came later. (And who, though liking to be considered as of the remote past, belong properly to the age of petrol and steam.) For one thing the party started much earlier: the horse-drawn brakes were creaking out of the Quad well before six—which meant, since Mass was a fixed beginning to the day, that the boys must have got up at an unearthly hour. There is a place on the Kilmersdon-Mells road which I can remember being still called Whiskey Hill, because it was at this point of the journey that a flask used to be handed round to the senior choristers. They probably needed it at that hour in the first week of June. But Whiskey Hill must date back some way, because though I can recall, as a small boy, watching the somewhat hushed and muffled early start ("Tell them to shut up in front . . . don't they know that the rest of the school is supposed to be asleep?") I do not remember hearing afterwards that the journey was interrupted for the drink. Another difference between the old and the (relatively) new was that the brakes were used for chariot races, and that horses appeared in the group photographs taken on the lawn. It is one of my regrets that the Longleats which I attended were not of the horse age.

At what time the brakes got back in the old days I do not know: we used to arrive and climb down from our high-off-the-road buses while the rest of the school was going to bed—which meant that boys were leaning out of dormitory and wash-house windows saying "What was it like?" The classes next morning were a weariness of flesh and spirit. There seemed to be nothing to show for Long-leat but blistered hands, cut feet, dirty towels.

As an epilogue it should be noted that the Longleat holiday has, since the Second World War, been discontinued. The band, the sacristy, the successful candidates of last year's exams get their free day, but they make their own arrangements and go off wherever they choose. Soon there will be nobody left in the school who has been on a Longleat party, and a unique experience of Downside life will consequently be forgotten. But perhaps those who benefit by the annual holiday will, as they set out in search of their cinemas, continue to speak of "getting Longleat." And who knows but what some bronzed New Zealander, sitting centuries hence on the fringe of jungle known still as Heaven's Gate and sketching the ruins of a great house down in the plain below, may not share with the phantoms that linger there the ecstasy of Longleat . . . and even come upon a black and twisted pipe.

VI

Other outings there were, but these were always in private groups. With Dom Rupert Brace Hall a carefully selected party of us went each year to Orchardleigh, the home of a Major Duckworth, where a Grecian Temple took the place of Longleat's Gothic Pavilion, and where we always seemed to eat too much lobster mayonnaise to make the long bicycle ride back comfortable. On our last visit, in 1923, we took with us just as much lobster mayonnaise but we came back by car. The Ochardleigh parties seemed always to be well timed, falling in the middle of a heatwave. Water-lilies, blue and silver dragonflies, the cool tiled pavement of the Greek garden temple . . . these are the gracious things which return to the mind at the mention of Orchard-leigh.

Another nearby estate was that of Bonham, where Lady

Hoare, having given us permission to picnic in the grounds, once sought us out and invited us to tea. We were a small party of four, and it was a great success: scones, strawberries and cream, China tea—served on the lawn against the background of the exquisite Palladian house. The Hoares, with whom my brother afterwards became great friends, lived a strangely withdrawn life within the boundaries of their park, so it was all the more generous of them to take an interest in a handful of untidy-looking youths who were not even their co-religionists. This elderly couple, who belonged to the Edwardian world and not to ours at all, died on the same day in 1947, and the house was left to the nation.[1]

Fonthill Abbey, the property of the Shaw-Stewarts, was another place where we were allowed to bathe, row, and picnic. If Longleat favoured the Gothic, and if Orchardleigh and Bonham favoured the Greek, at Fonthill the styles were permitted to jostle. So closely did they jostle that a building which from the outside must surely be taken for a chapel by Pugin would turn out in fact to be a Pantheon. Nymphs, urns, sundials, follies and ruins abounded in the Abbey's grounds, and round every clump of trees you expected to see a centaur come dancing on his cloven hoofs and wearing on his head a Gothic mitre.

[1] At the beginning of the 1939 war an aerodrome was built quite close to the Hoares, attracting a good deal of enemy action. During the summer of 1941 or 1942, Lady Hoare was giving one of her rare tea parties to a few friends who lived in the neighbourhood, and while the conversation tinkled round the cups and cucumber sandwiches on the shady side of the house—as it had done twenty years before when we had been there for tea—the sound of gunfire was heard overhead. After hovering in the background for a little while, the butler announced impassively: "There is an aerial bombardment in progress, m' lady, over the Park." "Oh well, in that case, Benson," said Lady Hoare, "if you will take the tea things round to the west terrace, we shall be able to watch." And there they sat, these old ladies and gentlemen, going on with their tea and conversation, while the great trees of the Park splintered and crashed under the weight of steel.

The bathes at Fonthill lasted so long that we were usually late getting back, and I can remember now the feeling, on walking up from the lake, that no combination of natural and architectural interest could well be bettered than here. Perhaps at sixteen one begins to absorb beauty and fantasy and natural wellbeing in a single act of grateful discovery. I know that never before had I been so conscious of the sheer joy of living, and I think that these places which we went to—and went to together in a carload of friends or with all the agreeable agonies of a bicycling party—had a good deal to do with it. How shortsighted would that system of education be which prevented boys from being trippers. Time is not wasted when one trips.

The only other estate of this sort which was visited by Downside boys was Chantry. Owned successively by two families who were Catholic, and lying nearer to the school than the places mentioned above, Chantry was much frequented on days when we were free. The fact that the chapel in the grounds, which ranked as a public oratory, was served by one of our monks proved an additional bond, and for as far back as I can remember the smaller boys, who were entitled to the Longleat holiday but who were considered too junior to take their place among the elect, were sent off in buses or on bicycles to Chantry. Here they over-ate and over-bathed—for all the world as if they were at Longleat with their seniors. At Chantry there was an artificial grotto, and from an eminence of this piece of ornamental garden planning a boy called Holland fell and broke his arm. After this it was forbidden to risk one's life except by drowning. There were no dryads nor fauns at Chantry, but in the chapel there were statues of such variety and size that when it came to assembling the personnel for the Christmas crib St. Joseph was so big that the cows in the stable assumed the relative size of small

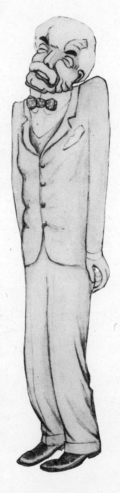

CAPT. LE SEUR

dogs, and for one of the Epiphany kings St. Joan, with her back towards the congregation, did service in a cope and crown.

VII

During the summer of which I have been particularly writing, namely 1922, either the zest for reading and painting must somewhat have waned or else other activities claimed my whole time, because for one thing the book list is considerably smaller and for another I remember nothing about Mr. Goosens until he appears again (with his home-made varnish and trick methods of mixing oils) in the autumn term.

Apart from student hours (as they would now be called) in the classroom, cadet hours on the parade ground, spectator hours in the Pavilion, there were a great number of strenuous athlete hours in the nets and on the golf course. Since I must be one of the few cricketers in the world who are content not to bat, my services are welcome in the nets, and during the 1922 season I bowled with a hopefulness which now surprises me. Much as cricket appealed to me in theory, and I still read it up with the enthusiasm of a Mr. Carter of Alexandria days, it was a game at which I never excelled in practice. So golf came in to restore my confidence.

Each Tuesday evening, and sometimes on Sunday afternoons as well, a regular foursome, of which I was one, used to go by car to Masbury where we would play till the last possible minute on a course which was neither good enough to attract serious golfers from afar nor bad enough to allow indifferent golfers much sense of superiority. In fact it was ideal for our sort of play. Golf was one of the few things at which I was able to hold my own against Maurice Turnbull, and in order to maintain this dizzy eminence I played indefatigably during the holidays and even received lessons from a professional at North Foreland. But at no club in England did I enjoy my golf as I enjoyed it at the homely little club on Masbury. Golf at this period I connect always with beans and bacon, because it was after platefuls of this food that we were picked up in the Quad by Mr. Fry's open Ford. Supper on Tuesdays was served early for some reason, and as the fare in the refectory never varied in its cycle, the association between a long evening of golf and a rushed meal of beans and bacon is immediate. Other refectory associations are: sausage and singing practice, curry and algebra, fried fish and corps.

Though Friday corps is inevitably identified with Friday fish, it must be admitted that there were occasions when the fish was boiled and not fried. On the whole we preferred it fried. The general opinion was that the fish which was bought for frying belonged to no particular species but was just *fish*—bought by the yard and chopped into lengths like ship's tobacco. The other kind, the boiled variety, was unashamedly cod. Coming up the steps to the refectory each Friday, we would see, as we filed through the doors in silence to our tables, the great water-heated metal dishes on the carving table in front of us . . . and upon these dishes *fish*. Behind the carving table, and holding an enormous fish-slice point downwards as if it were a baton of office or a sultan's scimitar, stood Mr. Fred Williams the butler. But Mr. Fred Williams was more than a butler; he was the maestro of the refectory and pantry. A short man, and in those days a stout one, he stood there with an air of circumstance. "The world is my oyster" said his expression plainly—as he gazed out over the tawny gravel surface of the fried or the shiny silver wetness of the boiled. One day as we pressed through the double refectory doors in our corps uniforms for luncheon—it was a boiled day and not a fried—we saw that over the cod's staring eye with which we had grown familiar in the course of years, glaring in its glazed but somehow vaguely obscene manner above our heads, an early-comer had placed a black shade. The elastic thread was neatly, and at a rakish angle, round the head; the mouth, drawn down at the corners as is the way with the mouths of dead cod, expressed helplessness and self-pity; the curved sides of its body were as if caught in the climax of a sigh. The eye-shade had evidently escaped the notice of Mr. Fred Williams, for he was still in his aloof pose when the signal was given for grace. Oddly enough I never discovered who the boy was who had conceived so strange, and yet so absolutely right, a fancy.

Fish, for the benefit of historians who may wish to record the fact, was called at Downside "alk." In fishcakes or kedgeree it was not called "alk." Nor did the term refer to kippers. So I suppose it applied only to the main dish at the luncheon on abstinence days. Certainly it was never "alk-pie," but then even fish-pie meant something quite different from what is generally associated with the name.

Mr. Fred Williams, with his bowler hat which always caught one by surprise in a Somersetshire lane, was a character. Particularly characteristic was his walk: elbows well out, and arms so far from the body as to suggest that the sides of his coat might be smeared with treacle. His was a face which I was able to draw in many aspects, and I did a series of Williams pictures called "Butling down the Ages" as a companion set to Tristram Hillier's "Geometrical Photography." There was one very elaborate drawing of Mr. Williams with a circlet of roses round his head, plucking a Jews' harp and dancing before Nero at a banquet. I think Dom Austin Corney has it still. Another was an Elizabethan Williams in a ruff and against the background of a college Hall. Yet another was a Roundhead

Williams, fiercely Puritan with a giant hymn book and foldover boots, frowning at a flagon of sack. The series was nothing like as good as Hillier's, but the designs show that what Mr. Lush was to my more talented friend, Mr. Williams was to me. And if Mr. Williams goes on butling much longer, as I sincerely hope he may, the idea of his doing so down the ages will soon not seem so fanciful as it did in 1922.

VIII

Corps in the summer always seemed less unpleasant than during the other two terms, and as by now I had crept up to the rank of corporal its exercises no longer greatly worried me. June and July were the months in which took place the Field-day, the General Inspection, the House Corps Competition. Each year the Field-day was to me a matter of the greatest interest, because I used to study the spirit in which it was variously approached.[1] There was always the small group of N.C.O. cadets who were keen: they would come laden with maps, field-glasses, first-aid equipment, and a spare haversack for this and that. There would be the much larger group who were not keen: these would come with lemonade in their waterbottles and light reading matter in their pockets. Jack Carroll, who was always very grand in everything that he did, would somehow manage to produce a thermos of coffee and some cigars. "Don't eat those beef sandwiches, my dear feller," he would say as we were sitting under a hedge at midday with the rather dreary little packet of provisions which had been issued to us in the Quad before starting, "have some of these." And then he would distribute some delicious little triangles of egg or tomato or even caviare sandwich, pretending that it was the most natural thing in the

[1] I have observed this very matter since, both at Downside of today and at the Oratory School, and the affinities remain unchanged.

world to be able to conjure a Fortnum and Mason luncheon out of what had appeared to be army rations. "I'm sorry there's no fruit, my dear feller, so until they make these pouches bigger we'll simply have to rough it." Then there were the intellectuals who used to bring their slim copies of the Classics in case the manoeuvres allowed them time for study; the aesthetes who brought Swinburne; the philistines who, having raided their Dayroom after breakfast, were secure from boredom by reason of the sporting pages which they carried inside their tunics.

The actual operations of the Field-day remain only vaguely in my memory. Each year's seem to have conformed to the usual pattern: surprise attacks, blanks let off at dangerously close range, enemy bolts looted and thrown into cow-ponds, and the inevitable summing up on the part of the planning authority. The white bands would be taken off our caps, and both sides would congratulate themselves upon having won. The only Field-day that I can recall with any clarity was one which was held at Cheltenham, because I had a bath in a hotel at the end of it. For some reason the time of the return journey was changed at the last minute, and I had to come back by myself.

Until the time when Sergeant Majors came and went with the rapidity of French masters during the War, we had an excellent man called Sergeant Major Reynolds to prepare us for the next outbreak of hostilities. He was Irish and from an Irish regiment. His method on parade was to speak quietly but very quickly at first, hardly opening his mouth yet articulating every word so that it could be heard all over the parade ground, and then, either with a word of command or at the sight of a detail which called for a correction, *burst*. It was most effective. The change would be so abrupt that a nervous cadet might be inclined to drop a rifle, and it was by no means unusual for a head in Number One Platoon to jerk back suddenly and a cap to fly free. One had to be constantly on the alert. I, being by nature inclined to wander in mind and now particularly on parade being caught up in the struggles of composition or of prayer, would find myself often brought to book. But worse off by far was one, Ian Calder, who called down upon himself so many sudden bursts from the C.S.M. that my little absentmindednesses were left completely in the shade. Ian Calder was once discovered marching by himself on the cricket field without the slightest knowledge of how he had got there. "I didn't hear anyone say 'halt'," was his explanation. Sergeant Major Reynolds could, when in good voice, be heard from within the Guest House when he was issuing commands in the Quad. This, I imagine, beats even Sergeant Major Cahill's record—and his was no mean carrying power.[1]

For camp (which my aunt Berthe used to call "your camping out") we went again to the place which we will call Mytchworth. Downside won the Band competition and the Gym competition, and this made us all very merry. It was moreover a camp which was run that year by the Irish Guards, and several of the officers were Old Grego-

[1] Sergeant Major Cahill came to us from the Irish Guards in 1924, and so is outside the range of this book. Thus it will have to be in a footnote that mention is made of a story (told by a lawyer and therefore presumably true) which was illustrated later in the pages of *Punch*. Apparently the C.S.M. had been practising a Cert A candidate in the word of command, and was superintending while the nervous and inexpert boy was moving his squad in a muddled zigzag across the cricket field. Finally the candidate fell silent and the squad marched closer and closer to the drop at the edge of the ground which meant a fall of some ten feet into excavated soil. "Say something to yerr section, sorr," roared the C.S.M., "even if it's only 'Goodbye.'" In spite of his fierce eye and his beard (for he was a King's Beefeater and was thus debarred from appearing clean-shaven) Tom Cahill was the kindest of men. I am sure that neither he nor Sergeant Major Reynolds, who was gentleness itself when the echoes of his voice had died away, had an enemy in the world.

rians. Charles Haydon was Adjutant. Charles on horseback shouting "Battalion" was a sight to be seen and a voice to be heard. The word was rendered "Tallanagh." Charles judged the sports, and though he did what he could for us in more than one event, there was no mistaking the fact that ours was not the best team on the ground. Had it not been for Francis Gordon who threw the cricket ball so far that it had to be fished out of the canal by one of the judge's runners, and the tug-of-war team which distinguished itself by appearing at the rope in ski-boots, Downside would probably not have been noticed.

When not parading or practising or rehearsing or washing up or cleaning equipment, we either crowded into taxis and went into Aldershot (to wash) or else relaxed at a nearby inn called The Admiral Napier. Over the fireplace at The Admiral Napier hung a framed print in sepia called "Kitchener's Homecoming," showing the General stepping from a train in Victoria Station while all around him were grouped men in tropical khaki waving pith helmets, and women in straw hats and long dresses waving Union Jacks. Each evening before we went back to camp, we reproduced in tableau Kitchener's homecoming. Some years later Jack Carroll made a special journey from London to The Admiral Napier and bought the picture. It must be very faded by now, but so long as the soldierly moustached faces of the men and the elated expressions of the women can be seen it cannot greatly matter if the print has suffered the ravages of time.

On principle it is obviously not a good thing that boys who have not yet left school should masquerade as regular troops and spend their evenings off in bar parlours. On the other hand looking back upon that hour after supper—and it cannot have been much longer than an hour because we had to be in camp by nine—I find it hard to condemn our youthful liberty. There was nothing to regret and much to

remember about these darts and shove-halfpenny recrea-
tions. If all such gatherings were as harmless, one would
not hesitate to recommend them as a practice. But they are
not.

After camp, which we left as usual in the early morning
and while flames were licking up the petrol-soaked timber
of some huts which would not be wanted any more, my
brother joined me in London (for he was too young to go
to camp) and we went abroad. Half across France my
brother did a thing which I suppose is common enough but
which I had never seen done before and have not seen
since: he sat on a man's bowler hat. The act was inadvertent, and we put things right eventually with the owner,
but after the first shock of joy it gave us some nasty few
minutes. The actual sitting on the hat was exactly as described in funny books: no more, no less.

On an earlier page I have suggested that interest in
things cultural suffered, during this summer term of 1922,
an eclipse. If the same need not be said of things religious,
the credit goes both to the wisdom of my advisers in this
field and to the fortunate discovery of a little book called
The Practice of the Presence of God by Brother Lawrence,
a Carmelite. I forget who it was who urged me to read
the book, but I know that on the bicycle rides which I
have mentioned above, as well as on parade and while
fielding in the deep, I made efforts to acquire some sort of
habitual recollection. I do not think I was very successful,
but it was something to be powerfully moved with the desire for it. At Longleat particularly I remember walking
into the woods with the determination to fix my mind
permanently on the thought of God, and at camp I tried
to evolve a technique for dealing with the many distractions which beset this programme. Perhaps because in
church one prays without specifically adverting to the generation of spiritual energy, the prayer-effort *outside* church

time remains more clearly in the memory. I can remember the security of religion as it came to one at Vespers, for instance, when everybody was smelling pleasantly of soap after game and a shower, but I can remember much more the individual appeal of it when the cumulative effect of Vespers, spiritual reading, and above all of course the Mass, expressed itself in an attraction which welled up and demanded attention at times not connected with religion at all.

During one of our picnic parties at Orchardleigh, when we had finished the lobster mayonnaise and were thinking that some stiff rowing on the lake might do us good, Dom Rupert lay down on the bank and said that he had to do his half-hour's spiritual reading. That in addition to his breviary—for he had not said his Office lying down on the bank but walking up and down at some distance off—Dom Rupert should bring with him on an excursion of this sort a work upon the spiritual life impressed me profoundly and gave me something to follow. I do not pretend for a moment that thereafter I went about with the reputed authors in my pocket—to be whipped out during a lull in a mock battle at camp or while playing in the goal on a hockey field—but I do look back with gratitude to the various sources of impulse which resulted in my studying the things that matter most in this life and the next.

VI: The Last Year

I

WITH THE RESUMPTION of the diary after its long suspension there can now, with the Michaelmas term of 1922, be a return to greater accuracy in the sequence of events. Not that the text will be burdened with dates, or that passages will be quoted which bear the stamp of the day to day entry. "Nothing much after supper (kippers), so played ping-pong and had a bath": this sort of thing is there all right, but it will be carefully suppressed in the present record.

At the start of every school year there is always the sense of surprise: either one finds oneself suddenly advanced or else one is amazed at having been overlooked. All at once in September 1922 I found myself in possession of a room, a fag, a number of exemptions, and a time-table which I could draw up more or less at my own discretion. I do not know that the room helped my work to any marked degree, because I very soon turned it into a studio, but the liberty which came with the self-planned time-table had the best possible effects: I laboured, admittedly at the subjects which interested me, as I had never laboured before.

On the first Sunday of the term, when by this time I was beginning to get used to walking about my room and was no longer afraid of my fag, I was made a School Prefect and all the excitement began again. Since I had not been a House Prefect the term before, the jump was considerable—from half-way up the table in the refectory

90

to another table altogether. I felt that if anything further happened, I should go clean through the roof.

For the first week the new School Prefect wafts about in a dream and forgets things. After this comes a period of great keenness and public spirit. Then as a rule, though perhaps remaining Olympian and self-conscious for the space of a term or so, he forgets his honours and becomes a person again. Provided a boy is not promoted to office for one term only, because this hardly gives him time to settle down in the position, the prefect system is as valuable to most senior boys as the fag system is to most junior ones. Obviously you get your measure of arrogance, pomposity, and sometimes injustice and cruelty among those who become prefects, but you would probably get this anyway and on the whole the system defends itself against excesses. For the case which can be made out against the prefect system—and such a case can indeed be made—there are a great many more which can be made out in favour. Certainly I have never seen anyone spoiled by this responsibility who was not already spoiled beforehand; and I have seen a great number rise to it.

Promoted at the same time—but to a higher level, since he was made Head of his house whereas I never became Head of mine—was Jimmy Reynolds. We now sat together on the Prefects' Table, we were in and out of each other's rooms, we had all things in common. We shared books, tastes, skill or lack of skill in games, friends, prejudices, and food parcels. We were together reproved by the Head of the School for laughing too much and thus lessening the prestige of authority. Another thing which earned us a sharp reprimand was our habit of playing French cricket on the lawn. "Not, for God's sake," was the final appeal, "within view of the Dayroom windows." Might we play Norwegian polo? No. Patagonian tennis? Certainly not. So we gave it up, adopting instead the more respectable pastime of playing short mashie shots into the goldfish pond behind the War Memorial.

If Jimmy and I spent much of our time together, our respective younger brothers were almost inseparable. Like us they were the same age, like us they had the same interests, like us they have kept up with one another since. Seeing them going about together, we used to wonder whether we could have looked *quite* like that five years before. "Surely not," Jimmy would reassure me; "not that school belt with the brass snake."

W. F. Reynolds (the younger brother), though gifted above the average in other things (especially painting), was no great hand at spelling. One day we found on Jimmy's desk in his room a note from Billy's pen which ran: "von Zeeler iss no langer mi frand." It was addressed on the outside to "Reynolds Wone." For how long our brothers kept up their quarrel I do not know, but from that time onwards Jimmy and I have called each other by the name of Frand.

It is curious the way in which the acquisition of a room can make to one boy the whole difference to his life at school, while for another it is merely an alternative to working in the library. Jimmy, as Head of Barlow, used his room not only for study but for official purposes. For recreation he more often used mine. He never made of his room a shrine or a castle of defence. His was a sensible matter-of-fact room with the correct pictures on the walls, the correct authors on the shelves, the correct implements of sport in the corner.

At that time boys who had rooms were allowed to furnish and decorate them in any way they chose, and the results were sometimes too markedly individual to be suitable. When the note struck was exotic beyond the bounds of reason, authority stepped in and the general effect was toned down. Today all this is changed, and those who are privileged with rooms have to conform to a standard: the furniture, curtains, carpet and even waste-paper basket are supplied. The present arrangement is better because it means that the boy who is not well off, or whose parents are unwilling to send their furniture, remains on the same footing as the boy whose means would allow him a greater display. Originality may suffer as the result of greater standardisation, but even within the existing system there is plenty of scope in the way of pictures and ornament.

So elaborate were some of the rooms in my year that one had to exercise the greatest care lest, in either making a hurried entry or turning round suddenly, one should bring crashing to the floor a complicated structure of damask hangings or a chain of alabaster lamps. Reginald Scrope's room was so dominated by the shade of pink that after a few minutes, if one was not used to it, one would feel quite overcome—as if by strawberries and cream. The bed, the window-seat, the cupboard, and the two armchairs with their cushions were all covered in their tailor-made pink costumes, and it took Tubby Scrope half an hour each morning to put the right covers on the right objects. Pink brocade creases easily, and it was not unusual to smell the warm damp smell of ironing in the corridor, and to hear a thudding as one hurried along to class.

James Murray's room was draped in black silk, *lined* with black silk, so that with its white silk curtains it looked like the inside of a dress coat. A singular economy of ornament characterised James's room, but what few specimens there were possessed distinction. James was a collector, a connoisseur, and everything about him, as about his possessions, was rare. He had a rare use of words—as distinct from a use of rare words—and his clothes, his reading, his opinions on people and life were rare. Not that he was at all flamboyant or that he was original for the sake of originality; it was simply that he was a boy of unusual sensibility and that he brought to life a scale of values and appreciations which, though perfectly natural to him, were not as a rule those of anybody else. In him were blended in equal proportions a remarkable maturity and an almost childlike freshness of perception. His talents and individual outlook brought him into the public eye more than he wished, and though he avoided publicity like the plague he was not able altogether to avoid popularity. Extreme diffidence is not always a safeguard, and, in spite of himself, whatever James did was news.

For one thing he possessed the faculty, more enviable than any other to the schoolboy, of apparently quite effortless success. Seldom seen doing any work, James passed all his exams. Never preparing a subject for debate, he spoke fluently at the Abingdon. Always seen hanging about and wasting time, he was better informed than anyone else on the current topics of the day. "If it is ever discovered than I *can* work," he told me once in a burst of unusual confidence, "life won't be worth living." He was a year or so my junior, but higher in form, and when I left he took my place as second Caverel School Prefect. Whether or not he roused himself to effort when placed in authority I was not there to see, but presumably he must have shown more signs of life as a prefect than hitherto or nothing would have been done at all. I have seen James hoist himself onto the lockers in the Hall on a whole holiday after breakfast, and sit there until the bell went for luncheon. His heels would tap the door of the locker immediately below him, and if anyone cared to stop and talk he would be good company. But there he would be all the morning, and as likely as not the same would be repeated in the afternoon. "But it is a free day, isn't it? I mean, we don't have to be doing things."

To be languid and apparently uncaring does not mean

to be slipshod, because nobody could have been neater or more exact than James Murray. It was because he was fastidious in words that he spoke little, fastidious in food that he ate little, fastidious in dress that it took him hours to change his clothes. In the holidays I used to receive from him—in the ratio of one to every four or five of mine—letters written in the dry humour of the Scot and the small precise script of the scholar. These letters were never longer than one page. When James Murray later on went up to Cambridge, he joined another friend of mine on a tour of the Italian lakes during the summer vacation. At Maggiore the two of them had to share a room for the night—a circumstance which must have gone against the grain with James—and my friend tells me that not only did James take an hour and forty minutes undressing and cleaning his teeth but at the end of it all settled down at a table with a candle to write a letter. At intervals during the night my friend woke, and there, sure enough, was James at the table fingering a spare candle with his left hand and bending over the text of his composition. "Still in his pyjamas?" I asked when the story was told to me, "wasn't he cold?" "Still in his pyjamas," was the answer, "pale green silk." In the morning when they were getting up—for James had eventually gone to bed—my friend asked if inspiration had come more readily in the small hours of the morning or if he was still delayed on the opening paragraph. "Some letters one writes and posts and forgets about," said James as he felt for his long narrow morocco slippers, "whereas with others one has to probe the quality and quantity of every comma." The letter was still on the table—one sheet and unfinished.

To get back, via Lake Maggiore, to James's room in the Lower Gallery, it is not surprising that something of this precision should show itself here. Each unit, whether a chest of drawers or a matchbox, was so exactly placed that any alteration of position would at once be detected by its owner. Order and proportion would then immediately be restored. The nice placing of things was no mere affectation: not only was James genuinely disturbed by an inch to right or left, but experiment proved that he could never be caught out. He would infallibly know if anyone had been testing him by so much as the reversal of a pen on his silver inkstand. "I have never understood," he would say wearily the moment he came in, "this mania for turning people's rooms upside down."

My own room, as I have said, was a studio, and of no interest consequently to the lay mind. My neighbour's, C. F. O. Bull's, was a sports department which in summer smelled of bat-oil and blanco, in winter of drying leather. I spent a lot of time in this room because mine was no place to sit and talk in—easels interrupting one's view, tubes of paint on the chairs, bed and floor. The wall between us was thin, and I could hear, from my desk, every time the cupboard door was opened, the clatter of bats, clubs, racquets, pads, rods, sticks and cues. It was like the valley of dry bones in the Prophecy of Ezechiel. C. F. O. Bull used to get me to bowl to him in the nets and to lend him money: the relationship was as easy as it was long sustained, and his name was added to the list of those for whom I gratefully performed the marriage ceremony on a later day.

C. F. O. Bull and I belonged to a club of uncertain aim called La Société des Gentilhommes Français, of which there were six other members and which had as its chaplain Dom Charles Pontifex, now superior of Ealing Priory. The club was founded by Tristram Hillier the year before, and whenever we could we had a dinner. A tie was made for us (after my design) by an Oxford firm, and since so small an issue was required it was found that each tie cost us seventeen shillings. But as I pointed out when the accounts were examined at one of our meetings, it was a very *strong* tie and could be worn for ever round the waist. Nor was this an idle boast, for after becoming a monk I wore mine for years under the Benedictine habit. The club had its charter (a large vellum scroll on which the rules were inscribed in Gothic lettering while caricatures of the masters adorned the margin), its secret signs, its passwords. On one occasion the Secretary, taking this scroll to a meeting, was stopped by the Headmaster and questioned as to the parchment which he carried. The Secretary was hard put to it to explain the thing away, and even when he had done so he had to face the Gentilhommes who were indignant at what looked like a needless violation of the society's secrecy. "Why didn't you eat it?" demanded the Gentilhomme Premier. I still feel resentful about this, because I was the Secretary.

After leaving school, les Gentilhommes Français had their club dinners always at Genaro's in Soho. For the last meeting, which was also my farewell dinner before entering the monastery, we had a private room on the first floor, and between the courses Signor Genaro himself came up to see how we were getting on. At least I have always assumed that such was his kindly motive, though at the time it was suggested that he did not like us throwing rolls and olives into the street below. If he objected, he certainly did not show it: not only did he brings us gardenias for our buttonholes but he toasted in champagne the success of my enterprise on the morrow. The hall porter at Genaro's, Billy by name, was a Catholic, and we used to have long spiritual conversations sitting on the pavement while waiting for a taxi. Many years later after I had been performing a wedding at Spanish Place, who should detach himself from the crowd on the steps and hail me as a brother but Billy? We had an old-times conversation while the guests were driving away to the reception. Genaro's and La Société will for ever be linked in my memory. It was before the little restaurant became smart; it was when everyone knew everyone else and when the waiters were as friendly and communicative as the diners. I am told that it has now been done up, that the prices have risen and that on any night of the week you can see important people there. If this is so, and if people in the houses opposite no longer lean out of their windows and wish you a good appetite in the accents of Salerno and Naples, then I have no regrets about not being able to go back to dine in that most hospitable part of London.

For one reason or another the eight Gentilhommes were seldom able to meet in full strength at Genaro's, but always there was a nucleus consisting of Mm. Hillier, Turnbull, Carroll, Walter, Bull, and van Zeller. The chaplain, though the dinners were seemly enough, never came. Only when we had our meetings within the precincts of Downside was Dom Charles present to say grace. On one occasion, after dinner at Genaro's, a musical play at the Adelphi, supper at the Café Marguerite, a party of six members made the journey to Brighton in a large but hesitant car. At several points on the journey the car slowed down of its own accord, trembled for a space, and then broke out into a sweat which gathered on the bonnet and rolled off finally behind the mudguards. A little beyond Lewes it stopped altogether, and C. F. O. Bull judged that the licence had expired. Somehow we got to Brighton in time for breakfast, still of course wearing dress clothes, and the return journey was made by what is often mistakenly called easy stages. After a light *al fresco* luncheon in the Park we made for our homes where a variety of welcomes awaited us. The episode is cited in order to show why Dom Charles decided not to extend his duties as chaplain to the meetings which were held in London. It is curious incidentally, in view of our frivolous bent, that we did not go to night clubs. Perhaps it was that night clubs, whatever they are now, were not very reputable in the early twenties and that their kind of fun was not really ours. It is gratifying to reflect that in some ways we were particular, if in most we were pleasure-loving. Only once did I go into a night club and that was to get someone else out.

Though each member of La Société was allowed by the rules to bring a guest to its dinners, no one ever did. I once asked my uncle Marcel, knowing that he would be perfectly at home with the Gentilhommes and they with him, but he gracefully declined and joined us one Sunday at the Florence for luncheon instead.[1] There was a strong sense of brotherhood about the Gentilhommes, so perhaps it was as well that we never had guests.

But to get back to when we were still at school, to the autumn of 1922, when La Société was still in its infancy and when most of its members were enjoying the freedoms of the Lower Gallery and the Attics. I cannot speak for the Lower Gallery because I never had a room there, but certainly the occupants of the Attics had nothing to complain of in the way either of service or of supervision. Our rooms were cared for by a "daily" (with an intermittent assistant as will be described below), and beyond this we were left almost entirely alone. Masters came up to give private tuition to one or two boys during the course of the day, and very occasionally at night the foot of authority used to be heard upon the stair, but there was no system of official visitation or spying, and it was the custom for everyone, master or boy, to knock. One could be as cut off from the rest of the school as one chose,

[1] I have described the Sunday routine in *Family Case-book*, where a chapter is devoted to the uncle mentioned above.

and it was sometimes with a feeling of returning to civilization after a period on a desert island that one left this quiet—and sometimes not so quiet—retreat for the hurly-burly of the Hall. I know that on coming upstairs again and getting back to my painting I experienced a sense of appropriateness, of being completely in my element, which in the corresponding occupation of writing I have never felt to quite the same degree. To be able at will to tap a source which you know to be exactly related to your nature is not a satisfaction which is granted to many. Nor is it one which can be counted upon to see you through your lifetime. For my part I have known this sense of correspondence, of harmony, of fitness, only when among my paints and brushes at school and, much later, when employed in liturgical worship. It is a curious fact that some things you enjoy doing, not because they are appropriate and familiar but rather the reverse. You like doing them precisely because they are not in character, because they represent a breaking away. The pleasure which these latter bring is not so lasting as the other. All I am saying here is that for some people there are certain ways of spending time which are in accord, absolutely, with their temperaments. Fortunate are those who discover what the particular ways are.

For the first week of the winter term the needs of the Attics were attended to by a Mrs. Fussel. But Mrs. Fussel got ill, and her place was taken by someone of whose name we could not at once be sure. We called the newcomer Mrs. pro-Fussel. When it became clear that Mrs. pro-Fussel was no mere *loca* but was attached to the Attics staff for good, we called her, for we still could not make out what was her name, Mrs. post-Fussel. Eventually Arthur Woods was able to tell us—for it was always he who found out these things—that Mrs. post-Fussel's name was Mrs. Preece. This Mrs. Preece was an exceptional woman, deserving more than a casual mention.

Born and bred in London, she had been a maid in various private houses until she had married Joe Preece and settled on Lord Acton's estate in Shropshire where her husband was employed on one of the farms. There were two children, a boy and a girl, and because the Catholic school was some distance from where the Preeces lived, a change was considered necessary. (Mrs. Preece had become a Catholic as the result of a chance visit to the Brompton Oratory where she had seen an Oratorian saying Mass in such a way that she decided then and there to ask for instruction.) The family moved to Stratton-on-the-Fosse where the children went to school at the Servite convent. Mrs. Preece was fifty when she took up part-time work in the Attics, and as I always seemed to be having free prep periods when she was doing the rooms I came across her a good deal. She had decided views about everything and everybody, ideas which were very much her own and which were expressed in a highly characteristic idiom. For example she showed her approval of Mr. Goosens, whom she saw constantly in my room at this period, by saying that if he were to start singing in the heavenly choirs tomorrow there would not be a single angel who would know he had just arrived. "Not but what he isn't far more useful here below, livin' in Bath and all, and doin' good to men and women of sin. Though a fat lot of use any of us are, come to that." Whether this last sentence referred to singing in the heavenly choirs or rescuing the inhabitants of Bath from lives of sin, or whether it was simply a comment upon the futility of the human race generally, I could not determine. Bath for some reason spelled licence and dissipation to Mrs. Preece, and often I heard her comparing it unfavourably with the capital. "Say what you like about London," she would challenge me, "but I'm a Cockney and I know. Bath? Bath? Babylon more like." Then I would steer the conversation round again to the less disturbing topic of Mr.

Goosens, saying something vague and sententious about
unselfishness always being worth it in the long run, and
that Mr. Goosens possessed a big heart. "Big heart? I'd
say he has," Mrs. Preece would confirm, banging the
handle of the mop against the window-sill so that a cloud
of dust flew out over the carts and crates in the yard below,
"big as the Crystal Palace."

Unlike many of her occupation, Mrs. Preece was tolerant
of laxity in regard to tidiness, food and fresh air. She had
no objection to our keeping cake, fruit, jam and condensed
milk in our rooms, though this must have added to her
work of cleaning, and she seemed to think it quite natural
that some "young gentlemen" should prefer to live in
disordered squalor rather than in "what they was used to
in their homes." "Not but what I don't like to see things
shipshape when I finds them," she said to me once, stepping
boldly over a mountain of games clothes, corps kit, golf
clubs, books and bed clothes, "but I seldom do in these
parts." The fact, all too evident from the tins which she
cleared away each morning, that we ate sardines late at
night did not shock her sensibilities either as a cook or a
mother. "No harm if you fancy them—then or any other
time," was her dietetically reassuring observation.

Nor did Mrs. Preece reprove me for the atmosphere
which most people found distressing on entering my
room—an atmosphere congenial to me and one which
moreover I had some difficulty in maintaining. Only by
pinning to the windows a notice which forbade their
opening on any occasion other than that of Mrs. Preece's
two minutes mop-shaking was I able to secure anything
like the temperature I wanted. The notice went up in
October and came down on April 3rd. In cold weather
I had to hire fags, at considerable cost, to fill and refill
basins of boiling water which were then dotted about on
the floor, and which not only made one's collar limp

with their steam but which rendered progress across the room hazardous to the unwary. The radiator system in the Attics has since been strengthened, so perhaps now I should not have to go to such lengths to insure my circulation, but in those days the measures which I took were surely justified, and by Mrs. Preece approved.

Mrs. Preece possessed, in addition to other and more important qualities which will be touched upon below, a well developed critical faculty. She knew at once when Arthur Woods and I had been over-ambitious in our choice of subjects for painting. In other words she told us when we were turning out rubbish. In the same way, though having no music, she could tell which of the gramophone records we played were good and which were trash—which was more than I could. In the matter of dress, though not pretending to anything very special in her own costume, she had again enough taste to distinguish between the parents who were smart and those who were either not trying or who had failed to compete. She told me that she liked it when my mother came down because "she gives the place a tone, and in Stratton we don't half sit up and take notice when it's a question of clothes . . . quite right, too . . . money may not be all that important, but style *is* . . . and that's what she's got, style from the heels up." It was very gratifying. I was glad to be able to tell Mrs. Preece that my mother came from London, as did her clothes, and that none of us had any associations with Bath and its wild life.

Mrs. Preece was still doing the Attic rooms when two years later I came back to Downside to be a monk, but shortly after this she must have given it up because long before I was ordained priest she was in bed with cancer. Her illness dragged on painfully for two years and though I saw her almost every week, sometimes when she was suffering so severely that she could not speak, I found her perfectly resigned to what she had accepted as coming from the hand of God. On the days when she was not in pain she would make her shrewd humorous reflections as I had known her to do so often in the past. Always interested in the "young gentlemen" she pressed me for news of their subsequent movements, successes and indiscretions: I could never supply her with enough, and used sometimes—may heaven forgive me, for it was in a good cause—to invent a few triumphs for her particular friends and attribute a few adventures to those whom she admired for their enterprise. When my aunt Yolande visited Stratton, she too made a practice of calling on Mrs. Preece, and together they would talk about London, food, clothes, and me. I can hardly imagine two women more different by nature, but because they both loved people—special people and people in general—they got on perfectly. It is characteristic of Yolande that she continued to send Mrs. Preece various little delicacies long after I had written to say that she was not eating anything but was being kept alive by injections, and equally characteristic of Mrs. Preece that she always asked me to write back and say how much she had enjoyed them. When Mrs. Preece died of her cancer, and she did not let it kill her without a struggle to the last minute, I could not find it in my heart to be sorry at her going. Hers had been a drawnout agony, and though she had taught me much, and would have taught me more if she had lived, I had learned enough to go on with about how to approach the problem of pain. And certainly I was never for an instant sorry on her account: if there is anyone whose suffering sent her straight to those heavenly choirs which she claimed for Mr. Goosens it is Mrs. Preece. I know too whose Cockney intonation it will be that I shall hear if to me is granted a share in the hymn of eternal praise.

II

As already stated on an earlier page, the help which Mrs.
Preece received in looking after the rooms in the Attics
was spasmodic. It came from an enormous red Irishman
with blue eyes and a forest of white hair whom we will
call, in case his life has been miraculously prolonged and
he is jealous of his rights, Mike. Who and what Mike
really was I do not know. He cannot have been all that
he pretended to be, because in the life of any one man
there would not have been room for it. He claimed to
have fought—though it must have been for the love of
fighting and not for the love of England—in Natal during
the Zulu War of 1879. He had been a lay-brother, though
never getting as far as vows, in a Franciscan house of
studies. (This he might well have been, because you could
never catch him out in anything to do with religion.) For
a while he had been a member of Driscoll's Scouts, which
seems to have been a little private army which toured
Europe and Africa, like a cricket team, in search of any sort
of war or revolution which happened to be going on. He
had worked in a mine following the first rush south for
gold; he had travelled, as a trick rider I think he said,
in a circus; he had, when he could not get round the
world any other way, been a sailor. On his arms and chest
were tattooed strange designs which suggested India; he
was convincing about China and Japan. Accordingly he
was the kind of man who in the sixteenth or seventeenth
century would have been written down as a soldier of
fortune—except that this sort of Irishman belongs to every
century and is always a soldier of fortune.

Entirely without guile, Mike was at the same time the
most shameless liar. Never deliberately getting out of
his work, he seldom did a stroke. Possessed of a piety

which could on occasion be pressed to its most ornate extent, he indulged in language which sometimes stood in striking contrast. In spite of his white hair and large experience, Mike was ageless—finding instant response in us who were of a different race, upbringing, background and generation. People who do not know the meaning of selfconsciousness are at home in every society, with men and women of any age. If as well as their confidence they have humour and vitality, there is nothing that can stop them. They sweep all before them in a great roar of good spirits. Such a one was Mike. From this it might be judged that Mike had little respect for authority, was apt to be familiar, did not know his place. Quite the contrary: with us he was always, in the best sense of the word, the servant. "Yerr clean larndry, Mister Woods, sorr." There was not a salute to accompany this, but there quite well might have been, and I seem to remember the clicking of heels.

Mike possessed, among his other gifts, a fine singing voice. He possessed also a considerable repertoire of songs (or, as he preferred to call them, "airs"): Irish ballads and jigs, marching songs from the American Civil War, sea chanties, and some very catchy numbers from the Victorian music-hall. "I wonder now, Mrs. Preece, would you be familiar at all with this one?" At the end of the Attics corridor there was a good deal of brasswork which needed cleaning and which had something to do with the fire escape apparatus. While Mike rubbed a leisurely polisher up and down the spout of the hose, and while Mrs. Preece with great sweeps of her strong arm applied Ronuk to the linoleum floor, there was song. "Isn't this the way it used to go, Mrs. Preece? Will we try the air together? Just once through and then perhaps a cup of tea below." Mrs. Preece had, more often than not, at least a nodding acquaintance with whatever melody was started up, and while we boys were bending over our Chaucer, our Cicero,

our Cambridge Medieval Histories, the combined voices
would float down the corridor penetrating the thin walls
and translating us from Stratton-on-the-Fosse to such
unknown territories as Virginia, Bunker Hill, The Old
Mole, The Tivoli and The Empire. Then the bell would
go, Mrs. Preece would get up from her knees, Mike would
fold his shammy leather over the top of the Brasso tin for
all the world as if he were smothering a dearly loved
temptation, and the two of them would move off—
"below"—in search of tea.

Unfortunately tea was not the only beverage for which
Mike frequently felt the need. His native porters and
spirits drew him every bit as much. (For weeks we tried
to imitate his way of saying "porter" but never managed
to get near it. The word is quite different from what we
in England use when speaking of the man in the station
who carries your luggage.) In fact I believe it was this
weakness of his which proved Mike's undoing at Downside. In all he was with us only a few months, six at the
outside, and it is therefore all the more melancholy to
reflect that but for an unguarded thirst we would have
been the richer for an altogether distinctive personality
in our gallery of lasting Downside figures. Outside the
Attics he was hardly known at all in the school. What
the immediate provocation was that occasioned his going
I do not know: I can only hope that the incident which
I am about to relate did not bring down the axe of sever-
ance. I hardly think it can have, for the measures which we
took to shield our friend seemed effective enough at the
time.

While having a shower one Tuesday after the Corps
parade I was told by my fag that he had noticed, when
collecting my clothes, a man asleep in my chair. I asked
what sort of a man. "Just a chap," said the fag, "big
chap." My thoughts flew at once to my father, but wedded

though I knew he was to his hour's sleep every afternoon I could hardly believe that he would have chosen so unsuitable a place for it. I was further reassured when I reflected on the practical side of the matter: he was not due in England for another eight months, and his arrivals were normally timed with the greatest care. I dressed, and made towards the Attics.

Looking through the glass transom over my door, I discovered the sleeper to be Mike: he was overflowing the chintz confines of my largest chair, and I could see at a glance why it was that he slept so soundly. Flattered as I always am to find that people should choose to shelter under my wing in the moment of distress, I was in this instance more conscious of humiliation than of satisfaction, and since Mike's condition was one which filled me with shrinking I tiptoed down the passage and sought the advice of my colleagues in the Attics.

At first the suggestions made were not helpful. "You must obviously move your things out and sleep in the Gym," was one. "You could always roll him up in your bedclothes, of course," was another, "and let him down through the window into the yard." After a lot of this, Arthur Woods, reliable as always, undertook to remove poor Mike—who while the situation was being reviewed in Arthur's room could be heard snoring his head off in mine. It was decided that the only safe time for the operation would be during supper when there would be nobody about to ask questions. So just before the appointed time we provided Arthur with a light meal—as if he were a raiding party in a war story—and wished him godspeed. We, the rest of us in the Attics, went down to supper.

Throughout the meal which followed I for one was on tenterhooks, wondering what was happening upstairs —and also wondering, I admit, whether my physical squeamishness had not withheld me from performing what might well be some sort of necessary corporal work of mercy. Immediately after supper we raced up the turret stairs, past the open door of my room which revealed a crumpled but gratifyingly empty chair, to where Arthur sat waiting for us at his desk. "Well?" we asked with one voice.

It turned out that Mike, once wakened, was perfectly amenable to movement—provided it was not rushed— and that the two of them went down the spiral staircase in dignified silence until they reached the mat at the bottom, where Mike sat down and prepared himself for further sleep. Pulling our errant friend to his feet, Arthur, who was now rather hot, led him away to the servants' room at the back of the Sixth Form Stairs and here, in an atmosphere of boot-polish, he was left. At his elbow, in case he should feel thirsty later on, were left a bottle of Eno's, some water and a glass. His escort had thought of everything.

"He wasn't nearly as bad as we thought," said the charitable Arthur, "so the whole thing was comparatively easy." "Did he talk at all when you had got him down there?" I asked, hoping for a piece of dialogue which might be committed to memory. "Not much," was the reply, "but before I came away we said the Hail Mary." "In Irish?" asked James Murray with that slight lift of the eyebrows which was more eloquent on his tired, sad, handsome face than the most expressive of smiles, "or Swahili?"

Next morning during the first prep period I heard Mike's footsteps pass my door and stop outside Arthur's room. The interview must have been a brief one because very soon afterwards the footsteps returned along the passage, and a chastened Mike appeared, after a discreet knock, in my room. "Mister van Zeller, sorr," said Mike clicking his heels and standing stiffly to attention, "ye have seen me in my hour of shame and degradation. Be warned by a sinner against the evils which lie in wait to thrip ye op. I'm thanking ye, sorr, for your forbearance." Except for the name at the beginning, this speech was word for word the same as that delivered to Arthur Woods. But it lost nothing on this account. It was still magnificent. The phrase "to thrip ye op" became a familiar one in the Attics.

Shortly after the above mentioned incident, on December the ninth, 1922, to be exact, Mike left for good and Mrs. Preece had to manage the Attics rooms alone. In spite of having conceded the fancy that Mike is the kind you will find on every page of history, regardless of place or period, I still like to think of him as in the service of a medieval or renaissance nobleman, smiting the paynim and the Moor. His last actual campaign, to date, at the time when we knew him, was not against the heathen and the infidel but against the Black and Tans after the Sinn Fein Rebellion. Granted however that Mike goes back in spirit to the Crusades there is nothing to prevent him going forward in the flesh to the Spanish and even (who knows?) to the Hitler War. Perhaps at this moment Mike is engaged, eighty-eight if he is a day, in guerilla warfare on one or other distant field. It is not impossible that he should be behind the Iron Curtain. Or is he in a prison camp? "Tis a grand air when yer all jining in together. What's this the name of it again? But wait while I give you one that will take ye back to the Alhambra in the days of Mister Dan Leno. How's this the way it goes? I think I have it yet." And ghosts, gay and brassy, dance lightly through the cannon smoke of Communism. No, I suppose Mike can hardly be alive . . . all the more reason then why I should try and preserve something of him in these pages.

III

My diary tells me, though I would have remembered
it anyway, that for Christmas and the New Year I went
to my aunt's in Surrey. Here, at Nutcombe House, I seem
to have spent my time playing pencil and paper games.
But I also went to a number of dances and Christmas
parties, both in the neighbourhood and at a distance. The
Vane Tempests, living near Guildford, were friends of
ours, and I remember the thrill of being able to hear the
voice of Adolphus ("Dolly") Vane Tempest at the tea
table where before I had heard it only on the stage. Dolly's
appearances, at the tea table or indeed anywhere else, were
all too rare. Retiring young from the stage, he retired
more and more from the social life to which he was by
nature and training so well suited. Whether he was scornful of entertainment or merely tired of it I did not know
him well enough to judge, but when dragged by force of
circumstance to play the host or guest he played with such
a grace that all were charmed. Dolly's son, Francis, was
at Downside, but because of the difference in our ages—
he was more a contemporary of my brother's—we met
seldom during the term. It was generally understood that
Francis would one day become Lord Londonderry, for he
was related to the existing peer, but I saw him quite
recently and he was still Francis Vane Tempest.

In 1924 or thereabouts, Dolly came down to Downside
to see his son, and though I was at that time in the novitiate I was allowed to spend the afternoon with the two
of them walking in the grounds. Dolly was unusually
communicative on this occasion, not only telling me some
very good stories about Mrs. Patrick Campbell, Charles
Hawtrey, Sir George Alexander and Beerbohm Tree, with
all of whom he had acted, but discussing with me the
question of his son's future. This must have been very

annoying for Francis, who of course was present, but it was very encouraging for me. Why Dolly should treat me as an equal, taking me into his confidence and pressing me for my opinion, when Francis was old enough to be consulted himself and I young enough (with a margin) to be Dolly's son I cannot make out. Be this as it may, it was not easy for me to get back into the atmosphere of the novitiate again that evening: my mind was like the famous curtain at the Coliseum—where down the great sweep of the stairs came all the leading figures of the English stage. But it was only for a single day, only after a single matinée performance. Very soon another curtain came down, screening Squire Bancroft in his grey top hat and Ellen Terry with her hand upon a flower, and no great harm was done. The great marble stair was, with the novitiate brush and pan, quite quickly cleared.

That earlier Nutcombe Christmas I walked through the woods to Midnight Mass at Grayshott, arriving in time both to go to confession before the altar boys began whispering in the sacristy and to secure a place near the stove. It was an hour's walk each way, and the combination of the frost cracking under one's feet, the moonlight washing the valley in a silver mist, the sense of Christmas and the hush of waiting made it an adventure of singular sweetness. I have always, as I have said, been short of musical perceptions, but on this occasion I was so far transported by the singing at Midnight Mass that I hummed what I am pleased to think was the *Adeste Fideles* all the way back from Grayshott Church to Nutcombe House. Another member of the congregation whom I remember to have taken part with much feeling in the hymn, and who had also taken care to find himself a place near the stove, was Wilfrid Rooke Ley, who in after years made a name for himself as a broadcaster. Even then in 1923, he had something of a reputation in the literary world, and what with his beard and cloak and

F. MOORAT, ESQ.

shapeless black hat he undoubtedly looked the part. One year at Grayshott I counted seven Downside boys among the congregation, and this not at Midnight Mass but on an ordinary Sunday. The congregations were smaller then than they are now, so the percentage of Gregorian attendance was high. I hardly thought when I used to go to Mass there that I would return time and time again to preach retreats at the convent next door.

Hindhead is near enough to London to allow frequent visits to the theatre, and we used to go up a good deal, travelling at speed in my aunt's Daimler. "Can't you go faster than this, Mooney?" "No, madam, not if I'm to keep out of prison." Speed was a sensation which my aunt rated high. While flashing through the villages of Surrey my aunt and I used to tell each other stories about imaginary people whose houses we could see from the road. With each journey to London the stories grew, and without a smile we would recount the latest piece of news which had come to us from our friends. Almost we came to believe in the characters we had created, and on one occasion when I was not in the car my aunt Rita told a certain Mrs. Stern, to whom she was giving a lift, how Major Tapworthy "who lives in that big red house over there" had been very rude to Madame Zukopulos at the meet which took place in her own grounds "at the left just here before we come to the crossroads." Mrs. Stern was much puzzled, and only when she expressed surprise at my aunt's knowledge of these people's private affairs did Rita say with a sudden coming-to-earth expression on her face, "Oh, but these people don't *exist*, you know; my nephew and I have invented them." Then, characteristically, she added: "Madame Zukopulos is a Greek widow; very rich."

During the Easter holidays too, though this is to get slightly ahead of the sequence, I stayed for the last two weeks at Nutcombe. Dances were now beginning to supplant the theatre in my scale of enjoyment, and though one London ball is very much like another I remember with extraordinary distinctness a dance which was given in Prince's Gate and which I came up from Nutcombe to attend. Several factors rendered it memorable. In the first half hour a partner with whom I was sitting out a dance on the stairs said to me: "Of the many different kinds of poisonous young men one meets at dances and parties, the poisonous Downside young man is far and away the worst." Within three months she was engaged to a Downside young man, and in later years I had the satisfaction of having two of her sons under me in my house. That was one feature. Another was the presence of Somerset Maugham, who looked quite different from what I had expected him to look. He looked, and was, nicer. The third circumstance which took this particular evening out of the ordinary catalogue of a season's engagements was a car smash on the way from Prince's Gate to South Audley Street when the dance was over. I was being driven back by an Old Etonian in whose flat I was to spend the night, and a big Vauxhall ran into us in the wide open spaces of Hyde Park Corner. It was the most unnecessary of accidents, leaving us to do the rest of the short way on foot. My host was a barrister, and while we were sitting about before going to bed—it was now about three in the morning—we were joined by another barrister, Patrick Redmond Barry, who had been to a dance somewhere else and was delaying the moment of going to bed. He had been Head of the School when I was a small boy at Downside, had fought with the Irish Guards during the War and gained the M.C., was now reputed to be the best dressed barrister at the English Bar, and in later life was to become a K.C. and finally High Court Judge. And here was this inhabitant of Elysium actually talking to me! My partner of a few hours ago would not have looked pointedly at *him* and made her indictment. And if she had, the son of a former Lord Chancellor of Ireland would have known how to deal with her. Far from being the remote, almost mythical, figure whom I had remembered walking backwards and forwards—again and again, and with perfect composure—to receive one bound volume after another at the hands of Abbot Cuthbert Butler on Prize Day, Paddy Barry turned out to be both self-effacing and excellent company. His advanced humility on this occasion was accounted for by reason of an embarrassment from which, when he looked in at South Audley Street, he was still tingling. His hostess at the ball which he had just left was a Frenchwoman with very little English, and Paddy Barry, having scraped together the French which he had learned at Downside from Mr. Wylie, decided to play for safety and combine his gratitude and farewell at the end of the evening with something short. "It seemed to me," he explained to us, "that the neat, if unambitious, formula of *au revoir* might meet the case, so I learned this up with considerable care—only to say, when it came to the point of delivery, *aujourd'hui.* I bowed gracefully from the waist, and fled in shame. And here I am."

Next day, when my aunt had ticked off the items on her shopping list and I had left cards in Prince's Gate, we made the journey back to Nutcombe. "Faster, Mooney, please" —as we sped past Major Tapworthy's Georgian mansion and the noble gates which belonged to Madame Zukopulos —"are you sure you can't make it go a little faster?"

It is curious to think that twenty-five years ago we were, in leaving cards on people after they had given a dance, doing something which has now so completely gone out that young men of this generation are found to ask what was the meaning of the practice. We wore white kid gloves at dances in those days, and carried dance programmes with their small white pencils swinging on a cord. Nothing in the world can so effectively bring the lump to memory's throat as the sudden discovery of one of these little rectangular dance programmes.

IV

The Lent term which came between these two holidays at Nutcombe House was cold and wet. Not cold enough for skating, and too wet for more than intermittent hockey. I had hoped to wriggle into the Hockey Eleven as goalkeeper, but a certain Simon Turner played with far more dash in that position and there was not room for the two of us. I had nothing to complain of, however, because in other directions I was advanced beyond my deserts. Drum Major in the O.T.C. and Master of Ceremonies on the sanctuary were more than enough for my vanity, and in the absence of other claims—for I had abandoned boxing completely by this time and played squash only in the holidays— I devoted myself to much reading, painting, and talking.

On days when the weather was too bad for anything else we played "quad hockey." It spelled death to shins, windows, and shoes. Even today when the true West Country rain falls in rods, lashing the stone walls of the Quad, I hear the swish of a tennis ball heavy with wet as it hisses through the air with its comet-tail of water after every bounce. For quad hockey it was the tradition, and the practice is still kept up, to wear decorative costume.

Coming in after an hour or so of quad hockey one would flop down, wringing and exhausted, on the bench outside Dom Austin's room and kick off water-logged shoes, peel off soaked stockings. One's shorts clung, cold and slapping, to the leg. Straight in front of one, through the door of the Junior School Dayroom, one would see a crowd of small boys sitting on the floor, on chairs, on tables pushed together, on chairs on top of tables, listening breathless to Dom Edmund Kendal in the middle of it all telling a story. Now that one was in one's last year it seemed a long time ago since one had fought for a place in that arena. And here was the whole thing going on exactly as before—so indifferent was time to one's advancement! How one had enjoyed these wet afternoons when, after a run and a shower (or, better still, instead of a run and a shower) one had been sent up as a messenger to the monastery, there to ring a hand-bell at the far end of the Petre Cloister until some monk should come along who would promise to tell Dom Edmund that an audience awaited him. The moment Dom Edmund appeared in the Dayroom there would be much jumping about, and as he was led to his place in the middle there would be this: "O sir, tell us the one about how you walked the tight-rope over the waterfall . . . No, sir, the one about the secret plans strapped round your chest when the bandits were roasting their prisoners . . . O sir, can we have a bit more about . . . O sir, last time you'd got as far as the North Pole, sir, and you didn't finish . . . Yes, he *did*, you fool, shut up . . . O *please* go on from where the dynamite was just going off and you were tied to a barrel of rum in the hold . . . No, we've *had* that, you frightful fool, and in any case it wasn't rum but some stuff called tokay or something. . . ." And here they were, saying exactly the same things whenever there was a break in the story-telling.

He was, on fine days and when his services were not required by the Junior School, a Doctor of Divinity and a scholar. But really of course, as the reader may have gathered, he was the Dick Barton *de ces jours*.

v

It was during this Lent term that Dom John Kane began to attach himself to the Attics. No one could have been more in keeping with the Attics spirit, and we looked forward to his visits whether during class time or out of it. He had taken a first in Classics at Cambridge, and bore a reputation for great learning. He too possessed a sense of humour, but, unlike Dom Edmund, never laughed. The most you could get out of him was a dry chuckle; more often a rather twisted smile would appear, and no hint at all of humour in the large heavy eyes. Dom John was young—still in the early thirties when he died three years later—and Irish. He taught Roman History to one or two members of the Attics, and his voice would reach the rest of us as he shouted the names of his pupils. His ordinary delivery was quiet enough, but every now and then he would rouse his listeners with a bellowed pounce upon the name of one of them. "*Whoods*" we would hear at intervals, never quite knowing whether it came from Father John Kane or from Woods himself imitating Father John Kane. "*Whoods, whake up.*" In the ordinary way, Arthur Woods was no mimic; Father John's voice, however, he reproduced to perfection, and though he frequently attempted the accents of the departed Mike there was never any real problem about distinguishing which of the two kinds of Irish he was giving us. "Will I leave that bit of sweeping till tomorrow so?" was Mike. Father John was quite quite different. An example of the Father John sentence was the comment made in a Sixth Form report: "This boy has a good, indeed a first class, butterfly mind." Another came in answer to a boy who asked "What do you mean exactly, sir, about getting the *feel* of a period in classical history?" "Well, if you blindfolded Mr. Watts and put him down anywhere within ten miles of this place," came the instant reply, "you know very well that he would be able to tell you where he was, and that he would be able to grope his way home from hedge to hedge. This is called having the feel of the countryside. A person who has the feel of a period can *smell* his way through it to whatever he is

looking for." Mr. Watts also taught the Sixth, and if anyone knew Somerset it was he.

Father John's early death was a great loss to Downside.
He had been in the school as a boy, and knew it in its
every shade of mood. His was not the mind of a leader
but of an observer. Wisely and wittily he looked at life
and commented. The close-meshed intellect, such as Father
John possessed, is seldom the kind which either expresses
or inspires enthusiasm. It is, nevertheless, a store from
which other, and lesser, minds may draw. I am glad to
think that we of the Attics were not slow to avail ourselves.

VI

There was no retreat that term because we broke up early
on account of a measles epidemic which followed a mumps
epidemic which followed flu. Since I was not expected at
Nutcombe at my aunt's until the scheduled end of term
I went off with Jimmy Reynolds on the Wednesday in
Holy Week to stay with him in Westmoreland. The family
had moved to Levens Hall from Dove Park in 1921, so
this was the first of my many visits to this hospitable
household in the new home. Our departure from Downside had been decided upon so suddenly that we found
Levens empty except for the servants, and the Headmaster's letter to Lady Reynolds explaining the early break
up of the term was lying on a table in the hall. For four
days we had the horses, the cars, the tennis courts and the
huge house to ourselves. It was like Alfred Noyes's fantasy
about the two survivors of the world moving through a
suddenly depopulated but well appointed Europe. If it had
been a little earlier in the year we would have had the
shooting to ourselves as well, but even as it was we
managed to find things to do.

The only person whom we saw anything of was Jack
Shand who was lodged in a cottage on the estate, who

had served in the Brigade of Guards during the War, who smoked fifty cigarettes a day, who was the best shot, the best horseman, the best looking man I have ever met. He was then a bachelor and something of a recluse: a person to be speculated about. Unfortunately he so completely over-awed me that I was dumb in his presence. This was distressing because had I not been so self-conscious I would have derived much benefit from Jack Shand, who had all the qualities which I admired in my father and none of those which roused me to opposition. But as things were I did everything wrong, tripping up over the carpet, pressing the syphon too hard and spraying the room with sodawater, making insignificant remarks in such a way that they sounded as if charged with sinister meaning, and finally banging my head against a door and having to be patched up with sticking plaster. Gaucheries of this sort were called by Jimmy and me "kick-things," because when one remembered them afterwards—sometimes years after-wards and usually in bed—one kicked oneself with curled toes. Seventeen is the age for doing kick-things, and though I find myself doing a lot of them still, the ones which make me lash out under the sheets are mostly connected with some frightful piece of social blundering which I perpe-trated in 1923. And many of them, as I say, are to do with Jack Shand. The maddening part of it in this par-ticular case was that Jimmy was never guilty of a Jack Shand kick-thing, and was always perfectly assured. He said he could see mine coming—"I knew *ages* before that you were going to sneeze and that you hadn't got a hand-kerchief"—but this I do not believe. Thus instead of following Jack Shand about, as I usually did in the case of my heroes, I sedulously avoided him. So at least he was spared.

Levens is less like a stage set than Kentwell which had so dazzled me the year before. But it has a greater appeal, a more subtle character. Much has been written about this historic house, so I had better not enter into competition with the experts. All I dare say is that it is the most completely satisfying house I have ever stayed in, that its grounds are exactly planned to suit the architecture, that its interior matches the feel of the outside, that its decoration and furniture look as if they had been chosen by the walls themselves. Everything, without doing violence to style or comfort or period, *fits*.

In later visits to Levens I was able to meet not only some interesting people in the literary world, among whom Stephen McKenna stands out in my memory as being the most individual, but also some of those who have appeared already in these pages and who were now brother officers of Jack's in the Irish Guards.[1]

Arriving as we did in the middle of Holy Week, Jimmy and I were able to plan a programme of religious observances which we intended to follow in the parish church of the neighbouring town of Kendal. Accordingly on Jimmy's motor bicycle we sped in and out of Kendal at frequent intervals, missing nothing which we would have attended at Downside and adding much in the way of casual penance. Our faces froze and cracked in the icy morning air, and Jimmy's eyes watered so much on the journey that not only did I, clinging on at the back, get

[1] Charles Haydon, who has been mentioned before and who was at this time a frequent visitor to Levens, used to come to an arrangement with me whereby his, and my, more humble way of life should not be put to shame by the grand manner in which we, as guests, were taking our temporary part. Thus when Charles called to me from the tennis courts or while mounting a hunter, "If you are going into Kendal, I wonder if you would get me a hundred Abdullas," I knew at once that what he wanted was a packet of ten Gold Flake. And again, while out shooting, if I should say in a loud voice, "Two brace of pheasant, Charles, which is not bad for me," he would know that I had shot a couple of rabbits while nobody was looking. In this way, with our system of code messages, we did not lose quite so much face.

splashed with it but the parish priest remarked to me upon the devotional piety of my friend. But if Jimmy had not the gift of tears with which to edify, he certainly had the gift of energy with which to inspire. I, already at least in my own mind two parts a monk and therefore a long-ceremony subject, was left nowhere in comparison with the zeal of my friend. "*Now* where shall we go, my Frand?" putting away his bulky Liturgical Missal and jumping imperatively upon his self-starter, "I expect if we went on to the convent we could get in another Stations of the Cross." So my stiff limbs would arrange themselves astride the bracket of his bicycle, and off we would go, bumping and splashing and skidding, to our next devotional halt. Not only on these exceptional occasions did my friend insist on frequent church-going but in the matter of week-days as well was he emphatic. Indeed it is owing to Jimmy's ruthless alarm clock and motor bicycle that I acquired the habit of daily Mass in the holidays.

These few days on our own were not to be forgotten, and it is characteristic of my friend that he dressed for dinner each night and made me do the same. Then, late on Easter Sunday, the family came back, and it was all, for me, a little bit frightening. Frightening but stimulating and challenging . . . so that it was with a wistful ache that I made the long journey south the following week from Westmoreland to Surrey for what remained of the Easter holiday.

VII

Now comes the last term, and the most crowded of the twenty-six that I spent at Downside. For me the easiest course in the treatment of this phase would be to follow the sequence of the diary as it stands, but for the reader it would be tiresome to have his attention switched to and fro and back again from games to classes, from corps to people, from books to sententious reflexion. Subject matter, then, rather than chronology will, as it has done hitherto, determine the divisions.

A factor which greatly influenced the enjoyment of this last summer term was the permission granted to Jimmy to bring back his motor bicycle. (It might be noticed in passing that we did not allow the word "bike.") We could now go off on short recreation days to Masbury to play golf as years ago we had gone off to Sir John's to skate. We went on longer days as well, playing the full eighteen holes on Sundays and Tuesdays. By this time our game had so far improved as to justify foursomes which included the professional, an excellent and unassuming man named Ham, and Mr. Cunningham.

Ham played a robust, masculine game of golf, swinging his iron with determination and power. He despised the mashie as being—why on earth?—a ladies' club, and for getting out of the rough he brought to bear a whacking great lean-back niblick as heavy as a sewing-machine. The rough would shiver and splinter and quail under his blows, becoming rougher still when he had finished with it. C. F. O. Bull said that nobody could be called Ham, and that the letters must stand for "*Homo appropinquationum magnarum*"—referring to the force of his approach shots. But this theory was disposed of by the arrival of another Ham, a brother, who played no golf and cared nothing for approach shots, long or short. "*Haud aequalis magistro*" said C. F. O. Bull with prompt but not very good Latin. The brothers Ham are still alive, but what they do now I do not know.

One day, a heavy overcast day, as Jimmy and I were nearing a village on the motor bicycle, a policeman came out of his little dolls-house police station, looked up at the sky, turned inwards towards the porch, bent over a string of black seaweed which was hanging on a nail, pinched a pod of it between finger and thumb, reflected for a second, unrolled his waterproof cape, put it on, and marched smartly down the little gravel path onto the street. "Did you see that?" Jimmy and I said together. The whole thing had taken less than ten seconds. It was like those finger-and-thumb cinemas which one used to get in the nursery—a block of drawings moving swiftly and jerkily to their climax—and the setting was so exactly in keeping with the toyshop that we could hardly believe we were in Somerset and not in Hamley's.

All this golf meant correspondingly less cricket and tennis, but we satisfied our consciences by playing enough of these two games to be of use to our respective houses: we knew that the school cricket and tennis teams could afford to do without us. And let it be added that as non-regular players none could have been more faithful to the cricket side than we. From the pavilion we watched every match; we bowled in the nets; we even, when asked politely, scored. This was still in the days of the old cottage pavilion with the slate roof and the rotting floor and the pictures of early teams wearing belts and black socks. (Photographic groups of a by-gone age in cricket show that not only in the matter of clothes and whiskers did our fathers differ from us as they went out to bat, but that when they sat down to be photographed they differed every bit as much: they lolled, they leaned on each other, they looked away from the camera, they let their legs sprawl about under them. It was presumably all part of the idea that they should be caught striking a natural pose. To us, brought up on regimentation in this sort of photography, nothing could seem more un-natural. We may have declined in almost everything else, but at least we are better about our team photographs.) Today the cottage pavilion is not even a store for bats and stumps; it has gone. Even the grass bank on which it was mounted has been removed, pushed farther back, and the cow-pond nearby into which you could throw, if nobody of consequence were looking, your bottle of lemonade, has also gone. The cricket field today makes a graceful sweep, but conservative souls will be found to mourn the passing of ancient things— just as members of a yet earlier generation will be found to mourn the uprooting of "the cabbage," a tree which towards the end stood well within the ever-enlarging boundaries of the cricket field and which, so the story comes down to us, on one occasion enabled a player to score forty-eight runs before one of the fielding side, having at last found a ladder and disappeared into its branches, cried "How's that?" from some incredibly high position invisible to the spectators, and, throwing the ball which had been wedged between two branches into the field, secured from the umpire the verdict "caught."

The score-box which stood to the north of the ground and which looked like a very primitive mobile coffee-stall was now, at the time of which I write, in the process of being exchanged for the elaborate affair which is still standing. For various reasons the process of exchange was gradual, and not until after my time at Downside was the present professional arrangement working properly. There were still some among us who preferred to throw tin number plates about in the open rather than sit inside a dark pillar box wheeling a caterpillar belt so that figures followed one another at the appropriate openings. For a while there was a telephone service, legitimate this time, between the pavilion and the new score-board but this was abandoned when either the human voice was found to serve instead or else the telegraph staff grew to be more proficient. There is a story about the pavilion telephone which is reputed to be funny but which I can never remember. Nor at the moment can anyone else. But since it must be more or less on the lines of the story about the House Prefects' telephone its omission cannot matter.

From field sports the mind turns to water sports, and scenes on the river in Bath come back with agonising clearness. Leaving out—because it does not belong to this period, and in any case I was not there—the legend of how Morgan Duncan shot the rapids in a punt, there are adventures on the Avon which would fill a boathouse with books. All our rowing expeditions seem to have been connected with trouble of one sort or another: swan trouble, oar trouble, leak trouble, paying the man trouble, even police trouble, and always getting back late for roll-call trouble. The swans used to be fed out of Jack Carroll's inevitable Fortnum's luncheon basket; the oars and punt poles used to get broken over a game which we invented called "water-jousts" (and which involved a whole crop of minor troubles of its own); the leaks meant baling out water at panic pressure with one's own or someone else's hat; paying the boat people for damage caused serious embarrassment, as did explaining matters satisfactorily to the policeman who was summoned on one occasion by the boatman in charge. The boatman had a voice like a saw-mill and a great red hard face like a fire-bucket. Compensation is a costly business, but fortunately there was always Jack who could be relied upon to toss a purse of gold where needed.

A frequent member of these river parties was Tony Du Port, who had been a friend of mine since Junior School days. In the matter of water sports we had been rivals for years, his swimming being better than mine, my diving better than his. As we were almost the same age, we were always in the same division: he, the swimmer, wanted more than anything to excel in diving; I, the diver, craved those extra few yards to the minute. But that is the way of these things.

Tony and I had only one joke between us, and that was

not properly a joke at all. We kept it up over the whole course of our school careers, and if we met tomorrow we would repeat it. It began when, aged ten, we had both been waiting outside the Headmaster's room for a beating. Dom Leander was interviewing a delinquent who had gone in before us and we were indulging in gloomy speculation. "What sort of padding," I asked, "do you use?" "None," he replied, "I don't believe in it." "Do you rub on cocoa-nut oil ever?" I asked again. "Hopeless." "Do you bite on blotting-paper? . . . I hear that's very good." "No." "What then?" "Between each shot I say to myself," confessed Tony Du Port, "these words: 'It's only life,' and somehow it doesn't seem worth bothering after that." This struck me—perhaps because I was necessarily in a nervous state at the time—as wildly comic, and though I have never quite recaptured the view of it which seemed so funny I record the observation now because it aptly expresses that particular boy. The phrase "it's only life" was shared by us and us alone: we applied it to moments of high triumph as well as to our times of trial and punishment. I remember in the summer of 1923, while we were standing together on the edge of the Petre Bath waiting to dive in for the final lap of the House Relay—Tony was in Roberts, I in Caverel—we reminded each other, against the roar of the spectators who were jumping up and down and shouting their heads off, that it was only life. It was a philosophic reflexion which came in useful when we were considering the hopelessness of the questions in an examination paper, and was signalled across the hall accordingly. The last occasion of its use was in the Quad on the day when we left school—he to go into the army, I to go into business. The phrase had the makings of a joke but it was not one. Du Port had the same pondering look in his eyes which I had remarked in the expression of my philistine friend with the brown shoes at the Tate, and which I have noticed since in the faces of those who are either uncommunicative or inarticulate. I have not got it at all, but then—as Rupert Chamberlain said—I talk too much. Du Port was not stupid like the other, but he was silent for the most part, and vaguely haunting still is the memory of his look.

VIII

Quite early in the term, during the first fortnight if we must be accurate, an extra place was laid on the Prefects' Table, and we were informed that an Old Boy would be coming to spend the next eight or nine weeks in our rather rarefied midst while he was working for a Foreign Office Exam. Not knowing him except by sight, for the six of us prefects were considerably junior to him, we resented the prospect of being saddled with Martyn Hemphill[1] in what was necessarily a confined and intimately contemporary society. Our delight therefore was great when a single meal in the company of our guest changed all this. He not only adapted himself to our more juvenile ways but in some respects outdid us in them. In every school there should be someone who can make prefects forget their lofty station for a while. We thawed out, we relaxed. Our guest was more experienced than we, and very much more clever. Under his tuition I came to read dramatic criticism, book reviews, political comment. He showed one where to look, and lent one the books which were coming out. He appeared to have read everything. For me he completed the course which was begun by Leonard Parker and Kevin Hayes. Max Beerbohm became my oracle. Before long it was clear that Martyn Hemphill would have to be put up for membership to La Société. He was elected unanimously to this and to the Kennels Club as well. To both groups he brought the rare Balliol air which was what they mostly lacked.

[1] Now Lord Hemphill.

ADOLPHUS ("DOLLY") VANE TEMPEST

Martyn Hemphill matched his intellectual vigour with bursts of violent activity, and I recollect with agony his calling me in the early mornings for an ice-cold bathe in the Petre. We used to race each other to the pond, shake off our pyjamas, and plunge in—even when the water had been newly changed and was as clear as gin and as cold as a rock pool in Norway—the first to hit the surface winning a prize.

Another though a very different Old Gregorian to return for a period of residence in the school was Dick Stokes. He was working in Bristol, and so was able to make Downside his temporary base. We saw less of him on the Prefects' Table than we did of Martyn Hemphill because he came back only in the evenings, but for a period of about two weeks we had him with us in our heatwave practice of sleeping out on the lawn. Each evening we would drag our mattresses from whatever part of the building we happened to be occupying—not all of us enjoyed, as I did, the privilege of sleeping in our own rooms—and for hours we would stay awake talking under the starry sky. Under that starry sky which Richard Sykes so much disliked to have over him. From our guest we heard stories of the War, stories of Downside as it had been ten years before, forecasts about Downside and England and the Colonial Empire. I wish now that I could remember what kind of a future it was that he painted for us; I do not think it was a very happy one. The only thing that remained in my mind was the fact that he objected to the third prayer which was said in English after Mass. He held that it was absurd to pray that St. Michael should "thrust down to hell Satan and all wicked spirits" because this was going to happen in any case whether we prayed for it or not, and it was a waste of good prayer breath. "I knock off at the end of the second one," he told us.

The heatwave that year was prolonged beyond all the

wildest hopes and against the opinions of the weather prophets. The practice of sleeping in the open meant that I wrote more bad verse than I had written for years—much of it had to do with 'hay-heavy scents of harvest' and skies 'warm in their purple wash'—and that I was bitten to bits by ants. What with composing and scratching, my nights were shortened. Lying awake one morning at dawn I was horrified to see a line of peahens bearing down upon our little encampment. The ungainly birds sped swiftly down the slope from the sunken road and I could hear the flutter of their feathers. Putting my head under the bed-clothes and propping up the pillow as a shield I waited, cold shivers running down my spine, for the rushing of claws over my body. I wondered whether the loathsome animals would peck at us through the sheets or whether they would just hurry on. Perhaps they would re-form the other side and repeat their charge . . . again and again until we went mad. So I waited, lunacy very close, but nothing happened. Complete silence. Eventually I mustered the spirit to look over the trench-top of my pillow, and there they were in a line looking at me. Then quite suddenly, as if at a signal, they turned and walked away. They seemed, I thought, a little embarrassed. I never told my sleeping companions of the disaster which they had so narrowly missed because I knew I should never have been believed. But it was perfectly true—seven peahens with wings outstretched coming closer and closer, crying their ridiculous call which sounds like "buzz-*pip*."

During this sleeping out interlude, one mattress with its complement of sheets and blankets was unaccountably lost. The circumstance puzzled everyone for days, and the owner had to buy a new lot out of his private funds. The moral was not difficult to point: bedding should be taken in at once and not left until after breakfast. I marvel now at the spirit which thought it worth while to bundle all the paraphernalia of sleep up and down stairs morning and evening for the sake of wakeful nights spent wrestling with discomfort. But I am glad we did. I am glad too that we judged, nobly, that this particular labour of transport was not within the duty of the fag. Then the weather broke— with the delicious suddenness of a storm—and we were woken one night with raindrops the size of fried eggs splashing on our faces. Matches went out in a sizzle as soon as we struck them. We trailed, wet to the skin, across the Quad, and spent the rest of the night on the lockers in the hall. I do not know why we did not go to our rooms because they were not far away, but I know we did not. We watched the rain beating down upon the Quad, and thought how comforting it was that the ants must now be drowning in their thousands.

The evenings for the rest of the term were warm enough to spend talking till a late hour on the flat roof outside Arthur Wood's room. Here three or four of us would gather before going to bed, and drink glass after glass of Eno's. The amount of Eno's which we got through that summer must have been prodigious. The prefects divided naturally into two groups: those who played bridge down-stairs, and those who drank Eno's on the roof. The first group never spoke unless to discuss a hand, the second never stopped talking. More often than not the subject was religion. I can remember almost word for word some of the conversations which took place between Arthur Woods and myself after the others had said goodnight and we were left alone. I was lucky in my friends: they kept me up to it.

For these nightly sessions Arthur used to wear over his pyjamas a kimono which had dragons and storks em-broidered all over it. I, despising all form of dressing-gown as much then as I do now, wore a pair of tussore silk trousers which belonged to my father, a broadcloth dress overcoat which I had found in a trunk at Lower Belgrave Street and which must have been left by one of my uncles or my grandfather, and a pair of elastic-sided "jemima boots." The coat had a silk collar, and I was told that I looked like Dr. Watson. Sherlock Holmes would hardly have approved of the absence of shirt and socks. Eno's, religion, colours and outlines fading into one another as the last summer light died out of the sky, the square of a lighted window on the other side of the Quad, a light breeze playing about one's neck . . . and then Arthur finishing up with "O Lord, I suppose we want to know too much." Arthur's kimono would rustle in the dark, I would knock over an Eno's bottle (because I am awkward of foot), and together we would creak indoors with our wicker armchairs, and so to our respective rooms to bed. I felt then, and I feel now, that had Arthur decided as I had done to become a monk he would have been happier both in his last year at school and later on. But perhaps he did more for souls as an airman than he would have done as a priest. I do not think he minded being killed.

IX

"Motor bicycle for sale at £17" said a notice in Mr. Fry's garage window. I wrote home at once to Alexandria asking for seventeen pounds. My letter was carefully worded—James Murray helping me to weigh the commas and turn the phrases so that on a second or third reading new shades of meaning might appear—and I sat back to await a cheque. During the interval which it then took to receive an answer from Egypt I tried out the bicycle on an experimental ride to Masbury, and found to my delight that it could move along the road in a not unbecoming manner. It was not a swift machine, particularly if the wind were contrary, but at least it did not stop. In my letter I pointed out that to possess this means of transport would free me from the expenses of hired cars and would not tie me down to other people's arrangements for the afternoon: economy and independence must, I felt, recommend themselves at home. The letter was addressed to my mother, who would then, when she had fully appreciated the advantages, pass on the request to my father. It was my father's custom not to write to his sons except on the rarest possible occasions. I myself had heard from him only four times in my life: once when I was unexpectedly recovering from pneumonia, once when his yacht *Waterwitch* won an important race, once when he had objected to a letter which I had written to my mother in a fit of homesickness, and once when he wanted me to do a job for him at the frame-makers who were responsible for sending his pictures to Burlington House. So when I received a cable from him saying "Since you have bought it you had better sell it again letter following" and signed "Cis," I wondered what the next communication would bring. In my letter I had hinted (with James Murray's assistance) that the bicycle was already mine, and that the cheque was all that was needed to satisfy commercial opinion on the matter. It was characteristic of my father that he should sign himself by a name (a corruption of Francis) which I was not allowed to use; it was equally characteristic that when the significant letter came it should contain no reference to either money or motor bicycles.

My father wrote exactly as he talked, and this fifth letter to me was so characteristic that I felt it to be worth quoting in my diary. It was short and all about an old Downside boy who had called on him. "Awful chap came to see me saying he was a friend of yours. Wears a ring. Wants me to put him up for the Club which I'm flatly unwilling to do. I wish you wouldn't send your friends wriggling along to me on their beastly stomachs asking for things. Your mother thinks he is the limit too, I may say."

I replied at once saying that there was no question of my having sent this Old Gregorian, that I had never even spoken to him, and that I would not recognise him if I saw him. But I knew that it was no use and that I would be saddled with him. And so indeed I was. Thereafter he was always "That frightful feller, friend of yours, with the ring."

My mother told me years later that whenever the young man called—which he did repeatedly because he was a dogged young man and very anxious to join the Club—my father showed his impatience by looking at his watch every two or three minutes. My father carried his watch on the inner side of his wrist, and in order to look at the time he used to shoot out his arm suddenly in an upward direction with the fist clenched and in a way which often made people think that he was about to strike them. The movement, resorted to so frequently and accompanied by my father's loud and discouraging voice, so startled the young man that eventually his resolve was worn down and he gave up coming to the house.

My father's watch, attached to a heavy gold chain which was fastened by a system of hidden springs, was laid aside only when my father entered the water to bathe or bath. Frequently the clasp, which was his own design, would spring free and the watch would jump away from the wrist —only to be caught after a flight of barely three inches by a little gold safety chain. My father liked nothing more than to keep people guessing.

Patent devices, little inventions which enabled you to do simple things in a complicated way, formed a useful and frequent outlet to my father's energy. In 1912 he designed a special kind of toothbrush, which he said was both more economical and more convenient than what was being sold in the shops. The handle and brush were made separately: you fitted the brush into a socket at the end of the stem. The idea was that when you had worn out one brush you replaced it with another, retaining the stem or handle. The handle was made of light metal, designed to withstand the ravages of time, and was stamped *Silsileh*, 1912. Silsileh was the name of the house which we had in Alexandria. The whole household was issued with toothbrushes, of which there were a considerable number made, and for years afterwards the phrase "surely these refills can be used for something" was constantly heard. The refills were, however, too small to be used for anything. Even during the short period when they were used, as planned, in the mouth and attached to the end of their metal holders, they were not a success. The brush was always either so loosely held in the socket that it came apart and you had to spit it out for fear of swallowing it, or else so firmly fixed that you broke the handle when you tried to change it for another. So in the end the orderlies, who in any case cleaned their teeth with the stubbed end of a stick of sweet cane, employed their *Silsileh* 1912 toothbrushes for polishing their buttons, while the rest of us hoarded them against a grimy day. My father, from a stern sense of duty, clung on to his *Silsileh* 1912 until after the First World War, and then, while on leave in England, bought himself, albeit shamefacedly I thought, a bone toothbrush at Boots'.

But it was a pity about the motor bicycle. Had I been a little more anxious to acquire it I could have paid the required sum out of my own money. Just at this time I was better off than I had ever been before. Not only had Rupert Chamberlain left me something—in an envelope and not in a will—but I had sold a camera for fifteen pounds. It was a pity that I did not buy the bicycle, because instead I spent the money, during my last weeks at school and in the week of camp, rather vulgarly.

Looking back at the three months of my last term at

school I find it hard to believe that there were any disturbing factors whatever. Even in writing the diary I seem to have forgotten the shadows: all is sunshine and Strauss waltzes. If seventeen is the age for lying on the grass and talking about the elemental things of life, then I used that last term well. I marvel that I could have watched so many games of tennis, listened to so much music, discussed so many topics, laughed at so many jokes—and never reproached myself for idleness. I have lost this facility for leisure, and cannot now comfortably waste time. All the more, therefore, do I value the memories of that summer term when I could still, without having to mention it afterwards in confession, do nothing.

Not only was there nothing in the school routine to dread—because even corps was now, at the level at which I came in contact with it, more of a pastime than a penance as hitherto—but there were a number of things positively to look forward to. Apart from the privileged reactions which the Prefects and members of the Sixth Form enjoyed—such as private bathes and having meals out—there were isolated entertainments which stood out like diamonds in a tiara. Just when the daily round was beginning somewhat to pall, there would happen either by chance or by design one of those incidents which, for colour and fantasy, make a man's judgment so fallible when reviewing the years which he has spent at school.

For instance, there was the day when the commercial traveller came to sell a fire-extinguisher. It was a very hot afternoon, and we of the Attics had gone down to James Murray's room in the Lower Gallery because here it was reputed to be cooler. Overlooking the Quad, and surrounded by James's silk walls, we pursued our studies. Through the open windows opposite there broke every now and then a gust of laughter—a master was going down well—and sometimes there would be a shout of reprimand. It was like flames spurting suddenly from a banked-up fire and dying away as suddenly again. Then into the Quad rattled and roared a silly little car with a silly little man in it. The back of the car was full of metal cylinders; the man had come to sell to the Headmaster a silly little fire-extinguisher. A greater act of hope cannot well be imagined.

To our surprise the Headmaster allowed himself to be fetched from his room to witness the effect of the extinguisher upon the little man's car. "Watch, Reverend, you just watch," said the traveller as he soaked his car, cushions and all, in petrol and set it alight. Out came the extinguisher at once, and in no time the fire was in control. Not a cushion, not a tyre, not an inch of rubber was scorched. We, gazing from behind James's damask curtains, were spellbound. So also, standing in the Quad, was Father Trafford. "Do it again," he commanded. The little man repeated the performance with equal success. "And again," cried Father Trafford. "And again"—as the poor little man, his coat off now and very hot, ran round his car setting fire to it and putting it out. "Hypnotism," whispered Cyril Bull to me, "that's what it is . . . chap's a fakir." It was then that I made one of the few good jokes in my life, and it was not seen. "It's Elias the Thesbite," I said, "in reverse." I then quoted in full the passage in the Third Book of Kings where the Prophet mocks the sacrifices of the priests of Baal and demands the repeated soaking of his own holocaust before the fire of the Lord licks up the offerings in a single flash. But my friends, having never come across the incident, thought me to be improvising. I suppose even this was a compliment. By the time I had declaimed some fifteen verses of Scripture there were heads at the windows of the classrooms, and Father Trafford was shouting at everyone and enjoying himself enormously. We in James Murray's room came out from our hiding, and joined the group in the Quad below. "It's a knock-out, Reverend, now isn't it?" said the little man breathlessly. "Forty quid."

Then there was the Prince of Wales's visit to the school in July, when the Prefects were presented and I slipped while in the act of shaking hands, my studded corps boots skidding on the polished floor. Though the panic of preparing for the Prince's inspection of the Guard of Honour was in some ways an agony, it was memorable. Jack Carroll was still being fitted into his uniform by a team of fags when the advance party of outriders drove into the Quad to herald the arrival of the royal car. My own fag had been up late the night before polishing the silver on the Drum Major's baton which it was my function to swing, twist, throw and catch on these ceremonial parades. The dents in the surface of the orb at the top had been beaten out by a firm in Bath, and now no evidence remained of my inexpert wielding in the past. It shone, on this day of all days, like the North Star. Roland could not have been more proud of his horn than I of my gleaming rod. But as I came clattering down the Turret Stairs to be in time—having left myself hardly more margin than Jack Carroll—I tripped over it and it rattled down into the Quad before me. By some miracle it was intact at the end of this unfortunate dénouement, and not even the Prince, whose eye for detail was said to be unerring, detected the new hollows and scratches. The Prince, who must have disliked the whole performance but who carried it off with grace, made a short speech from his car before leaving, and then swept down the drive while the boys roared their throats out and the ladies drawn up on the tennis courts cried. Miss Symes was there, in her straw hat with cherries, but she was far too blind to see a thing. All the other village figures were present, and it did one good to see so many sworn enemies sinking their differences in the radiance of royalty.

In the same month John McCormack the singer (Count McCormack as he became later) gave a "musical evening" to the school. The sheer pressure of sound seemed to me terrific and not altogether agreeable, but I am told that I have no right to judge upon matters musical. Standing at the back of the Gymnasium, ready to get out, one felt that the wall-bars were bending away from the centre of melody, as they might in a Disney film, and that even the box horse was sweating and shivering. The impression I had was that he was singing down to us, and that he would have been better appreciated had he planned his programme for a more sophisticated audience. *The Last Rose of Summer* was certainly a mistake—though possibly this was by request. Some César Franck and Handel (*Aria* from the Semele) were the only other numbers that I can remember. Arthur Woods went through the programme afterwards for the benefit of a select audience in the Attics, and though in his rendering of the famous singer's Irish he might equally have been doing Mike and Dom John Kane, his performance was brilliant. Bad impersonation, brilliant burlesque. Arthur used also to imitate me, and I am told that it was not as bad as some of his other impersonations. Only once have I heard myself convincingly reproduced, and that was by a parrot belonging to the landlady where I lodged while working in Liverpool. Each morning after breakfast I used to call out to Mrs. Archer before leaving the house, and tell her what time I expected to be in and where to ring up if I should happen to be wanted during the day. One morning I did not do this, and to my extreme mortification I heard her loathsome bird cry out in the most affected voice, "Oh . . . er . . . Mrs. Archer . . ." Was it really as bad as that? I buried my face in my hands and hurried out into the street.

Another feature of the summer term was the celebration, the last celebration for us who were leaving at the end of the month, of Club Day. After a suspension of many years, this annual event had recently been revived, and since it was unique in character it deserves mention in these pages. Club Day has, alas, been dropped once more, so the reason for preserving its memory here is all the stronger. It was a village and not a school function, involving a mass procession of men and women with banners and a band, a speech of welcome from the Abbot standing on the steps of the Old House, an answering speech from the President of the Club, a presentation of money from the Community to the Club, a lot more processing, and then, in one of the playing fields lent by the school authorities for the purpose, an afternoon of games, sideshows, sing-songs and beer.

Since the "day" of Club Day went on till well after dusk, and since the whole thing was strictly out of bounds for the school from the moment that the procession left the Quad, it was the enviable privilege of the Prefects to be taken by the Headmaster after evening prayers to the Club Day field to see how the Club was getting on. By this time the field would be showing signs of wear, and always the members of the Club would seem to be getting on very well indeed. It was the Headmaster's custom to allow each of the six prefects to bring a guest, so with Martyn Hemphill we numbered fourteen as we came upon the celebrations that year. My guest—for I knew that Maurice Turnbull would be chosen by one or other of my colleagues and James Reynolds was there already in his own right—was Arthur Woods.

All the way up to the Club Day fair, Arthur impressed upon me the absolute necessity of securing a cocoa-nut for Miss Symes's birds. "I promised her that she would be set up in cocoa-nuts for years," he said, "and that no bird would ever call in vain." "What the birds see in the beastly things I cannot imagine," said James Murray wearily, "they taste to me of clean sheets."

The side-shows were the great attraction but there were other things as well, hurdles and obstacle races, and it was interesting to note how much livelier the band was now than earlier in the day. In the quest for Miss Symes's cocoa-nuts one of our number showed such energy that he threw the wooden ball high over the canvas screen at the back of the pegs, and a man playing skittles on the other side was hit between the shoulder blades. The injury was not serious because the skittle player was later seen to be taking part in the grand finale, the tug-of-war. Those who tugged for this picturesque climax to the day's festivities tugged a swaying and uncertain rope, and I was glad that Mike had left us before the thirsty hilarities of Club Day could claim his patronage.

In the end we collected between us thirteen cocoa-nuts. Arthur and I called on Miss Symes next day carrying a suitcase which rattled and rolled. "Out with the hacksaw," cried Miss Symes in ecstasy as soon as she could make out —which she was able to do only by peering so closely that her loosely tethered head was almost inside the suitcase rolling about among the cocoa-nuts—what they were. The three of us spent the rest of the afternoon cutting the hard hairy objects in half and then attaching the sections to those trees in the garden which Miss Symes judged to be the most "visible." "Because it would be awful if they didn't *see* their lovely cocoa-nuts," said Miss Symes, who assumed in every living creature the shortness of sight which was hers. The milk of the cocoa-nuts she saved for making rock-cakes which we had the next time we went to tea and which tasted quite disgusting—like bedclothes in fact. When I visited Miss Symes's house two years later there were cocoa-nuts hanging from the eaves of her little porch, so it looks as if our successors were as assiduous at the Club Day fête as we had been the year before.

X

The House Corps Competition that year was, in spite of me, won by the house to which I belonged. Having spent my corps life in the band I knew little of the mysteries of arms drill, so when given the position of "right marker" I was more than often at a loss. For example on the command "fix" I would march boldly into the open (which was correct enough) and continue so doing in the expectation of the word from the platoon commander to halt (which was not). This little weakness which I never seemed able quite to overcome took me sometimes far afield— landing me, it might be, in the shrubberies beyond the tennis courts—while my men behind me, rigid with their left hands upon their waiting bayonets, marvelled at my stupidity.

No, the O.T.C. (as it was then called) was really no hardship any more. Even the route marches, boring though they were, had their moments of entertainment. It was one of the rules of La Société that the members salute when passing an inn or public house, so along the whole marching column the voice of authority would be heard censuring what appeared to be unaccountable lapses of discipline. One N.C.O. after another would bellow a reprimand as each of the seven members in turn smacked the butt of his rifle and sharply turned his head to right or left. Some of the Gentilhommes even thought fit to hail in this way passing brewers' vans, but such salutes were felt to be a refinement and not in any degree obligatory.

In my capacity of Drum Major I had sometimes occasion to demand extra band practices and even dress parades. Once towards the end of term when we were getting up a lot of new tunes to play at camp—not that I myself could play any of them, or even that I could be certain as to which was which when played—I put a notice on the O.T.C. board requiring a full meeting at a certain hour. Of this notice the concluding sentence, typed by my efficient fag but dictated by me, ran as follows: "Also I want all the drums, fifes and bugles to be brought, cleaned, to my room for inspection immediately after the practice." As I was pinning the notice to the board, I heard one of the junior members of the band, a fair boy called Donald Armour, say, "O, my God, it seems hardly credible." "Well, why not?" his neighbour in the crowd charitably suggested,[1] "they've got to be cleaned, and I suppose he's got to see them." "I don't mean that," said Donald Armour, "what I object to is beginning a sentence with an adverb used conjunctivally." Such was Donald Armour, and when in later years he wrote a novel called *Swept and Garnished* I searched the text in vain for an adverb used conjunctivally. His letters to me, which I am glad to say continue to this day, may be a more fruitful source of investigation and indictment, but I am at the disadvantage of not being able to read his writing.

Boys at the top of the school lived, in those far-off days before economic and social crises disturbed the surface of what was inherited from an older tradition, a somewhat unspartan life. The whole picture has entirely changed since then, and in a great many ways it has changed for the better, but in the early twenties the privileged at school were privileged indeed. To us now the life they led seems almost feudal. To live in the grand manner, even on such a scale as is possible at school, is never cheap. But it is always worth it. Probably we never reflected whether it was good for the character or not to be able to send a fag for the barber when one wanted a shampoo and to have the whole operation performed in one's room; one did it, and one was envied by those lower down in the school who

[1] The neighbour was Adrian Green-Armytage, in case anyone should wish to verify the story.

would do it too one day. But they do not do it now. Any boy who wants a shampoo today will have to go into Bath for one, and this he never does because he quite rightly wishes to spend his money on something more worth while. Service, in the early twenties, was taken for granted, was expected, was not denied. I do not recall that the school tailor came up the Attics stairs for fittings, but I remember well that a representative from Nokes in Bath used to come out by car and see me into the shirts which he was making for me. There he would stand with pins in his mouth, not daring to move very freely for fear of knocking over an easel, and talking about some agreeable shades which he had witnessed only recently in the windows of the Burlington Arcade. Perhaps the extreme in this kind of thing was reached when Hugh Ryan had his corps uniform, the ordinary rough tunic and trousers of a soldier in the line and not the resplendent garment of the under-officer, made by a tailor off Piccadilly. The uniform arrived in a powder-blue box, which had *Billings & Edmunds* embossed in raised lettering across the top, and in the sleeves was packed the softest tissue paper. To such heights of purposeless exquisiteness I myself never aspired.

Particularly at camp did the tendency towards fastidiousness and grandeur assert itself. Not always felicitously. I remember that one year when the luggage for this annual excursion into the simplicities of army life was piled up in the Hall on the night before starting, the Headmaster asked me why I had decided to leave my polo sticks behind. When, on the morrow, we finally set off towards Mytchworth it was as if a Maharajah were on the move.

Even when we arrived at our destination we were spared the worst excesses of roughing it with the other schools: we had servants to do our washing up and I think I am right in saying that our first parade in the morning was altered from the scheduled hour to a more reasonable time later on in the day. All this was very wrong of course, but very, very sweet. No amount of privilege, alas, could exempt us from the principal parades of the day, and we used to come back from route marches and manoeuvres as tired and dirty as the cadets of any other contingent. So primitive did I find the shower system to be, and so cold the water, that I bribed the camp cooks (who were regular soldiers and not above this kind of thing) to heat up more water than would be needed for cooking and to let me have the extra amount every afternoon on my return from battle. Thus it was a brave and comforting sight, a sight to which I looked forward throughout the day during the ardours of the military exercises in which I was involved, to see, as we came swinging through the camp gates to the sound of drum and fife, a little procession of cooks carrying on their heads steaming dixies of water to my shower bath. Watching these strong men, with their grey singlets stretched tight over their massive fronts, I felt that my money was being well spent. And so, I am glad to say, did they.

The cooks at camp performed other services besides cooking and providing for my comfort. For a small sum they were prepared to relieve the camp buglers of the duty of blowing their innumerable calls. Downside was publicly commended by the Colonel for the excellent performance of its solo buglers, so here again the money was not wasted. The cooks went even beyond the terms of their engagement, and taught to various members of the band mnemonic rhymes by which the different calls could be distinguished. Certainly these rhymes, indelicate though some of them may have been, were not likely to be forgotten.

It was the duty of the first chaplain of the camp to say the public Mass at the Church Parade on Sunday, and this was attended by the Catholics of all the contingents in the command. Father Ryan, S.J. of Stonyhurst celebrated and Dom Ambrose Agius, our own chaplain, preached. The altar was put up in a grove of fir trees. The scene was not one to be forgotten. Dom Ambrose's sermon was all about the duty of preserving the tradition for which the Old Boys of our Catholic schools had died in the war which had ended five years before. It was a good sermon, and now, when five years have passed since the end of the war which came next in history, there seems all the more need for a repetition of its doctrine.

The only other thing which I remember about that Sunday—apart from how thin the Sanctus bell sounded, tinkling away out there in the open—was the length of time it took to have our lines inspected. Lieut-Colonel Howard Vyse was thoroughness itself, spending a little over three hours on that unexciting duty. As we stood in the sun behind our kit and folded packs there was talk, in spite of the morning's sermon, of mutiny, murder, and desertion, but we were so highly commended at the end of it all—the cooks had been at work on the lines while we were at Mass —that even the most rebellious were mollified and in the best spirits as we drove off into Aldershot to give each other farewell dinners.

But these pages about camp are not strictly within the terms of the title of this book. Wrenching back the text, therefore, to a time when we were still at school there are yet a few bitter-sweet memories which are bursting to express themselves. Even study, seen like this in retrospect, has an aura about it and becomes a thing to be remembered with pleasure. I remember one night, fortified by Eno's and ginger biscuits, working until it was light enough in my room to pull down the little chain of the gas. I remember going for solitary walks with books under my arm, and lying in the sun at a place called Hunkle Spunkle where we used to smoke and where there was a stream.

Perhaps the human constitution needs less sleep at the

age of seventeen than later on, because morning after morning I used to get up at the sound of the monastery bell for Matins, work for an hour, and then go out for a walk—wearing what Jack Carroll called my sanctimonious face. This early morning walk was part of a spiritual course which I had set myself and was designed, with its application to holy thoughts, as a preparation for the monastic life which I had every intention of embarking upon as soon as I could extract the permission from my father. With the same object in view I practised at this time a somewhat elaborate brand of penance. In fact I must have been insufferable, imagining myself a sort of Saint Aloysius with a Benedictine twist. The inability to obtain my father's consent, together with the prospect of having to substitute a cotton office for a monastery, caused me at times such acute fits of despondency that often I despaired of ever being a monk at all. Knowing my mercurial temperament, I did not see myself waiting till I was twenty-one and independent. During the sittings when I was painting my fag's portrait —like Renoir I looked for what was paintable as well as for what was efficient from my staff—I mentioned these hesitations, and in order to stiffen my resolve, he, himself a draughtsman, copied for me Watt's picture of the young man in St. Matthew's Gospel who turned away sorrowful. The encouragement which this serious and somewhat sentimental gesture gave me was enormous, so it shows that people should always act upon such generous impulses— even at the risk of appearing a little foolish. Some years later, when I was at last planted firmly in the novitiate, my one-time fag came down to his old school, landing in his own plane on the cricket field. I hoped he would approach the authorities and get leave to speak to me. I wanted to be able to tell him of the part he had played in keeping my nose to the monastic grindstone. But since either his nerve failed him or his request was refused, I can make the acknowledgement here. He now has a boy in the school.

XI

It was the custom then, and perhaps is the custom now, for the School Prefects to be granted leave of absence once in the term from Friday evening until Monday morning. Some of the more sober-minded and industrious members of the body did not avail themselves of this opportunity. I did. I chose to go to Oxford, where my visit was timed to coincide with the Commem Week Balls. I suppose I must have gone to bed during some of the time that I spent in Oxford, but if I did it cannot have been for long. I attended three College Balls, seeing each one through to the photograph finish in the grey of morning.

It was during this Oxford Friday-to-Monday interlude that I came to know two people who influenced me considerably, F. F. ("Sligger") Urquhart and Lionel Hedges. I was taken to breakfast with Sligger, a Fellow of Balliol, on the morning after my arrival—having just had time to bath and change into day clothes—and was immediately accepted by my host as part of the circle. "You need not introduce your friend, because we have met before," he said to whoever it was who had brought me, "I have been waiting for him to call for about five years." This was a graceful recognition of one who was not even an undergraduate but only a schoolboy. He had, as a fact, though I was amazed at his remembering it, given me a lift in a dog-cart during the War when I was walking to the station at the age of eleven. I had been going up to London for some reason, and but for Sligger's thoughtfulness would certainly have missed the train at Chilcompton. He had been on a visit to Downside and was being driven by old Mr. Isaac Perry in the Abbey pony trap. That this should have simmered in Sligger's busy mind flattered me as much as did the manner of his referring to it. I saw quite a lot of him after this, both at Oxford and at Downside.

With Lionel Hedges it was quite different. He was a Blue and a wit, and how I came originally to meet him I do not now remember. But a strawberry and cream tea on the lawn at Trinity, at which I met also R. C. Robertson-Glasgow (who, like Lionel Hedges, was playing cricket for Oxford), remains vividly in my memory. When the tea party was over Lionel asked me to his rooms where we went on with our conversation while he changed into Bullingdon dress clothes. We arranged to meet next day for luncheon, but I was somehow prevented from keeping the appointment. Fortunately I still had Rupert's little legacy to draw upon so instead he dined with me at the Clarendon—before we both went on together to whatever Ball it happened to be. I felt that Rupert would have approved of the way in which I was making use of his present.

As a mimic, raconteur, entertainer, Lionel Hedges was without rival in a world where the stock-in-trade of humour was by no means scarce. His early death was felt by others besides cricketers. I have unfortunately not come across anybody who was taught by Lionel when later on he became a master at Cheltenham but I can imagine what an exhilarating experience his classes must have been. The champagne-like quality of his talk would have stimulated a village idiot into glittering displays of fancy and repartee.

Moved as much by personal inclination as by the gratifying suggestion of my Oxford friends, I entertained for a time the possibility of seeking admission to the University. I wrote home about it, and though my father did not reply, I learned from my mother that grave misgivings were expressed as to how I might figure as an athlete. "I could not bear it if he did not get a blue . . . he would only be a disgrace to his college and to me." There was also the financial question. "He would have to do it properly or not at all; I couldn't have him saving on the butter. He is wildly extravagant and would get into debt. I should be ruined. We should have to sell the *Waterwitch*, the younger boy would have to be taken away from school and made to work in a shop, we should have to go everywhere on foot and eat our meals off dirty tablecloths." My father saw things always in their sharpest outline. In alluding to my brother as the younger boy and to me as the elder, my father was not being pedantic. It was simply that unless he thought about it he could seldom remember our names. In order to help with the name difficulty he invented nicknames for both of us, but since these were invariably transversed there was in fact no appreciable progress.

So in spite of the Oxford project, which looked at one moment as if it might develop into a first-class family crisis, I received no sixth letter to add to my collection. After all I had been sent the fifth only that very term, and could hardly expect another. I believe that for a long time after both my brother and I had been going to school in England my father used to express surprise to find that we could read. Though meticulously accurate about his own affairs, my father was surprisingly vague about other people's—and particularly about the age at which people started doing things. I remember his telling me before I went to school at all, and when I was therefore only eight or nine, that if I ever came down to breakfast unshaved he would see that I was soundly thrashed. Possibly he was looking ahead ten years and warning me of how I would then lay myself open to his anger, but I suspect that it had suddenly occurred to him how unpleasant unshaven young men looked in the early morning and had thought that I was of an age to take steps about it.

Though there was much talk and correspondence about Oxford, it soon became clear to me, and to anyone else who thought about it for a moment, that I would never be able to get in. University authorities do not accept people who possess only the barest knowledge of Latin and Greek, and who are still wrestling with the subtleties of long division. I had read a certain amount and I could paint in an amateurish sort of way, but I did not *know* anything. Nor did I show any particular inclination to study the things that bored me. Even if I could have bluffed my way through Smalls, I should have been exposed later on and sent down. So perhaps it was as well that I decided not to fight my father on the issue, exhibiting instead an attitude, rare for me, of filial cooperation. But though nominally working in a Liverpool cotton office for the whole of the year following, I spent all the time I could among those whom better brains and ampler fortunes had placed so enviably. Oxford, as I have suggested earlier, was the cake out of reach.

XII

Then the last week of school life. The tension, and subsequent exhaustion, of exams; the emptying of drawers and cupboards of their letters, photographs, papers, score-cards, clothes, golf-balls, and familiar rubbish; the litter on the floor of what either will not fit into the packing cases or may reasonably be expected to find a buyer; the sense, sad and pleasurable at the same time, of doing things which will never have to be done again; the round of rather formal goodbyes, with their glasses of sherry, in the village and to members of the staff; the unexpected discovery of new friends in the school whom one had somehow never noticed before—relationships started all too late and doomed to fade in after life—and the agony of wasted opportunity.

Then, finally, the actual day before leaving. Trunks carried, bumping against the wall, by willing fags in "going home" suits. The Hall vibrating with fuss about labels and tickets and advance luggage and bicycles. Servants to be tipped, addresses to be exchanged, old menus and team photographs and programmes to be signed. The anxious boredom of the afternoon, with the two speeches to be made later on in the day—one to the school and one in the House dormitory—and with no opportunity of distracting the mind with a game because all except what one stands up in has been packed. The nervous artificiality of the last meal, with its uneasy talk and still more uneasy silences. The last scheduled feature of the day, and in some ways the most uneasy of them all, is the Auld Lang Syne (the words for this being "We're here because we're here") which is performed by the entire school (except for the Irish boys who have gone off, roaring, in a special bus to Bristol six hours before). There we all are, a little self-conscious at first and saying that this is really rather nonsense and ought to be dropped and that nobody wants it, but crossing our arms nevertheless and joining hands—joining hands, moreover, not with any two who may happen to be standing near but with associates of choice.

"I wonder who started this thing, and why . . . *here because we're* . . . don't forget I've been vaccinated and this business hurts . . . *because we're here because* . . . do look at that frightful fool opposite us who is doing it too fast and spoiling the whole thing . . . *we're here* . . . and who on earth have that lot got with them? . . . *because we're here because* . . . not on my foot, blast you . . . *we're here* . . . what? I can't hear . . . *because we're* . . . yes, much, but that's because the school's twice the size it was when we came . . . *here because we're here* . . . I suppose it would be a pity to let the thing lapse after all these years . . . *because we're here because* . . . can't shout any louder you fool . . .

here . . . last lap, thank God . . . *because* . . . hey, you're slipping . . . *we're* . . . just one more, up and down, quick . . . *here* . . . well, this must be a record . . . *herebecausewerehere becausewereherebecause* . . . all over." Three cheers for the Headmaster, for the Head of the School, for Downside. Speeches. Visits to people's rooms. Bed at about half-past two. The end. After the weary, strained, drawnout penultimates, the closing scenes come always in a rush.

Epilogue

"THE LIVES we need to have written for us," says Ruskin, "are of the people whom the world has not thought of— far less heard of—who are yet doing most of its work, and from whom we may learn how best it may be done." Almost all of those whose names are mentioned in this book are unknown; few, however, have shown themselves, either in the boyhood or later, to have been mere passengers in life. I have tried to suggest that some among the elder ones have not only justified themselves as men who, in the words of the above quotation, have "done the world's work" but have been patterns also from whom "we may learn how best it may be done." This, namely the stimulus which the biographical element is meant to provide, is the only merit of a book which contains so much about the author. The book (believe it or not) is biographical in design, autobiographical only by accident. The characters described in it are not lay figures, posed to suit my composition and clothed in garments of my own. Immortals in the accepted sense they may not be, but influences—to others, I hope, beside myself—they are.

For me as I place the lid on the typewriter and begin, pencil in hand, to revise the script, there are so many strictly personal pictures which appear in the margin of the pages that I cannot in the least see how the text will look to any reader who is not myself. My hope, possibly a forlorn one, is that the subjective is lost in the objective and that the author is seen only as the signature in the corner of the canvas or as the grinning spout-head scarcely discernible on the abbey wall.

Yes indeed, for me there are more pictures than pages. I see many more of what I have left out than of what I have put in. The factual is always easier to account for than the emotional, and when a writer reads what he has written he knows very well that though he may have told what he has done, and what others have done, he has not even begun to tell what he has felt and what he has known others to have felt. As well it is so—or all books would be unbearably heart-to-heart.

Put it this way. I can look back with an easy eye, for instance, at that group of village children who are throwing stones with aimless but evidently enjoyable earnestness onto the frozen surface of Sir John's at Emborough. My skates are slung round my neck, and the bootlace which connects them is cutting into my skin. As I swing, with metallic clatter, onto the bicycle which is to take me back in time for a hot shower before class I glance over my shoulder (with difficulty on account of the skates) and see a bonfire burning itself out red against the darkening background. I hear the stones ringing and klonking on the ice. Underneath me I feel the crunch of the tyres upon the frost; crisp and powdered leaves are sticking to the earth. Or, again, I am almost horizontal in an armchair while Jimmy Reynolds, a frown on his face and his voice charged with feeling, is reading aloud to me Chesterton's *Ballad of the White Horse* or Thomas Malory. I see the sun of early dawn reflecting red on the windows of the Abbey. I hear the Upper School coming down from games on a December afternoon: the light already going, the *plup* of a football being kicked and the smack of a football being caught from a pass, the scrape of rugger boots at the Five Pins, the hiss of hot water from the showers and the steam coming through the windows into the Quad, the fags hurrying and leaving doors open, the Prefects singing and using other people's soap. Oh yes, all this is easy. I can remember and give you this. What I can remember equally well but find much harder to express is the spasm of loneliness at the shutting of a door, is the sense of shame on receiving a snub, is the elated feeling of not having made a fool of myself when I might have done, is the satisfaction of having written the right kind of letter. You cannot write a book about these things. But one such impression, for what it was worth, I will attempt to put down.

It was on a whole holiday when I was in the Middle School. I had been "gated" for some piece of indiscipline which I cannot now remember, and was occupied over an exercise book in what was then the Studyroom. Someone came in with his packet of sandwiches and asked me to lend him a thermos flask. As I handed over the key of my locker I knew that this was a "moment," a moment of light, an experience. It had nothing whatever to do with the person who wanted the thermos flask, nor was it connected with what I was writing or with what, being deprived of the holiday, I was missing. Romance did not enter in. It was simply that I knew myself to be—for want of a better word—alive. It was like leaving a dream and walking on solid ground. It was the discovery of the present moment. It was a physical experience in the sense that I understood for the first time the true and even sacred significance of material things; it was a spiritual one in the sense that I realised their absolute *in*significance in comparison with the things of the soul. When one sees that there are two distinct worlds in the created order, when life is viewed quite clearly as an outward and an inward, one has been brought to a point from which there is no going back. From now on one tabulates, remembers, relates. It may be a pity that one should so tabulate.

Perhaps it would be a good thing if one were not to remember so precisely, if one were not to relate. Much better, from all accounts, to be entirely objective. But the better or worse does not here arise; the point is that one has now a perspective, an approach, a vision. "It all hangs together," I heard myself saying inside, "and here I am watching as well as fitting in." This must seem nonsense to anyone who has taken it all for granted, but on me it still acts with the force of novelty every time I think of it. Now *that* was the moment, if I had only had my wits about me, to sit down and write the book which I am writing now. It would not have taken the story beyond 1920, but it would have ended up as more of a pattern. Instead I went back to my exercise book and marvelled at the unique nature of my outlook—wondering whether everyone else in the world possessed his own, and equally unique, outlook. The conclusion which I arrived at did not dismay me in the least, and I have been acting upon it ever since.

People write books about the past, at all events about their particular slice of it, not for the sheer joy of recording the part they have played in it—though this comes into the process of course—but for the much deeper satisfaction of touching a nerve or a memory or a fancy in the minds of other people. By digging down into himself, a writer finds his affinities. Mutual understanding is based on self knowledge.

When I read in Maurice Baring's *C* that the central figure on leaving school "suddenly became conscious, and for the first time, that he was the part of something large, of a corporate body, of a long tradition, a note in an end-less series. 'Bright with names that men remember, loud with names that men forget' they sang, and he knew that, if his name was not destined to increase the blaze of the long record, it would, at any rate, be one of the obscure notes that contribute to the volume of sound . . . now for the first time in his life he learned the difference between the tears that are luxuriously shed in tasting an emotion that does not belong to you and the tears of recognition that respond to the call of actual experience . . ."[1] when I read this I know that waves of understanding are flowing out from the author, and it is in the attempt to let something of the same sort flow out from me that I have ventured upon the ambitious project of writing this book.

[1] pp. 98, 104.